Australia

The Present and the Past
General Editors: Michael Crowder and Juliet Gardiner

This new series aims to provide the historical background necessary for a proper understanding of the major nations and regions of the contemporary world. Each contributor will illuminate the present political, social, cultural and economic structures of his nation or region through the study of its past. The books, which are fully illustrated with maps and photographs, are written for students, teachers and general readers; and will appeal not only to historians but also to political scientists, economists and sociologists who seek to set their own studies of a particular nation or region in historical perspective.

*Australia   *John Rickard*
*Modern China   *Edwin E. Moise*
France   *Jolyon Howorth*
Ireland   *J. J. Lee*
Japan   *Janet E. Hunter*
*Russia   *Edward Acton*
Southeast Asia   *David P. Chandler*
Southern Africa   *Neil Parsons*

*Already published

The Present and the Past

Australia
A cultural history

John Rickard

Longman
London and New York

Longman Group UK Limited,
Longman House, Burnt Mill, Harlow,
Essex CM20 2JE, England
and Associated Companies throughout the world

Published in the United States of America by Longman Inc., New York

© *Longman Group UK Limited 1988*

First published 1988

British Library Cataloguing in Publication Data
Rickard, John
  Australia. – (The Present and the past).
  1. Australia – History
  I. Title   II. Series
  994   DU110

ISBN 0-582-49329-3   CSD
ISBN 0-582-49330-7   PPR

Library of Congress Cataloging-in-Publication Data

Rickard, John, 1935–
  Australia, a cultural history.

  (The Present and the past)
  Bibliography: p.
  Includes index.
  1. Australia – Civilization.   I. Title.   II. Series.
DU107.R48   1988   994   87–21393
ISBN 0-582-49329-3
ISBN 0-582-49330-7 (pbk.)

Set in 10/12 Palatino Roman

Produced by Longman Singapore Publishers (Pte) Ltd.
Printed in Singapore.

Contents

List of Maps

List of Figures

Acknowledgements

I wish to thank the following institutions, organisations and individuals for permission to reproduce figures which appear in the text:

Angus and Robertson Publishers (5.3 (illustrations by Hal Gye from *The Moods of Ginger Mick* by C. J. Dennis, © Angus and Robertson Publishers 1916)); Art Gallery of New South Wales (2.2 and 7.7); Art Gallery of South Australia (3.5 (Gift of the South Australian Company 1890)); Australian Consolidated Press Limited (7.5); Australian National Gallery (3.9 (b)); J. S. Battye Library of Western Australian History (4.2 (66717P), 4.6(a) (1083P), 4.7 (24396P) and 8.2 (25258P); Arthur Boyd and the Robert Holmes à Court Collection (10.2); British Museum (Natural History) (1.4, 2.1, 3.2 and 3.3); John Fairfax and Sons Pty Ltd (6.2, 8.1, 8.3, 8.5, 8.8, 9.3, 9.4 and 10.3); History Department, James Cook University of Northern Queensland (4.6(b)); Jimmera P/L (7.3); La Trobe Library, State Library of Victoria (2.3, 3.7, 4.4, 4.8 and 5.4); Longman Cheshire Pty Ltd (5.1, 6.4, 7.8 and 8.6); Melbourne University Press (7.2); Mitchell Library, State Library of New South Wales (4.3 and 4.5); David Moore Photography Pty Ltd (8.7); Museum of Victoria (1.2 and 1.3); National Gallery of Victoria (3.8 (Felton Bequest 1956), 3.9(a) (Felton Bequest 1932), 5.2 (Gift of Edwin V. Adamson 1982); 9.2 (Purchased 1956) and 9.5 (from negatives presented by Stuart Tompkins 1971)); National Library of Australia (3.6, 5.5, 6.3, 7.1, 7.4, 7.6, 9.6 and 9.7); Sidney Nolan and Lauraine Diggins Fine Art Pty Ltd (10.1); John Oxley Library, Brisbane (2.4, 3.1, 4.9, 6.1 and 6.5); Press Association Ltd (8.4); and Sydney Dance Company and Branco Gaica (photographer) (10.4).

Preface

This is a history of Australia written from a cultural perspective. I have assumed a broad, anthropological understanding of culture: thus the aim has been to tell the story of Australia through an examination of its evolving values, beliefs, rites and customs. To some extent this has been a means of avoiding the conventional, consecutive narrative of events which is already provided by other histories. Familiar signposts such as Eureka, the birth of the Labor Party and Gallipoli have not been ignored, but they are read here for different messages. Although there is an overall chronology to the book, the cultural orientation has enabled a freer, thematic treatment.

A benefit of the anthropological emphasis is to encourage a pursuit of the totality of the culture, however difficult that might be. Much Australian history has been preoccupied with the quest for national identity – a preoccupation which is itself revealing – and has, as a result, often concentrated on that which is seen as being distinctively 'Australian': so a self-fulfilling model of national growth is embraced which defines and limits the narrative. My assumption has been that a provincial culture is by definition derivative, and that it is necessary to keep in view the continuing relationship with the metropolitan culture. The paradox is that if one focuses on the derivative, one gains a new perception of what might ultimately be seen as 'distinctive'. Thus, for example, the Californian bungalow was an architectural importation, yet in its local adaptation became a recognisable part of the culture of suburban Australia, along with the backyard, the garage down the side of the house, the corner shop and the picture theatre. It is from the *arrangement* of such elements that a distinctive suburban milieu emerges.

Similarly, it is only when one has grasped the relationships between the different parts within the whole – between, say, city and bush, working class and middle class, Protestant and Catholic (each of which can be seen as having a culture of its own) – that one can gain any sense of something called Australian culture. I have attempted in this history to chart the emergence of certain cultural accommodations which have become characteristic of Australia. I do not want to reduce culture to the artificial unity implied in 'the Australian way of life': rather, this is an historical inquiry into the ways in which Australians have related to their environment and each other.

The reader will notice that the book is weighted towards the twentieth century. It may seem cavalier to dispose of the period 1788–1901 in two chapters, but the decision is a deliberate one. Part Three, which covers the period 1901–1939, is the centre of gravity for my analysis: it gives meaning to both that which precedes and follows it. It also seems appropriate, as we edge our way towards the year 2000, to remember that this is the century in which the great majority of Australians have lived.

It should also be self-evident that this is a white view of Australian history. I have attempted to juxtapose Aboriginal culture against the culture of the immigrants, and to accord the continuing Aboriginal presence proper recognition. But this is still – perhaps inevitably – contained within a European-focused narrative: an Aboriginal history of Australia would be a different story.

I have, from the beginning, been aware of the effrontery involved in embarking on a project such as this. Occasionally when I self-consciously mentioned that I was writing a cultural history of Australia it would invite the cheap crack, 'That will be a short book'. The problem, of course, is just the opposite: so much has now been written about Australia, particularly in the last ten years. The interpretation offered here is very much a personal view, and as the narrative approaches the present day I have allowed my own speculations more play. Nevertheless my debt to many historians is enormous, and I have drawn freely and unashamedly on the insights they have brought to Australian history. The measure of this debt should be evident from the Bibliography.

While, too, I claim some originality for this book, it is not without its predecessors. In some ways its model can be found in the first of the modern short histories of this continent, W. K. Hancock's *Australia*, published in 1930. In Australian historiography this has long been regarded as a crucial book, which was profoundly to influence later perceptions of Australian society. Less obvious, however, is the extent to which Hancock's concerns were cultural.

Like this *Australia*, fifty-eight years later, it was thematic in its approach; nor did it shrink from contemporary analysis. I did not set out to emulate that classic; it was only when I was in the midst of writing that I recognised what might have been an unconscious source of inspiration.

A precedent of a different kind is offered by Geoffrey Serle's *From Deserts The Prophets Come*, recently republished as *The Creative Spirit in Australia*. This was primarily a history of 'high' culture in Australia, and sought, for the first time, to integrate the various arts into an historical narrative. Given the broader cultural focus of my own study, the approach to the arts must necessarily be different. While I have sought to place the arts in their social context, my narrative use of writers, artists and intellectuals generally is historically selective. That one writer is mentioned and another ignored is not in itself an estimate of their relative importance: rather, it may mean that the writer included serves a purpose in illustrating a chosen theme. My account, therefore, cannot be depended upon as a critical guide to the arts: it does, however, attempt to relate the concerns of 'art' to the wider culture.

I have been helped by many people in the writing of this book. I discussed the project at seminars at places as far-flung as London and Perth, but I owe a special debt to my colleagues at Monash University, particularly Marian Aveling, David Chandler and Graeme Davison whose comments on the draft were both useful and supportive. Ann McGrath, Andrew Markus and Peter Spearritt were also kind enough to make suggestions, and Nicolas Peterson showed an anthropologist's patience with an historian in reading chapter one. The editors of the Present and the Past series, Michael Crowder and Juliet Gardiner, were there to remind me of the need to interpret Australian to the non-Australian reader, and offered encouragement as deadlines beckoned. But above all I must thank Richard White who made many suggestions for the improvement of the text, a contribution all the more generous considering the use I had already made of his own work. That I have not been able to meet all his criticisms is not a comment on their value, but rather on the difficulty of reshaping an intractable narrative.

My chapter written for the 1938 volume of the bicentennial history, *Australians*, was of great assistance to this present book, as was the work of other contributors; likewise the discussions engendered by that project were incidentally of benefit to my own. I must also thank Monash University for the study leave which was essential to the writing of this book. Within the University I am grateful to

Gary Swinton for the execution of the maps, and Tony Miller for some of the picture reproductions. Bess Brudenell, who typed the manuscript, was, as ever, both helpful and patient.

Finally, I owe a not so obvious debt to two good friends, Ray Lew Boar and Alex Crawford: I was staying with them in their Cotswold cottage, 'Rabbit Hill', when I first toyed with the idea of this book. In that remote but congenial English setting it seemed somehow easier to conjure up the nerve to contemplate writing a history of my own country.

John Rickard
Monash University

For John and Juan

Part 1

Sources

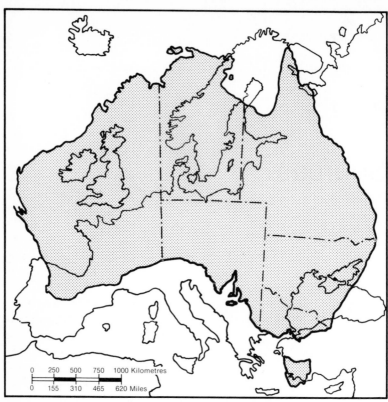

Map 1   The comparative sizes of Australia and Europe

_1

Aborigines

For the Aborigines the earth had always been there. It required no explanation. Myth interpreted the shape and appearance of the world the Aborigines knew and inhabited. Rocks, trees, waterholes, animals, birds: such objects, intimately experienced, were integrated through myth and ritual into a spiritual universe of extraordinary richness.

There were – are – spirit beings which expressed themselves in creating or actually becoming the physical detail of the Aboriginal world. In doing so they gave meaning to the land and to life. These spirit beings had an independence and unpredictability which were also beyond explanation. So they might appear male or female or draw on the sexuality of both; and human might, at will, become animal; nor was their force diminished if they transformed themselves into the features of the landscape.

So the rainbow-serpent, which is found in most Aboriginal mythologies, is commonly depicted in its terrifying, animal form, with a kangaroo-like head and crocodile teeth, ears or crown of feathers, long, spiked body and fish tail. Usually inhabiting waterholes, the serpent is also the arching rainbow in the sky. Thus the rainbow-serpent is a symbol of water and life; sometimes it is also an ancestral being. For the Gunwinggu it became Ngalyod, a woman, who, with her husband, Wuragog, travelled the country carrying her digging stick and net bag. When Wuragog sought to lie with her, Ngalyod was apt to return to her serpent form, but their union produced children who were the first Gunwinggu. For the Murinbata the rainbow-serpent became a man, Kunmanggur, who made the musical instrument, the didjeridu, from a bamboo stalk. He blew on it hard, and with the reverberation of its strange music several flying foxes flew out of its end. Kunmanggur decided to make people, and when he blew again a boy and girl emerged.

In some myths the spirit beings who created the familiar world of the Aborigines came across the sea from another place. So in the Djanggawul epic song cycle two sisters and a brother came from somewhere far away, but the journey celebrated is from Bralgu, the island of spirits. Reaching the mainland they continue their journey, making wells and trees, and through such acts investing the land with meaning. Then, following proper ritual preparations, children are removed from the wombs of the sisters. The world of the Yirr-kala people had begun to take shape.

It is myths such as these which are the source of what Aborigines call the Dreaming. The myths are not fables of 'long ago', for the Aborigines have, in the European sense, no concept of history. The past does not so much precede the present, as lie contained within it. The Dreaming paths mapped out by the spirit beings continue to determine the pattern of Aboriginal life, for the Dreaming is a relationship between people and land which forms the basis of traditional society. The myths serve to unite the creativity of the source with the continuing reality of life. So a man can say of a particular site, with certainty rather than wonder: 'This is a place where the dreaming comes up, right up from inside the ground.'[1]

The frequent association in myth of origins with canoe journeys over sea is historically suggestive. The Aborigines have been in Australia at least 40,000 years. Human evolution could not have taken place separately in Australia, for there is no evidence of the existence here of the ape-like predecessors of *homo sapiens*; therefore the first Aborigines must have come from elsewhere, most likely South-East Asia. Sea-levels were then much lower, and although the Australian continent was never joined to Asia, New Guinea was part of a mainland which was relatively close to the chains of islands pointing from Java and Borneo. Most islands were within sight of each other, and even over the last and longest gap it is likely that smoke from natural bushfires on the Australian continent would have been visible. Whatever the background to this migration, and whatever the precise route followed, the journey required a combination of technical skills and high motivation. Setting foot on the unknown land the first inhabitants had to learn to understand a new, though not totally unfamiliar, environment. Northern Australia shared some of the plant life of Indonesia, but its animals were strange and different. The newcomers had to, like their spirit beings, 'make' the country in their own image.

How long it took for the Aborigines to spread out over the vast island continent is not known, though it might have been as long as

10,000 years. Preferring at first the kind of coastal terrain familiar to them, they were unlikely to have sought out less hospitable regions until forced to by circumstances. Twenty-three thousand years ago another drop in sea-level united Tasmania to the mainland, and almost immediately, it seems, Aborigines ventured into what was then a harsh, cold environment, with glaciers paving its mountains and icebergs floating along its coast. Ten thousand years later the sea rose again, and the Tasmanians were marooned, but in what was now a more congenial environment. As for the desert regions of central Australia, so often associated with the archetypal Aborigine, these were probably the last to be occupied: there is no evidence of habitation far inland older than 26,000 years. By 1788 it is thought that there might have been a total Aboriginal population of about 750,000.

Over many thousands of years, therefore, the pattern of Aboriginal settlement emerged. Eventually there came to be possibly between 500 and 600 dialects and languages. These might be spoken by as few as 100 people, or as many as 1,500: each such group was a society unto itself. The world was largely defined through a particular people's relationship with its land. Myth did not need to explain the life and culture of other people, since they impinged only incidentally on this world. To travel beyond your country was to go outside your world – it was hazardous spiritually, as much as materially. Aboriginal culture is, then, many separate cultures. Even physically, Aborigines vary considerably: the Tasmanians, for example, were distinguished by woolly hair and reddish-brown skin colour. Although the similarities remain important, the diversity of Aboriginal experience is one born of 40,000 years in a continent of great physical variety, from lush tropical rain forest and fertile, grassy plains to desert wastelands and wild mountains.

'Tribe' is an inappropriate word to describe an Aboriginal community. There was no chieftain, and the community came together infrequently, and usually only for ceremonial purposes. Yet within each society relationships were governed by a complex web of structures. At the base was the family – a man, his wife or wives (for marriage was not necessarily monogamous) and their children. For purposes of daily hunting and foraging the family was part of a band, usually comprising no more than fifty people. But beyond the family a range of groupings was organised according to descent, relationship to the land and particular sites within it, and totemic association. The total community was usually divided into moieties which had important social and ritual functions. So all were aware of

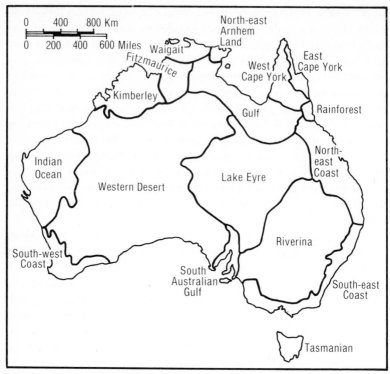

Map 2   Aboriginal cultural regions (source: Nicolas Peterson, *Tribes and Boundaries in Australia* (Canberra 1976))

their position in society, and accordingly the nature of their relationship to other members. In some ways this was restrictive – marriage, for example, was governed by an elaborate hierarchy of rules – but it also made for ease and security. This did not mean that Aborigines were mere captives of custom: there was still much scope for negotiation, bargaining and making decisions. But the entire society was like a family in which the individual member had a clear knowledge of the obligations and responsibilities of social intercourse. So it was possible to live your whole life without meeting anyone who was, literally, a stranger.

A casual observer watching an Aboriginal band absorbed in its daily concerns could hardly guess at the complex social structure which conditioned it. Even the movements of the band from camp to camp reflected a pattern born of a long spiritual and material association with the land. To describe the Aborigines as nomads is misleading if it suggests aimlessness, and indeed in the more fertile regions Aboriginal communities were much more settled. In the south-east there were even villages of stone dwellings, close to lakes and rivers where there was good fishing with elaborate systems of weirs, channels and nets. But even where, as in the arid zones, greater distances were crossed, the essence of these cyclical movements was to 'look after' the country, both in terms of husbanding its resources and caring for its religious sites. The gathering of food was a material and not unpleasant necessity, but it also kept the Aborigines close to the spiritual source of their culture.

In the daily routine the men hunted, with much ingenuity, their game being kangaroos, wallabies, emus and a range of smaller marsupials; fishing, too, was often important. Women and children were primarily responsible for gathering vegetables, fruit, eggs, shellfish and honey; sometimes they hunted smaller game. Their tasks too, demanded considerable skill in recognition and selection. Various foods required cooking or preparation: meat was lightly cooked, often in earth ovens, while some tubers and the fruit of the cycad palm, for example, required quite complicated processing. The diet was one of surprising variety, though this was naturally affected by the seasons. The seasonal availability of a particular food might provide the occasion of a gathering: so in the summer when clouds of small brown Bogong moths took shelter in the southern alps many Aborigines, some travelling great distances, pursued them there for a time of sociable feasting. Food generally was shared: the band was a cooperative unit.

Although accustomed to moving about the country, the Aborigines had a strong sense of their home in the camp. Dwellings, although not universally used, were important citadels of shelter and rest, and even the humble bark hut featured as a motif in Aboriginal art. Widows and unmarried women gathered around one fire, bachelors around another, while each family usually had its own. Such an arrangement was more in the interest of order than privacy, and part of the vitality of camp life stemmed from its openness and communality. After the separate pursuits of the day the camp provided the focus for social and cultural sustenance.

So life went on, and somehow this society functioned with little evidence of overt government. Partly this was due to the interlocking network of social structures which set the rules for conduct. But partly it was due to the consensual mode of making day-to-day decisions, a mode encouraged by the realities of nomadic life. Respect was accorded older people, because their knowledge was greater, particularly in matters of ritual. Ritual, of course, was concerned with conditioning behaviour, so in this sense the old presided over the young. But their authority was not formalised, outside the context of ritual itself. When someone offended against recognised standards of conduct – say, in breaching a sacred tabu – the penalty was usually a customary one, though it might be carried out in a casual manner without ceremony. So a man who had offended might, when hunting in a group, suddenly be speared in the back by a companion: the nature of this act as punishment would be understood by all concerned.

In one sense men had more power and privilege than women. They could take more than one wife, while a woman was not similarly able to acquire husbands. Moreover a husband exercised certain rights over the disposal of his wife's sexuality. Men were more likely to exercise authority and to preside over ritual, and they assumed that hunting had more status and glamour than gathering. Yet women had their own ritual life, their own sacred knowledge; and their work as food gatherers was fundamental to the economy.

The relationship of woman to man was not, in practice, one of subservience. In one myth Minala, whose totem is the tortoise, is married to Wimu who is extremely possessive, and does not want to share him, somewhat to Minala's chagrin. He goes to seek the magic which will turn her into a tortoise, and thus rid him of her, but the determined Wimu follows and observes him, and later profanes his magic, with the result that it is Minala who becomes a tortoise. Wimu is now overtaken by remorse and wants Minala turned back into a man, but she is told that there is no magic strong enough: the only solution is for her to become a tortoise. Such a tale might be interpreted as a warning to wilful wives, yet ultimately it is Minala who is the loser.

It is notable, however, that while many of the creative spirits of the Dreaming are female, the myths seemed to feel a need – or, one should say, the tellers of the myths did – to explain a disparity between the status of woman as the source of life and her tribal situation. So in the Djanggawul cycle the brother steals the sisters' sacred basket and emblems, and thus appropriates a particular ritual. The sisters appear neither resentful nor humiliated, for they still retain important roles, but the myth can be interpreted as validating male control of a female-derived ritual.

The subtleties of relations between the sexes is futher revealed in the Aboriginal understanding of conception. Some accounts have misleadingly stressed the Aborigines' ignorance of the causal connexion between coitus and pregnancy; in fact it was the general

1.1 A sketch by the explorer, Sir Thomas Mitchell, of an Aboriginal woman and child: she carries a digging stick and dilly bag.

belief that there were both physical and spiritual aspects to concep-tion. On the one hand sexual intercourse was necessary to place a foetus in the womb, though one act alone would be insufficient to 'make' the child. On the other hand the foetus could only be animated by a spirit child entering the woman's body. This could happen in various ways: it might be foreshadowed by a dream of the father's, and would usually be identified by some particular symp-tom experienced by the mother. The place where this happened – the nearness, for example, of any sacred site – would help determine the totemic affiliation of the child. The spirit-children were them-selves part of the environment, often inhabiting the waterholes. So from the very beginning of life the integration of land and people was celebrated. While all Aborigines identified the physical and spiritual aspects of birth, different emphases can be detected. Among the Warlpiri, for example, older men tended to believe that the entry of the spirit-child into the woman was more important than copulation: women, on the other hand, perhaps influenced by the nature of their own experience, were certain that coitus was the primary factor. Men and women, while sharing a common religious heritage, might nevertheless have different perspectives on sexuality.

Of course in Aboriginal society it was hardly necessary for such theoretical differences to be resolved or even spelt out – they simply existed. Sexuality, in its day-to-day manifestations, was talked about openly, without shame or embarrassment. It was not something that children needed to be shielded from. Such discussion, gossip and banter were focused largely on heterosexual behaviour; homosexuality seems only to have played a minor role in Aboriginal society, and then largely as a transitional experience of puberty.

It was part of the balance of Aboriginal life that there was plenty of time for social activity. Except in times of drought, hunting and gathering did not take up many hours of the day, so that conversation, storytelling and ritual were easily accommodated. Ritual, however, had more than a social function, for it was vital to the maintenance of the community. Much care and time were taken in the preparation for and performance of rites. Some rites were dramatic re-enactments in song and dance of the deeds of the spirit-beings or heroes; some were concerned with replenishing the natural environment, and therefore were seen as fundamental to immediate survival; others were essentially rites of initiation or death. All were characterised by great energy and commitment; there was a real sense in which the community was revitalised by their performance.

Male initiation rites were complex, with many stages and practices; circumcision was widely performed, subincision to a lesser extent. Initiation often involved a symbolic death and rebirth. The boy would be taken away from the main camp, where the women would, for the time, remain, wailing in formal grief at their loss. In the distance elders swung bullroarers – a sacred, wooden object, common to most Aboriginal communities – the howling sound of which represented the voice of a spirit-being, perhaps the rainbow-serpent, which would duly swallow the boy and then vomit him back into a new life. Women's role in this male-centred rite (there were less complex puberty rites for girls) was nevertheless important. Initiation was a rite of communal significance, and from one perspective it could be seen as a structured dialogue between the sexes concerning the future of the community.

Music, dance, painting and culture were all essential to ritual. Indeed, 'art' was not something to be juxtaposed against 'society', in the sense that 'leisure' is often contrasted with 'work'. Art was fully integrated with the social process: it always had a utilitarian purpose, whether in terms of immediate function (as with a spear or a dilly bag) or ritual significance (as with body painting and sacred objects). There were no professional artists, and little distinction between 'art' and 'craft'. Certain skills were required of most people – in making implements, for example, and body painting – and if some gained particular reputations as artists, songmen or dancers, it was because of the opportunities their position in the community afforded them, rather than any special response to an artistic calling. To play the didjeridu called for the development of considerable technique to maintain a continuity of sound and produce, simultaneously, two pitches, but such a player, however important to his community, was in no sense a professional performer.

The importance of art was assumed: it needed no justification. Indeed, art was so important that there was a constant process of production rather than any sense of amassing artistic treasures. For communities on the move there was no point in *objets d'art*, except, of course, for the few essential sacred objects. Bark paintings might simply be left to decay or, if used in rites, deliberately destroyed, though sometimes a sacred object would be hidden at a site for later use. Sand sculptures, made for mortuary and healing rites, were as ephemeral as the sound of the didjeridu itself.

There were, however, the great galleries of Aboriginal art in caves and on rock faces, which were often part of the Dreaming and had, in that sense, always been there. So the Aborigines were certain that they themselves had not painted the extraordinary Wandjina figures, with their white faces and red haloes, found in the Kimberleys. For in the Dreaming the Wandjina came from the north, making waterholes and shaping the landscape; each Wandjina then painted his own image on the walls of a cave before making his home in a nearby waterhole.

Similarly the *mimi* figures of Western Arnhem Land seem to represent an ancient artistic tradition, though the Aborigines remained well acquainted with these curious spirits. The *mimi* were stick-like creatures, usually depicted in lively movement, running, dancing or hunting. They were so thin and light that they only hunted in still weather, for fear of being broken by the wind, but they possessed very keen sight and hearing. When an Aborigine came near they ran quickly to a rock and blew upon it; the rock

1.2   This almost life-size bark painting, from Oenpelli, Western Arnhem Land, shows a hunter in the act of spearing a kangaroo, which is depicted in x-ray style. The artist told anthropologist Professor Baldwin Spence, who collected the painting in 1913, that the hunter came across the kangaroo when returning from a search for honeycomb, with which the dilly bag around his neck is filled.

obediently opened and closed behind them. Sometimes medicine-men claimed to have glimpsed the *mimi*; and in the past the Aborigines were said to have acquired various skills from these spirits.

Ochres, pipeclay and charcoal were the main materials of Aboriginal art; sometimes blood was used. Hence the basic colours were red, white, yellow and black. Yet although the predominence of this colour range throughout the continent gave Aboriginal art a surface homogeneity, a variety of styles and techniques pointed to its essential diversity.

The Wandjina figures were so unusual that early European beholders imaginatively detected Egyptian influences. They were not only in a different mode from, say, stick figures such as the *mimi*, but seemed the product of different artistic concerns. Another distinctive tradition was that of 'x-ray' art, when the painting depicted the internal organs and structure of humans or animals. Some Aboriginal art made use of geometrical motifs and arrangements to such an extent that the effect was abstract.

The meanings of Aboriginal paintings or sculptures were usually intricate. The geometrical motifs might represent landscape features such as waterholes and rivers; they might also have other deeper symbolic meanings. To fully understand a particular work one would need to be a member of the particular group within the people from which it came. Although the graphic code language upon which artists drew might have some universal characteristics, precise meanings were localised in context. So a sacred object, the significance of which was located in ritual, might only be capable of full interpretation by a very few. It was not so much that knowledge was 'secret', in an elitist sense, but that an Aborigine's expectations of 'understanding' a work of art were conditioned by circumstance.

Traditional Aboriginal society was imbued with a religious view of life, and ritual and art were harnessed to its expression. Particular people acquired ritual responsibilities, but just as there was no chieftain, so did religion lack secular organisation. So personalised by culture and experience was the Dreaming that there was no *need* for such organisation to maintain it. Nor were the spirit-beings worshipped in a formal sense.

The nearest thing to a priest was, perhaps, the medicine-man (or 'cleverman'). At one level the medicine-man was a doctor who by ordinary or magical means cured illness; he might also be a sorcerer capable of using magic to harm or punish others. But above all the medicine-man was respected because he had access to the spirit-beings and powers of the Dreaming. Sometimes the medicine-man gained his position, at least in part, by inheritance; sometimes he might be chosen by the elders, or more particularly the existing medicine-men; sometimes he might experience a call in a manner which marked him out for the role. However selected, the novice then underwent a complex ritual transformation. Just as in initiation there was a symbolic experience of death and re-birth, so too the making of a medicine-man often required a ritual death, sometimes achieved by the candidate having the 'death bone' pointed at him, sometimes by his being swallowed by the rainbow-serpent. Once 'dead' he was then 're-made', limbs being removed, cleaned and replaced, and magical substances, such as quartz crystals, inserted.

The body was restored to life: the medicine-man had been born. In the course of this ritual transformation he had come into contact with the spirit-beings, even, in some cases, meeting them in the sky. So in some measure he now shared their powers: he was no longer constricted by time and space, and could do extraordinary things. Yet for all his singularity and the community's respect for his powers, the medicine-man was otherwise an ordinary member of the society, living out his life, in practical terms, in the same way as his neighbours.

Aboriginal religion was life-oriented. It contained no sense of sin or personal salvation, and death, while it did not destroy the spirit, offered no promise of a heavenly after-life. Death was, therefore, something of a puzzle. At one level there was a tendency, particularly if a person died short of old age, to blame the exercise of malevolent power – the sorcery of another people, for example. At another level myth sought to explain how death had come to the world. According to the Murinbata, Crow and Crab argue about the right way to die. Crab, a very old woman, shows how she would do it, crawling into a hole where she remains for some time changing her shell. When Crab emerges from the ground everyone is happy except Crow. 'That way takes too long', Crow protests. 'There is an easier way to die. This is what we should do.'[2] Whereupon he rolls his eyes, falls over backwards and dies instantly.

Similarly for the Maung, there is the myth about Possum and the Moon, when they were both men. They fight with yam sticks and Moon mortally wounds Possum. As he dies, Possum says that all who come after him will, like him, die for ever. Moon protests that Possum should have let him speak first, for although he, too, would die for a few days, he would return in the form of a new moon. Both Crow and Possum were responsible for Aborigines having to follow the example they had set. The option of renewal, offered by Crab and Moon, had been pre-empted. There was no particular moral to be drawn from this, but the myths suggest that while for Aborigines life was natural death was not – people had to be taught how to die.

Aboriginal beliefs did not altogether discount the prospect of renewal, but there was little sense of the human personality surviving death intact. The spirit was, in effect, dispersed. Part of it lingered in the land, always having the potential to haunt the living; but the main energy of the spirit travelled to the land of the dead, losing its individual identity, and awaiting some later re-birth. Death, in the personal sense, remained an austere reality. In most places the name of someone who had recently died could not be uttered: the tabu might apply for years.

The mythology of death points to a fundamental feature of Aboriginal culture – its lack of concern with motivation and 'morality'. It was not pertinent to ask *why* Crow or Possum behaved the way he did: the myths did not operate at this level. There was no attempt to explain the need for death. Rather, the mythology simply defined the alternatives as they existed, and nominated the fate which Aborigines had to accept. It is not surprising, therefore, that Aboriginal culture was not noted for proverbs or saws, for they would have had little point. Behaviour was not governed by moral precepts, argued out a theoretical level. Ideas about 'right' and 'wrong', or appropriate and inappropriate behaviour, derived from a complex interaction of social structures anchored in the land itself.

So the spirit-beings of the Dreaming were sources of energy and life, and performed great deeds, but moral majesty was not part of their aura. They were feared and marvelled at, and their ways had to be respected, but they were not adored. Often, indeed, there was a moral ambiguity to their behaviour. The *mimi*, for example, were sometimes credited with having taught the Aborigines their skills, yet they were also seen as being capriciously hostile to human beings, and likely, if given the chance, to take them captive.

There was no room, in such a culture, for a sense of tragedy. Suffering, like death, had to be accepted. But just as there is an almost abrasive matter-of-factness in the compelling myth of Crow and Crab, so, too, suffering was not an occasion for moral grandeur. The point of suffering was its material reality. It was made bearable by a religious understanding of the world which was underpinned by myth and sustained by ritual.

In its acceptance of the realities of survival, Aboriginal culture could to the outsider sometimes appear harsh. Infanticide was practised, though its exact extent remains uncertain. Babies with deformities were killed, and in the case of twins the weaker seems to have been discarded. If this was population control, it was only so in the immediate sense of the family and band meeting the difficulties of raising children in a semi-nomadic situation. Such decisions, ratified by the culture, did not pose moral dilemmas; in any case the spirit of the dead baby simply returned to its source. In some areas cannibalism occurred, usually associated with rites of interment. Token parts of the flesh of the dead body might be eaten by certain kin, who would draw strength from this communion. A dried piece of flesh might also serve as a kind of talisman, helping, for example,

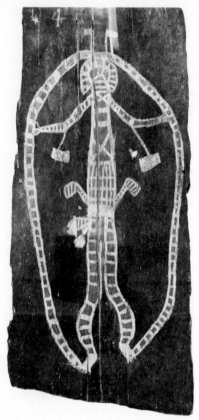

1.3   A bark painting of a Lightning Spirit from East Alligator River, Western Arnhem Land. The Spirit, which carries axes in its belt and sprouts them from elbow joints, is a threatening one. The oval composition represents the circumference of the clouds.

a man in his hunting. To describe such customs as uncivilised only obscures their cultural significance: they were not so much aberrations from an otherwise 'civilised' society, as logically compatible aspects of Aboriginal civilisation as a whole.

Aborigines had no concept of material wealth. Objects and implements had to be made all the time, to satisfy not only the requirements of daily life and ritual, but also to meet kinship obligations. There was no point in seeking to amass a surplus, for it would have been more a physical impediment than an instrument for power over others. Hence competition for wealth though not necessarily power was notably absent from Aboriginal culture. It was partly for this reason that society did not have the sorts of in-

stitutions of government usually needed to regulate such competition.

Disputes and fights were more likely to be concerned with
matters such as sexual relationships. The organisation of Aboriginal
life did not preclude opportunities for aggression. Sometimes rites
and ceremonies would allow for physical contest. Just as the Aborigine was proud of his hunting prowess, so too he respected bravery
and loyalty. Although territorial disputes would appear to have
been infrequent – bound to its own land, a people had little motive
for expansion – there were other occasions for dispute, particularly
deriving from the tendency to blame the sorcery of another people
for the ills of one's own. But just as the Aborigine's religion lacked
the structures of church and priesthood, so their society did not
encourage a warrior tradition. Violence and killing were not absent
from their society, but for the 40,000 years of their uninterrupted
occupation of the continent, the Aborigines had not found the need
to develop the structures and stratagems of formalised war.

Above all, Aboriginal culture was characterised by a fusion of
the material and spiritual. The tasks of daily life were themselves
imbued with religious meaning, while the function of the great
rites was to reaffirm and sustain the community's relationship
with the land. The technological simplicity of Aboriginal society
was matched by a cultural complexity, as much evident in the
subtlety and opaqueness of its mythology as in the intricate pattern
of its kinship systems. As a non-literate people the Aborigines
found their history in the power and beauty of art, myth and ritual.
The land itself was a kind of text, a scripture, which each Aborigine
learnt to read. And in their painting and sculpture the Aborigines
not only expressed their aesthetic sense but also wrote, and wrote
again, their cultural messages. In all of this there was the continuing
reality of the Dreaming. When they celebrated the spirit beings the
Aborigines were celebrating life in its diversity – Ngalyod, the
rainbow serpent woman, the Djanggawul paddling their canoe
from Bralgu, Crow and Crab, Possum and Moon, the yam people,
the *mimi*, all represented the spiritual energy of the universe. The
Dreaming ultimately unified everything, and from that unity the
Aboriginal people drew their strength.

Such a sketch as this of a 'traditional' society is bound to convey a
static quality – a sense of the endless repetition of daily routines, of
myths being retold and rites re-enacted over the centuries. In fact
Aboriginal society did change, even if the pace of that change was

necessarily slow, and even if much of it can only be inferred or guessed at.

The coming of the Aborigines had a significant impact on the environment. The Aborigines have been called 'fire-stick farmers'[3]: they set fire to bush not only to keep tracks clear and flush out animals for hunting, but also, it seems, as part of a larger strategy for regenerating the land. The persistence of this practice established a new ecological balance. On the west coast of Tasmania, for example, ancient rain forest gave way to heath and sedgeland. The centuries of fire contributed to the dominance of the eucalypt which adapted best to the Aborigines' land use.

Changes in climate compelled adaptation, just as the casting adrift of Tasmania committed the Aborigines there to a separate history. About 4000 years ago a tabu emerged, for reasons unknown, on the eating of scale fish, and the Tasmanians ceased making bone tools; they had, however, satisfactorily established their own accommodation with their island environment.

At the same time the mainland was witnessing some significant innovations. New small tools – points, backed blades and adzes – were introduced to the technology, and though it seems likely that these were imported, the possibility of local development cannot be entirely discounted. The dingo, or native dog, was definitely an immigrant, possibly 4000 years ago and thought most likely to have been brought from south Asia; the Aborigines readily incorporated this animal into their culture. The dingo was semi-domesticated, often taken from the bush as a pup, to become for a time a pet of the camp, later returning to the wild. On cold winter nights the warmth of the dingo's company was much prized.

It must also be remembered that the evolution of the settlement pattern of the continent, with its variety of languages and dialects, must have been a long historical process. Contact between different societies remained important. Although the spiritual universe of each people tended to be self-contained, taking little account of what lay beyond its own country, there were often overlaps, as in the case of a site which might have religious significance for more than one people. Just as two communities might be able to understand each other's dialect, so too they might share sections of a myth. At a practical level there were patterns of trade by which all benefited, pearl shell from the Kimberleys, for example, finding its way right across the continent.

Myth and ritual were not unresponsive to the changing needs of their guardians, nor could they be. Sometimes elements might be discarded, so that eventually cave paintings of past generations could lose their original significance, or be endowed with a new one. With each myth there were always varying versions and emphases, and often these suggest the continuing vitality of oral tradition. Myth and ritual existed always in the present, constantly reinterpreting the Aborigines' relationship to the land of their Dreaming. A tradition, after all, only reveals its strength by its capacity to adapt and modify.

So as the Aborigines occupied the continent, and came to terms with the changes of environment and climate, their culture evolved and adapted, in all its variety. Nor can it be assumed, as the coming of the new small tools and the dingo warn us, that once they set foot on Australia the Aborigines were isolated from the rest of the world. The cultural overlap between the Aborigines of Cape York Peninsula and the Papuans (the Torres Strait islanders representing an amalgam of both) provides evidence of extensive contact between Australia and New Guinea, though for how long a time before 1788 remains uncertain. The contact was strong enough, however, for Papuan technology and customs to penetrate some 300 kilometres down the Cape. We know of the regular visits of the Macassans from Indonesia to northern Australia possibly from the sixteenth century or even earlier. They took advantage of the north-west monsoon to guide their praus (dugout sailing canoes) to the Australian coast where they fished for the valued trepang or bêche-de-mer. The processing required, which included boiling and smoking, meant that they needed to establish themselves for a time on the shore, building, it seems, villages of leaf-thatched houses for their stay. Although there were instances of hostility from the Aborigines, there is also evidence that they were most interested in the visitors, their technology and customs. They may even have helped the Macassans in their work. The iron implements which the Macassans brought with them were sought after, and their dug-out canoes were adopted in Arnhem Land. Perhaps even more significantly, Macassan words entered Aboriginal languages, and the visitors had a noticeable influence on Aboriginal music and art. Thus Aboriginal culture responded creatively to both the Papuan and Macassan influences.

It would seem that the voyages of the Portuguese in the sixteenth century (when they may have sighted Australia) and of the Dutch in the seventeenth century impinged little on Aboriginal consciousness. In 1629, however, a mutiny by survivors of the wrecked *Batavia* resulted in two of the rebels being marooned on the mainland. Nothing is known of the fate of these, the first known European inhabitants of Australia. Some Tasmanian Aborigines most likely saw Abel Tasman's party when it 'discovered' Tasmania in 1642, but if so they discreetly secluded themselves. Aborigines certainly witnessed the Englishman William Dampier's forays in 1688 when he visited the north-west coast, but they kept at a distance and deliberately avoided contact. Irritated, Dampier concluded that they were 'the miserablest People in the world'. And when Captain Cook explored the east coast in 1770 the Aborigines' reaction was more one of suspicion than hostility. But perhaps influenced by the lusher environment of eastern Australia, Cook disagreed with Dampier's assessment:

> From what I have said of the Natives of New-Holland they may appear to some to be the most wretched people upon the earth: but in reality they are far more happier than we Europeans; being wholly unacquainted not only with the

1.4   Thomas Watling's image of the man in this Aboriginal family group has more than a suggestion of the noble savage. The inscription reads: 'Native Man standing in an attitude very common to them all. A Woman with a child in her lap broiling fish while a Boy is beating two sticks together and dancing to the sound.' Watling, transported for forgery, arrived in 1792.

superfluous but the necessary Conveniences so much sought
after in Europe, they are happy in not knowing the use of
them. They live in a Tranquillity which is not disturbed by the
inequality of Condition: The Earth and sea of their own accord
furnishes them with all things necessary for life; they covet not
Magnificent Houses, Household-stuff &c. they live in a warm
and fine Climate and enjoy a very wholsome Air: so that they
have very little need of Clothing and this they seem to be fully
sensible of for many to whome we gave Cloth &c to, left it
carlessly upon the Sea beach and in the woods as a thing they
had no manner of use for. In short they seem'd to set no value
upon anything we gave them nor would they ever part with
any thing of their own for any one article we could offer them
this in my opinion argues that they think themselves provided
with all the necessarys of Life and that they have no
superfluities. . . .[4]

If Cook's portrayal of the Aborigine suggests a romantic image of the
noble savage, he nevertheless grasped something of the atmosphere of Aboriginal society before European contact.

How the Aborigines viewed these occasional curious visitors is
difficult to surmise, though their ships, great white birds on the
horizon, sometimes provoked alarm. Their visits were infrequent
and fleetingly brief. They came and went away, leaving almost no
imprint compared with the Macassans. Life went on.

And then, in January 1788, these visitors from another world,
another dimension even, came again – and stayed.

2

Immigrants

On 18 January 1788 the first of the eleven ships of the First Fleet, the *Supply*, entered Botany Bay. At three o'clock Governor Phillip and some officers went ashore; Lieutenant King recorded that they 'just looked at the face of the Country, which is, as Mr. Cook remarks, very much like the Moors in England, except that there is a great deal of very good grass and some small timber trees'. Searching without success for fresh water, they were returning to the *Supply* when they made their first sighting of some 'natives', who were suspicious of the newcomers. Yet the Aborigines obliged by leading the party to 'a very fine stream of fresh water'. Phillip approached them with tact – and beads. These he placed on the ground, until one Aborigine approached 'with fear and trembling' to inspect the gifts offered. He seemed astonished by the clothed appearance of the Europeans. King conceded that 'it is very easy to conceive the ridiculous figure we must appear to these poor creatures who were perfectly naked'.

Within forty-eight hours the remainder of the Fleet had arrived at Botany Bay. Encounters between the Europeans and Aborigines continued to create interest on both sides. On 20 January King met a number of women and girls, who had earlier been even shyer of contact than the men. They came down the beach and gathered around the boats,

> and made us to understand their persons were at our service. However, I declined this mark of their hospitality but shewed a handkerchief, which I offered one of the women, pointing her out. She immediately put her child down and came alongside the boat and suffered me to apply the handkerchief where Eve did the Fig leaf; the natives then set up another very great shout and my female visitor returned on shore.

Generally the natives behaved, as Surgeon Charles Worgan put it, 'very funny and friendly', though they were becoming wary of the soldiers with their weaponry, and expressed concern when the visitors began to cut down trees.

Governor Phillip soon decided that Botany Bay itself was unsuitable for a settlement, and led a party in search of a better harbour: not far to the north they entered Port Jackson, a most cheering discovery, because it was, according to Phillip, 'the finest harbour in the world, in which a thousand sail of the line may ride in the most perfect security'. But before the Fleet could be mustered for its new destination, there was the surprising news that two strange ships had been sighted outside the Bay. Bad weather intervened, and the ships disappeared from view; on 25 January Phillip took the *Supply* to Port Jackson. The next morning the two foreign ships entered Botany Bay, and turned out to be a French scientific expedition under the command of the explorer La Pérouse. Civilities were exchanged, though the British were cagey about their own intentions. They did not necessarily accept La Pérouse's view that 'all Europeans are countrymen at such a distance from home'[1].

So while the French chatted with the British in Botany Bay, a few miles to the North at Sydney Cove Governor Phillip, with a detachment of marines and convicts, was engaged in the prosaic business of founding the settlement. At sunset there was a pause for a brief ceremony at the landing place where a flagstaff had been erected. Beneath the Union Jack, officers, marines and convicts gathered, while volleys were fired and the Governor and officers drank to the King and the success of the colony. Thus on a Saturday summer's evening, with minimal flourish and rhetoric, the British established the colony of New South Wales.

Why had they come? What had brought Phillip and his motley crew of soldiers and convicts eight months around the world to found this humble settlement at Sydney Cove?

There is a simple answer. When it became clear that the American colonies had wrenched themselves free of the Empire, Britain was faced with the problem of finding a new receptacle for the convicts which North America had formerly absorbed. The gaols were full, and convicts were herded into hulks on the Thames. Various possible settlements were considered, including a proposal to dump convicts on an island in the Gambia River in West Africa, where they would have been left, virtually ungoverned, to fend for themselves. When humanitarian concern about the tropical climate

2.1   George Raper's depiction of the chief settlement on Norfolk Island, April 1796. Ringing the settlement are the distinctive Norfolk pines, which, it was hoped, would provide the navy with timber. Unfortunately their wood proved unsuitable.

caused this scheme to be abandoned, Das Voltas Bay in southern Africa became the prime candidate, but closer inspection caused this site also to be discarded as too barren. It was August 1786, and an element of desperation entered into the making of policy. Ever since Cook's 'discoveries' of 1770, Botany Bay had had a few enthusiasts, particularly Sir Joseph Banks and James Matra, both of whom had been members of Cook's voyage. Distance, and the expense it entailed, had always seemed the obvious disadvantages of Botany Bay, but now sums were hastily done to show that the costs, carefully managed, were acceptable. Given this assurance, distance almost became an advantage, for the further from Britain the convict rabble was deposited, the less likely was their return after sentence had been served. Within one month of receiving the adverse report on Das Voltas Bay, the decision to send convicts to Botany Bay had been made.

This simple answer has not satisfied some Australian historians who have sought more complex and, at times, more romantic explanations. The British Navy's appetite for flax and timber is said to have motivated the settlement, as Norfolk Island, which lies some 2,000 kilometres north-east of Botany Bay, was allegedly rich in both. Commercial motives have been suggested, particularly the Government's desire to protect the Chinese tea trade. Closely linked has been the strategic imperial factor – the perceived need to exclude the French from what Britain regarded as its sphere of influence. Such explanations tend to regard the convicts (and their labour) as a mere means to larger ends.

It was natural that any advantages enjoyed by Botany Bay as a site should be stressed, for it was a basic requirement that the proposed settlement should be self-supporting. But to promote such advantages to a primary motivating role is risky history. There seems little doubt that if the report on Das Voltas Bay had been favourable, plans for settlement there would have gone ahead – in other words the 'advantages' of Botany Bay were not great enough to press its case until this competitor had been disqualified. In so far as Britain was, in the wake of the American Revolution, particularly sensitive about its imperial needs, the French rivalry cannot be discounted as a consideration, and the remarkable coincidence which saw two French ships visiting Botany Bay at the precise moment when the British were founding their settlement alerts us to the strategic dimension. Concern about French trespass was also to be a factor in the brief, abortive settlement of Port Phillip in 1803–04, and in founding the Swan River Colony (Western Australia) in 1829. Yet there is little evidence to suggest that the founding of a new colony would have been on the British Government's agenda in 1786 but for the immediate convict crisis. Botany Bay was settled against a background of gathering urgency, but the urgency was a domestic not an international one: to say that the imperial factor was taken into account accurately states the policy priorities.

It is revealing, nevertheless, that Australian historians should be so sensitve about the question of origins. For several generations the convict inheritance was an embarrassment, which, made bearable by the pretence that most of the convicts were harmless poachers or stealers of a loaf of bread, really served to discourage the pursuit of history. Then as historians braced themselves to face the facts of transportation, it dawned on many Australians that the primitive convict society of New South Wales was an extraordinary beginning for a nation, and more a cause for astonishment than shame. Yet even as Australian history began to flourish as an enterprise, it seemed as if the old uneasiness had not been entirely dispelled; indeed, as the myth of the convicts' innocence was dismantled, the sense of the nation's original sin gathered unconscious force. To submerge convictism in a strategy of imperial defence and commerce would forever exorcise the ghost of Botany Bay. Unfair as such an interpretation might be to the revisionist historians, who were concerned to place Australian settlement in a world context, it does nevertheless point to one truth. In a young country such as European Australia history lies very close to the surface. It can enrich lives by making sense of our surroundings and our dilemmas, but it also has immense capacity to disturb. When the time-span is so short we are all much more implicated in its crimes: the protective glaze provided by culture is thinner. So I, too, must remind myself that I am a mere six generations from the First Fleet, from a humble marine on the *Sirius* and the convict woman with whom he was to make his life in New South Wales.

Australia's first colonists, whether convicts or soldiers, were unwilling migrants, sent either to serve their sentence or their King. Most of the convicts, and many of their gaolers, stayed on; but the nature of their migration must be borne in mind when assessing cultural origins. No matter how many free immigrants were to come later, the cultural source of New South Wales, and the subsequently settled Van Diemen's Land, lay in the social problems of British industrialisation and Irish disaffection.

In all some 162,000 convicts were sent to Australia over an eighty-year period. Three-quarters of this total were sentenced in Britain, though this included about 6,000 Irish who had crossed the Channel in search of work. The majority of these British convicts were products of a growing urban criminal sub-culture. The surge of urbanisation flowing from the Industrial Revolution, and the corresponding dislocation of rural life, swelled the ranks of the migratory poor. As the problems of maintaining law and order increased, so did the opportunities for crime, both casual and organised. At the time when Henry Mayhew was reporting on the London poor, it has been estimated that the criminal element ('street people, thieves, beggars and prostitutes')[2] constituted at least 5 per cent of the city's population. The members of this group were often nomadic and without stable relationships, but were in some measure sustained by the sub-culture and its social code. Whatever the links between industrialisation and the perceived growth of crime, the criminal sub-culture which emerged was often self-perpetuating: the children of the street were soon socialised into its ways. The world that Dickens so luridly depicted in *Oliver Twist* is part of the cultural heritage of colonial Australia.

London provided a disproportionate percentage of convicts; others came from the new urban conglomerations of the north. Possibly two-thirds already had a previous conviction against them.

Most had committed some form of theft, ranging from burglary to shoplifting or pickpocketing. Sometimes the offences appear trivial, but the courts often took into account the offender's reputation and other crimes of which he or she was suspected. Of the rural convicts probably no more than 300 were convicted of poaching, and these were more likely to have been members of organised poaching gangs than hungry labourers. In a category of their own were some 1,000 political prisoners: the most famous, perhaps, were the six Tolpuddle martyrs of 1834, whose offence was their determination to found a trade union. Overall it must be remembered that three out of five convicts were transported after 1830, when the penal laws were being reformed; they tended to be more serious offenders than those despatched earlier.

Relatively few convicts came from Scotland, where the rate of transportation was much lower than in England: correspondingly, the Scottish convicts were usually guilty of more serious offences. The Irish, however, were different. About a quarter of the convicts were transported direct from Ireland, thus forming a significant and distinctive ethnic minority. The typical Irish male convict was older than his British counterpart, and he was more likely to be married; he was also more likely to have had some contact with religion. Although a substantial minority came from Dublin, the majority were rural offenders, and a significant number of these were guilty of crimes which stemmed from agrarian protest. There often seemed little redress for the misery and squalor of the Irish peasants, oppressed by what they saw as a foreign gentry and a foreign church, other than through the rebellious activities of secret societies such as the White-Boys. Even the many who were convicted of more conventional crimes were likely, when transported, to be fortified by a sense of cultural protest, for the law which sentenced them was an alien British law.

Convict society was predominantly male, yet women were always there. The First Fleet included 191 female convicts (and thirteen of their children), and the *Lady Juliana* which followed the Fleet in 1789 was specifically hired to transport women. Only one-sixth of the British convicts were women, in contrast to a quarter of the Irish. Taking into account Irish women sentenced in Britain, three out of eight female convicts were Irish.

Most of the women claimed to be single, and nearly all were listed as domestic servants; they were usually convicted of some form of larceny. Some were noted as being, as the phrase went, 'on the town', but prostitution itself was not an offence carrying transportation. The colonial gaolers saw the female convicts as a bad lot, but this condemnation often seemed to derive from the shocked realisation that these women contemptuously disregarded middle-class notions of feminity. The society in which they had moved had placed little store on marriage and family, but a disdain for such values was more reprehensible if exhibited by women than by men. If, in the colonies, the female convicts aspired to marriage it was for decidedly practical reasons.

While, overall, the criminal sub-culture of industrialised Britain was the most important source of convict values, the significant element of Irish protest must also be recognised. For all the apparent sameness of the convicts, when viewed in terms of offences, they were more diverse than their masters might have allowed. The political prisoners, whether British or Irish, added an ideological strain, and the educated convicts, though relatively few, often gained a special importance in the colonial setting. What all the convicts shared was the stigma which society had stamped upon them: they were outcasts, banished to the end of the earth.

Those who policed the penal colonies of New South Wales and Van Diemen's Land were also a mixed lot. The colonial governors were usually naval or military career officers, who had often grown up in the service. Only a few, like Sir Thomas Brisbane, came from families of rank: most had relatively humble backgrounds. Phillip's father was a language teacher, Hunter's a captain in the merchant navy; King (the Lieutenant whose first impressions of Botany Bay we have noted) was the son of a draper, while Bligh's father was a customs officer, and Macquarie's a poor tenant farmer. Such men advanced in the services through dint of application and benefit of patronage. The going was not always easy – Hunter, for example, was forty-three before he even got his commission – but the Napoleonic wars offered unusual opportunities for self-made men in the services. They were to provide suitable material for gover-norships of the Australian colonies, convict or free, which were hardly posts as prestigious as Canada or Jamaica. Lord Auckland said of Hindmarsh, when appointing him to South Australia, that he was 'zealous, good-tempered, anxious to do right, brave and well used to hardship – perhaps not remarkably clever, but altogether, not unsuited to the conduct of a new colony'.[3] For someone like Ralph Darling, who had worked assiduously at his army career as an administrator, an appointment to New South Wales, which hinged on the support of the Duke of York, was an advancement; his wife, Eliza, wrote enthusiastically to her brother, 'Come with us, if we should go to "Bottomless Bay" which is still our favourite scheme if it can be accomplished.' On the other hand, Sir Charles Hotham, who had enjoyed a more glamorous career as a naval officer and diplomat, was dismayed by the offer of the governorship of Victoria in 1854, and set off 'with a sorrowful heart'.[4]

The governor was not necessarily helped by his subordinate officers who could often be difficult and disputatious. Ross, Phillip's lieutenant-governor and a major in the marines, was a thorn in the governor's side; a subordinate described him as 'without exception the most disagreeable commanding officer I ever knew'.[5] The officers were the first subsidised settlers of the colony, benefiting both from land grants and the labour of the convicts assigned to them.

The rank and file soldiers, particularly those of the New South Wales Corps formed in 1789, often had much in common with their charges. Some were forced into the Corps as a result of court-martial sentences. It was a standard practice for offending soldiers to be offered service in the Corps as an alternative to imprisonment. And from as early as 1793 ex-convicts in the colony were being recruited. Most members of the Corps had been labourers, and in social background were not so very different from the convicts, except that more came originally from the country and smaller towns. It was not uncommon for officers to denigrate their soldiers – Wellington cynically called his army 'the mere scum of the earth'[6] – and colonial service, with its connotations of banishment and disease, was considered fit for the worst. Many were bludgeoned into enlistment by the same social and economic conditions which had educated the convicts in the ways of crime.

These were not seen as encouraging ingredients for a new society. From the very beginning the need was felt for free settlers. 'If fifty farmers were sent out with their families', Phillip wrote to Under-Secretary Nepean in 1788, 'they would do more in one year in rendering this colony independent of the mother country, *as to provisions*, than a thousand convicts'.[7] Phillip assumed that such farmers would not simply come, but would have to be 'sent out'; thus was already implied a central and continuing theme in Australian history. Just as the convicts and soldiers were conscripted colonists, so later immigrants had to be mobilised by various means; the Australian colonies could not, in ordinary circumstances, expect immigration to develop as a natural phenomenon. Why should any European emigrant consider a six-month journey around the world, when North America was so tempting, cheap and close? Moreover the seedy reputation of 'Botany Bay', peopled by Britain's social rejects, was almost designed to discourage free immigrants.

As early as 1792 a few free immigrants were given passages, grants of land and the promise of convict labour. In the trickle of migration which followed were some settlers who had carefully sized up the prospects for economic advancement. Land and labour were the chief enticements. Possessed of some capital they were prepared to ignore distance and depravity if the colonial rewards seemed good enough. The end of the Napoleonic wars in 1815 saw not only more limited opportunities for careers in the services but also an agricultural recession: emigration now came to be seen as an option by more marginal members of the gentry and middle class. So in 1829 Thomas Henty, father of seven sons and a daughter, calculated there were more opportunities for his family in distant Australia, for, as his son put it, 'what can we do in England with £10,000 amongst all of us.' The Hentys were also comforted by the belief that, as an Old Sussex family,* 'immediately we get there we shall be placed in the first Rank in Society'.[8] A colony as socially impoverished as New South Wales at least offered a gentleman the prospect that he would be one of the select few. The Swan River Colony, which was founded as a free settlement in 1829 and which at first caught the eye of the Hentys, was specifically designed to attract private settlers with capital.

In 1857 *Blackwood's Edinburgh Magazine* remarked that 'the Australian colonies and New Zealand absorb many of the younger sons of the gentry, who despair of obtaining adequate employment at home, owing to the great competition and overcrowded state of the learned professions'.[9] There was also that archetypal figure, the remittance man – banished, like a convict de luxe, to spare his family embarrassment. Yet it is possible, as the case of the Hentys illustrates, to exaggerate the gentility of many of the free settlers. Wakefield, the theorist of colonisation, who wrote his *Letter from Sydney* whilst languishing in a London gaol, identified the free settlers ('excellent people in their way, most of them') as 'farmers, army and navy surgeons, subalterns on half pay, and a number of indescribable adventurers from almost the twentieth rank in England'.[10] And overall their numbers were relatively small. After two decades of struggle Western Australia still only had a population of 5,000: the colony then opted to accept convicts. The sig-

---

* Were the Hentys gentry? Their biographer, Marnie Bassett, thinks so, describing them as 'middle gentry'. Geoffrey Bolton considers them 'a more marginal case', while the rigorous Paul de Serville locates them 'at the edge of the gentry in England'.

nificance of these early free settlers lay in the position they carved out for themselves as colonial pioneers, and the claims they made accordingly. Acutely aware of their own marginality in British society they nevertheless expected that in the primitive colonial setting they would naturally receive social recognition. It was, indeed, their relative thinness on the colonial ground that emphasised their social prominence.

Large-scale immigration to the Australian colonies hinged on the devising of schemes and programmes, and this in turn was dependent upon the rise of British sentiment in favour of emigration. At the beginning of the nineteenth century there was still a predisposition to regard emigration as nationally debilitating. But the population expansion associated with the Industrial Revolution, and the economic problems of the coming of peace in 1815, stimulated a new appraisal of the question. As early as 1798 Malthus, in his *Essay on the Principle of Population*, had sounded the alarm about the future facing an over-populated Britain. At first Malthus dismissed emigration as of little consequence in alleviating the problem – essentially his solution was to punish the poor for their sexual irresponsibility by denying them relief – but by 1817 he conceded that emigration might at least be a palliative. The Government began to make experiments in state-aided emigration to Upper Canada and the Cape, a particular champion being Wilmot Horton, Under-Secretary of State for the Colonies, 1822–28. By the 1830s emigration had become a major political concern, a subject for theorists and publicists. Economic depression in Scotland in the late 1830s and early 1840s, where Highland 'clearances' of the crofters coincided with a dramatic local surge in population growth, reinforced the priority accorded emigration; while the Potato Famine which devastated Ireland from 1845 added an even more compelling factor. Thus by the mid-nineteenth century emigration had ceased to be an issue in Britain and Ireland and had become, instead, part of the metropolitan culture. In such a context even the dubious Botany Bay, and its sibling colonies, could hope to reap some migrants.

In 1831 a government-supported scheme of female emigration to New South Wales was instituted, designed to redress the colonial sex imbalance and to take advantage of unemployment amongst women in the agricultural counties; from 1835 men were included. The Colonial Office, not the colony, selected the immigrants, though in practice this responsibility was delegated to charitable institutions. In both Britain and New South Wales the scheme met criticism. Those, like E. G. Wakefield, who were promoting what was called 'systematic' colonisation, saw such emigration as un-scientific and unbalanced, while the colonists complained of the quality and morality of the migrants chosen. Many agreed with the British parliamentarian who labelled such migration as no more than a plan for 'shovelling out paupers'.[11]

The introduction of the bounty sysem in 1835 was a first attempt to tailor migration to the colonists' needs. In theory the bounty was given to the settler to sponsor the migrants he required: in practice the English shipowners did the recruiting, so that the colonies still tended to be consigned to a passive role in immigration policy. Caroline Chisholm's Family Colonization Loan Society, formed in 1849, represented a more specific colonial effort to influence migration. Mrs Chisholm, an ardent campaigner for a family-based society (and, incidentally, a convert to Catholicism), sought to encourage family and female migration, particularly emphasising the need for single women to be morally protected both during the journey and upon arrival. So, too, the Presbyterian minister and controversialist, J. D. Lang, worked hard to promote the migration of respectable Protestants who would be suitable candidates for a prosperous peasantry. Their work helped win Australia a better press in Britain. Dickens, who supported Mrs Chisholm's family colonisation in the pages of *Household Words*, felt no qualms, moral or literary, in consigning two of his problem families, the Micawbers and Peggottys, to remote Australia.

But despite the efforts of the Chisholms and Langs, the initiative in migration planning in the period up to 1851 lay firmly in the mother country rather than the colony. Just as New South Wales had been founded as a receptacle for unwanted convicts, so did Britain develop emigration schemes as a means of alleviating its own social and economic problems. Crime and poverty were exported with little consideration for the kind of new society they might create. The British assumed that a convict society must be a debased one; there were few qualms about also sending paupers there. The difference was, however, that while the convicts had no say in their banishment, the consent of the poor was formally necessary. If, for British leaders, emigration was a matter of 'shovelling out paupers', for the 'paupers' themselves the decision to go was always an emotionally demanding one. Many colonists thus had mixed feelings towards their former home, welcoming the opportunity to escape from it, yet perhaps resenting the pressures placed upon them to leave familiar faces and surroundings. It might be surmised

2.2 David Davies' 'From a distant land' (1889) is a genre piece, painted by him when he was a student at the National Gallery of Victoria Art School. The emigrant reads a letter from home, while through the open door is glimpsed the postman and a fragment of the bush. Note the *Illustrated London News* stuck on the wall and the photograph of a woman, perhaps the writer of the letter. The emigrant is watched by a caged bird.

that those who were most helpless and destitute were least likely to summon up the courage to make the break; one contemporary commentator lamented that 'the idle, the dissolute and the disaffected' could not be induced to migrate.[12]

If New South Wales and Van Diemen's Land were characterised as colonies of convicts and paupers, the settling of South Australia in 1836 represented an attempt to place emigration in a context of systematic colonisation. Wakefield and his supporters dismissed the Swan River venture as ill-conceived, and indeed their criticisms contributed to that colony's difficulties. Wakefield argued that a colony should be visualised as neither a convenient space for surplus population nor a far-flung opportunity for investment, but rather as an 'extension of Britain': emigration should therefore constitute a mixture of all classes. Wakefield's ideal parcel of emigrants comprised all sorts of professionals and workers, including 'farming bailiffs', 'practical miners', botanists, publishers 'and even reviewers', 'clerks innumerable', actors, 'milliners and other female artists', and, as he put it, 'at least, one good Political Economist at each settlement to prevent us [in Australia] from devising an Australasian tariff'.[13] The colony should also be an extension of Britain in its sex ratio, and the ideal emigrant was young and married. Economically, effective colonisation required an equilibrium between capital and labour, which could be achieved by selling land at a price which would attract the potential farmer with capital but at the same time deter the labourer from himself acquiring it too easily. Land sales would finance assisted migration, and the 'sufficient' price would ensure the concentration of settlement which was necessary economically and psychologically.

South Australia in practice did not emerge as Wakefield's ideal colony, but it was nevertheless significantly different from its predecessors. It was unique in having no experience of convict transportation; its promoters also particularly aimed to attract Dissenters who valued civil and religious liberty. If South Australia failed to become, as George Fife Angas hoped, 'the headquarters for the diffusion of Christianity in the Southern hemisphere'[14], its population did include a high proportion of nonconformists who where significantly to influence its social and political character. The colony was to gain a reputation for political radicalism, and Adelaide came to be dubbed 'the city of churches'. South Australia did not replicate British society, and the appeal to Dissenters assumed that it should not: nevertheless its citizens did in a sense perceive their community as an extension of Britain, a province rather than a colony.

By 1850 the total population of the Australian colonies was still well short of half a million. In that year the Port Phillip District won its separation from New South Wales and became the colony of Victoria; Moreton Bay did not graduate as Queensland until 1859. Transportation to New South Wales had been abolished, though it was just about to commence to the Swan River Colony. Van Diemen's Land had to wait till 1852 for an end to transportation, when it immediately sought to expunge its past by being re-christened Tasmania. By mid-century the geographical pattern of Australian settlement, with its six focal centres on the periphery of the continent, had been established.

The discovery of gold in 1851, hot on the heels of the Californian rush, only modified that pattern, but its demographic impact was dramatic. Suddenly the whole nature of British emigration to Australia changed. It was no longer a matter of despatching criminals, 'shovelling out paupers' or methodically constructing an 'exten-

2.3 This picture by the French writer and photographer, Antoine Fauchery, creates a dramatic, carefully arranged image of the excitement of the quest for gold and the masculine swagger of its participants.

sion of Britain'. Overnight the colonies had all the immigrants they desired – and more. Within a decade the population had more than doubled. Victoria, where the most celebrated gold discoveries occurred, was the epicentre of these changes. A mere 77,345 on the eve of the rush, the colony's population expanded to 540,322 in 1861.

According to Carlyle, 'of all the mad pursuits any people ever took up gold digging was the maddest and stupidest'.[15] But mad or stupid, a gold rush was one of the great safety valves for nineteenth-century European society. Even if fuelled by rumour and hysteria, it offered the prospect of riches, an escape from the drab routine of conventional life to a frontier where the exciting lottery of fortune was drawn. Yet the gold rush also partook of the nature of a pilgrimage. Distance was of little consequence, as primitive or exotic places became shrines for fortune seekers. All kinds of people could be affected. In London the Pre-Raphaelite Brotherhood discussed migrating to Victoria as a group, though in the end only a few lesser members went. Gold had magic properties: it could not only make the poor man rich, but also create civilisation in the wilderness. It encouraged, too, the illusion of democracy, for all men seemed equal in the physical labour of extracting it from the ground.

The very nature of a gold rush as a social phenomenon ensured a wide range of immigrants. In the first year or two there were plenty of young single men, who hoped to make a quick fortune and had little intention of staying. Later, as gold created an image of colonial prosperity, the immigrants were more varied. Mechanics, merchants and professional men all saw opportunities beyond the lure of gold itself. The gold rush migrants were better educated than their predecessors, with more drawn from the ranks of the middle class and respectable artisans. They were motivated enough to pay their own fares, and, conditioned by the culture of the gold-rush, were, by definition, acquisitive. According to one historian 'serious-ness of purpose, readiness of emotion, craving for respectability, prudery and sentimentality marked out this generation'.[16] The rum-bustious atmosphere of the goldfields often disguised the bourgeois ambitions of the diggers. Many, too, brought the religious enthu-siasm of the chapel with them. They also brought with them social and political aspirations which had not been met in Britain, where Chartism had recently collapsed. In the wake of the revolutionary tremors of Europe in 1848 there was a new restlessness, which found natural expression in the fluid conditions of a colonial society.

Assisted migration did not altogether cease. Particular needs of the colonial labour market still had to be met. The gold rush also reasserted the male bias of colonial society, for although, as time went by, wives and children often joined diggers on the goldfields, there was an overall preponderance of men. Single women continued to be sought, particularly through Sidney Herbert's Society for the Promotion of Female Emigration, and with the increasing emphasis on respectability even that Victorian phenomenon, the 'distressed gentlewoman', was drawn into the net. Caroline Chisholm con-tinued her work, Dickens urging that family colonisation was the only remedy for the 'curse of gold'.

Yet gold seemed more of a blessing, in that it launched a period of economic expansion and optimism which generated its own immigration. The colonial success story glowed brightly for several decades. The heritage of convictism, though it could not be forgot-ten, was now overtaken by the here-and-now of prosperity. Only the economic collapse and industrial strife of the 1890s undermined that image, and halted the flow of immigrants. The Western Austra-lian gold rush of the 1890s was a local exception, and most of its immigrants came from the eastern colonies rather than overseas.

2.4 St Patrick's Day at Mount Morgan, Queensland, perhaps as late as 1912–13. This occasion was an important affirmation of colonial Irishness, serving a quite different function from the day as observed in Ireland. The sunbaked procession pauses for the benefit of the camera.

Schemes of assisted migration were briefly operating before and after the Great War, but Australia had to wait until after the Second World War for a period of sustained economic growth and immigration to match that of 1851–90.

The process of immigration can also be viewed from another perspective, that of national or regional origins. Up until the Second World War it was one of the myths of official propaganda that Australia was a racially homogeneous society, basically of British stock. Not only did this disregard the peculiar situation of Irish (who, against their will, were designated 'British'), but it also ignored the importance of the ethnic differences within Britain. England, Scotland and Wales all contributed to colonial society, but they were not reproduced in Australia as separate territorial entities. Britons travelling to Australia in the mid and later nineteenth century often remarked on the sense of cultural familiarity, but what they were experiencing was a kind of 'British' amalgam which did not exist in Britain itself.

Assisted migration reinforced the Irish colonial presence, dating from convict times. Although middle-class Protestants were wont to jeer at the single Irish women who were shipped into the colonies, characterising them as slovenly and stupid, they still engaged them as domestic servants. There were also Irish on the goldfields, and the leader of the Eureka rebellion of 1854, when the diggers mobilised in protest against the administration and briefly raised the republican Southern Cross flag, was one Peter Lalor. For various reasons the Irish in Australia retained for longer than other migrant groups a sense of their cultural identity. Nevertheless, although there were rural pockets with an Irish flavour, and although the inner suburbs of the cities boasted relatively large numbers of Catholics, the Irish spread out fairly evenly across the continent. Fewer Irish convicts were sent to Tasmania, and South Australia's Protestant origins gave it a smaller proportion of Catholics, but overall the Irish and their descendants came to constitute about a quarter of the total population.

The Scots made up for their relative sparseness among the convicts by later assisted and unassisted migration. In early years Scottish settlers were attracted to Van Diemen's Land, whilst later on they were noticeable in districts which offered prospects for pastoralism such as the Western District and Gippsland in Victoria and the Darling Downs in Queensland. They were generally better educated than other migrants, and many coming from the Highlands had useful farming experience. Yet they, too, were soon dispersed throughout the colonies, though as a proportion of the population they remained significantly higher in Victoria. On the other hand, the Cornish were often prominent in mining communities, particularly in the copper mines of South Australia and the gold mines of Bendigo in Victoria. And whilst European migration to Australia was small, significant numbers of Germans were attracted to South Australia and Queensland. Such differences between the colonies in ethnic composition were subtle, yet nevertheless had cultural implications.

Overseas-born in Australia, 1891. Percentage in each colony

Colony	English	Scottish	Irish	Welsh	German	Scandin-avian	Other European
N .S.W.	52.2	13.0	26.3	1.8	3.3	1.6	1.8
Vic.	49.1	15.7	26.5	1.5	3.3	1.5	2.4
Qld	45.5	13.5	26.1	1.3	9.1	3.1	1.4
S.A.	58.2	11.0	18.5	1.8	9.0	1.2	1.3
W.A. (1901)	43.0	11.3	21.0	1.7	3.2	3.1	5.7
Tas.	60.0	13.5	20.0	1.2	3.3	1.2	0.8

More noticeable was the introduction of a Chinese minority. Small numbers of Asian 'coolies' had been imported before 1851 as indentured labour for the pastoral frontier, but the influx of free Chinese immigrants, lured like others by gold, caused alarm. Mostly Cantonese, they came from provinces unsettled by European penetration: at first Victoria was most affected, and in 1859 they represented 8 per cent of the total population, but, because there were few women among them, a substantial 20 per cent of the colony's men. Subsequently several thousand moved on to other colonies, and total numbers declined as some returned to China. However, as an exotic and self-contained community, the Chinese provided, at a time of economic competition and social dislocation, a convenient focus for European fear and resentment. Thus was added a new element to the colonies' pattern of race relations.

It is a truism that migrants bring with them cultural baggage; on arrival they unpack it and use it to furnish their surroundings. But just as in a new land all sorts of compromises have to be made with a strange environment, so in a new society accommodations have to be reached with *other* migrants, of differing backgrounds, who may, at close quarters, be equally strange. In this sense the newness of the society lies precisely in the uniqueness of its composition.

To outline the patterns of immigration which formed colonial society is already to suggest many of its cultural tensions. So the convict origins of New South Wales and subsequent free immigration created a set of dilemmas. How were the penal requirements of a gaol and the economic health of a colony to be reconciled? How should convict and free co-exist? Similarly the male character of early colonial society, and the attempts made to provide a female balance, point to a sexual tension. The frontier elevated male values, which were to be the source of much popular mythology. Yet almost from the beginning women were perceived as a necessary civilising influence. They were what Caroline Chisholm called 'God's police', an image which suggests that while men indulged in the showy exploits of pioneering, women were busy creating the real social order. As for the tensions of British society itself, they took on a new meaning in the antipodes. Class attitudes lacked much of the institutional order which helped sustain them at home: social relationships had to be worked out in new terms at the colonial level. And the hostility between Irish and English, although virile enough to travel the globe, took on a new cultural significance when transposed to a colonial setting; for the conflict, although so distant from its source, was ostensibly conducted on more equal terms.

It is possible to see a colonial society as a fragment of its metropolitan parent, the nature of the fragment determining much of its subsequent development. Thus Australia has been seen as a child of the Industrial Revolution, its history characterised by an urban radicalism which has been inhospitable alike to American-style individualism and ideological socialism. While this contains a kernel of truth, it over-simplifies. The Australian fragment was neither a clone nor a miniature of the parent society: it was never, in representative social terms, the extension of Britain which Wakefield had hoped for. Rather, it constituted disparate elements of the old society, with substantial numbers of dispensable convicts and 'paupers' offset by an array of immigrants who, whether members of the middle class seeking land and professional opportunities, or gold-diggers bent on adventure and fortune, shared more of a sense of autonomy over their lives.

The colonial fragment was not created in one moment, say 26 January 1788, but by a process of immigration over time. And although the fragment soon took on a life of its own, it remained within the orbit of its creator and susceptible to its continuing influence. For colonisation is a relationship, even a *mentalité*, and one from which Australia has found it difficult to escape.

Part 2

Interactions: 1788–1901

3

The environment

'There are few things more pleasing than the contemplation of order and useful arrangement, arising gradually out of tumult and confusion, and perhaps this satisfaction cannot anywhere be more fully enjoyed than where a settlement of civilised people is fixing itself upon a newly discovered or savage coast.' Such were the sentiments expressed by the author of *The Voyage of Governor Arthur Phillip to Botany Bay* in 1789. The 'tumult and confusion' lay as much in the disorder of nature as in the pioneering assault of that 'civilised people' on the 'savage coast'.[1] Phillip and his colleagues brought with them decidedly eighteenth-century notions of 'order and useful arrangement'. However stultified the colony might have seemed in its first few hesitant years, when there was a real struggle for survival, it was remarkable how quickly the colonists made an imprint on the new land. Once the axes got to work a process had begun which would transform much of the continent, and, in doing so, undermine the society of its original inhabitants.

It is an enduring cultural myth that Europeans found the Australian environment hostile, alien, oppressive, and that they had great difficulty in coming to terms with it aesthetically. Part of the appeal of such a myth lies in its dramatic power, particularly in contrasting the largeness of the continent with the relative smallness, even today, of the European presence. It has found expression in the work of many writers (less so with painters). Yet the myth is far from accurate: it confuses not only the various levels of perception, but experiences which have quite different cultural contexts. But a myth, once established in the national pantheon, acquires a certain power to sustain itself; it becomes an all too convenient landmark for the creative artist or social interpreter.

It should not be surprising that colonists, used to the long, cold winters of northern Europe, found virtues in the temperate climate of the Australian seaboard. The winters were relatively mild, and there was plenty of sunshine. Watkin Tench, a member of the First Fleet, described the climate as 'salubrious', which was to become a favourite adjective. J. T. Bigge, who visited as a royal commissioner investigating transportation in 1819–21, thought that 'the great charm in the Colony of New South Wales ... is the beauty of its climate'; indeed he seemed to think it too good for the convicts, recommending that more should be sent to the sub-tropical north where labour would be more 'oppressive'. (But even when northern Queensland came to be settled, the colonists who ventured there did not complain unduly about the tropical climate; only later did its suitability for the white man become an issue.) To the explorer Sturt, travelling the Murray River, it was 'a climate, so soft that man scarcely requires a dwelling, and so enchanting that few have left it but with regret'; indeed, it was positively regenerative, for 'the spirit must necessarily be acted upon – and the heart feels lighter'. So, too, another settler declared: 'In England, we exist, here we feel we are alive.'[2] Australia soon gained a reputation for having a healthy climate, often prescribed by British and Irish doctors for the sickly or delicate.

The summer heat was a cause for complaint, though it was more on the grounds of discomfort than any ill effects. The residents of Sydney were puzzled by the sudden hot westerlies that would blow in, incongruously it seemed, from the Blue Mountains. The intrusive northerlies of Melbourne and Adelaide, which caused temperatures to rocket, likewise displeased the immigrants. It became the fashion for many of Melbourne's well-to-do to repair to Mount Macedon (where the governor maintained a residence) or even cooler Tasmania in the summer months. And when the infant trade union movement was fighting to establish the eight-hour day as a colonial institution, it argued that summer conditions were an important consideration. It took several generations – and the twentieth century rise of the beach culture – for summer to become the preferred season.

Another reservation about the weather was its capriciousness. Dramatic changes in wind direction and temperature were not uncommon, particularly in Melbourne which gained a special reputation for having unpredictable weather. Changeableness became a more serious concern when viewed over the long term. The settlers of New South Wales experienced their first drought in 1790. With no records and little information they were ill-equipped to cope with such a phenomenon; likewise the extent of floods took them by

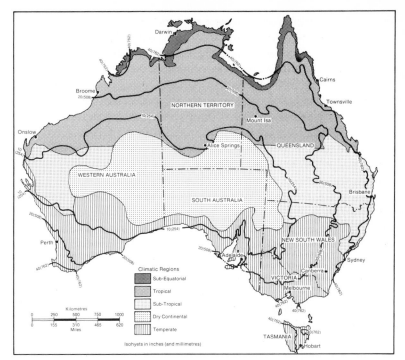

Map 3   Climatic regions

surprise. Later on, when settlement spread, a few good seasons would often encourage the farming of regions which proved un-economic when weather patterns changed.

This apparent waywardness of the climate did not detract, however, from the day-to-day pleasures of an environment which was generally temperate, and which gave opportunities for out-doors recreation unknown in Britain or Ireland. It was also a stimu-lating environment for anyone with an interest in the natural sciences. Australia, last of the continents, was likened by the convict painter, Thomas Watling, to a 'luxuriant museum'.[3] Cook had aptly named 'Botany Bay', and the involvement of the botanist Banks, who was president of the Royal Society 1778–1820, provided a focus for British interest in the flora and fauna of New South Wales. In 1798 Banks sent out his own botanist collector, George Caley, who reflected the sense of scientific mission when he assured his patron that 'every inch of ground I consider as sacred, and not to be trampled over without being noticed'.[4] Botany was a popular pur-suit for the amateur collector, particularly in an era in which there was such a close nexus between art and the natural sciences. The talents of an artist being required to record natural phenomena there was a sense in which art and science complemented each other; and the aesthetics of landscape were influenced by the scientific interest in the flora which constituted it. Banks himself noted in 1803 that there had been a marked rise in public interest in natural history as 'a favourite pursuit' since 1770.[5] Of the governors, Hunter was a keen naturalist (and sketcher), while Franklin in Van Diemen's Land founded a Natural History Society; Brisbane, on the other hand, was an ardent astronomer, and this was probably a reason for his seeking a governorship in the antipodes.

The collecting of this scientific data was something of an imperial enterprise. For example, the collections of the early botanical investigators usually found their way to the Royal Botanical Gardens at Kew or the British Museum, with the curious result that there was more information about the local flora in Britain than Australia. The British ornithologist and zoologist, John Gould, visited the colonies in 1838–40, bringing his family and a zoological collector, John Gilbert. On his return Gould began publishing the seven volumes of *The Birds of Australia*; Gilbert stayed on, travelling far and wide, and anxiously doing his best for his distant employer. In schoolmasterly tones Gould assured him that 'your good conduct will at all times be remembered and appreciated by me'.[6] The relationship between employer and employee had taken on the character of that between coloniser and colonised.

When it came to an aesthetic appreciation of the landscape there can be little doubt that most colonists found some satisfaction in the 'order and useful arrangement' which they imposed upon it. The young Lieutenant Ralph Clark, surveying the day-old settlement at Sydney Cove, remarked, 'I am much charmed with the place', adding, 'Our tents look pretty among the trees'.[7] The tents begat huts, the huts houses; soon there were farms, and estates with sheep and cattle. The native-born politician, W. C. Wentworth, who as a poet proclaimed Australia as 'a new Britannia in another world', could describe a journey twenty miles from Sydney in these terms: '. . . you are at length gratified with the appearance of a country truly beautiful. An endless variety of hill and dale, clothed in the most luxuriant herbage, and covered with bleating flocks and lowing herds, at length indicate that you are in a region fit to be inhabited by civilized man.'[8] So, too, an Anglo-Irish grazier could boast that with a few years of improvements his property, Pomeroy, near Goulburn, would be 'the gem of Australia in point of picturesque

3.1   This timber house with bark roof is the residence of the first Anglican minister at Roma in Queensland, about 1868. The minister presides on the front verandah, infant on lap, beneath a cockatoo. Little in the way of garden has yet materialised, but the bush is already giving way to settlement. The photographer, Richard Daintree, was a geologist with a special interest in photography.

scenery'.[9] For as J. K. Bennett said, surveying the landscape around Adelaide, there was no 'more interesting scene than to observe a country in the course of being rescued from a state of nature'.[10]

To exploit the land meant in some measure to understand it, if only in terms of the resources it offered. The primitive buildings of the new settlements reflected the first compromises between European technology and Australian materials. The untidy clusters of bark roofs became synonymous with pioneering, though thatching was also used; while twigs woven together, or wattled, and plastered with clay to panel walls, became the popularly known wattle-and-daub construction. (So, incidentally, did the brilliant yellow acacia, which often provided the twigs, come to be called wattle.) Later on the techniques of adobe, cob and pisé were adapted to colonial materials and conditions.

Brick and stone were the desired materials for buildings of substance. While stone was usually to remain something of a luxury, it was a mere three months before New South Wales produced

3.2   'Governor Phillip's House' as depicted by the artist who has been
dubbed 'the Port Jackson Painter'. The formal order of the building and its
garden is emphasised by the naïveté of the artist's presentation – the image
of a doll's house in an untidy landscape. Note the greenhouse to the right of
the house.

its first bricks. In May 1788 Phillip laid the foundation stone for a
governor's residence, and by July the colony's first 'permanent'
building was complete. There being no architect among the First
Fleet, a bricklayer by the name of James Bloodsworth was entrusted
with the job. The residence was originally planned as a modest three
room cottage, but as work commenced confidence increased, and
the result was a two-storey brick house on stone foundations,
roofed with burnt clay shingle tiles. Although hardly a sophisticated
building, this Government House presented the face of eighteenth
century British civilisation – neat, formal, making few concessions
to its surroundings. An early sketch reveals the contrast between
the bare symmetry of its facade and quickly laid-out gardens and the
straggly line of gumtrees on the crest of the hill behind. The building
housed the governor for fifty-seven years, until Gipps persuaded
the stingy Colonial Office that something better was needed, and it
was replaced by a handsome pile in the newly fashionable Gothic
style.

It was not long before Port Jackson had been transformed.
When he walked through the streets of Sydney on 12 January 1836

Charles Darwin thought it 'a magnificent testimony to the power of the British nation'[11], and he congratulated himself on being born an Englishman. Writing in the mid 1840s the convict novelist, James Tucker, looked back to the arrival of his transported hero, Ralph Rashleigh, at Sydney and recalled:

> There were *then* none of those elegant mansions or beautiful villas, with their verdant and ever blooming gardens, which *now* so plentifully meet the eye of the new colonist, affording abundant proofs of the wonted energy of the Anglo-Saxon race, who speedily rescue the most untamed soils from the barbarism of nature and bid the busy sounds of industry and art awaken the silent echoes of every primeval forest in which they are placed.[12]

Here the imagery of 'rescue' is reinforced by the alliance of industry and art in subduing and manipulating the environment. The later mythologising of the bush has obscured the extent to which contemporaries were impressed, like Darwin, by the overnight creation of urban civilisation in the antipodean wilderness. The Melbourne of the gold rushes was an even more dramatic phenomenon than early Sydney: according to William Kelly 'Melbourne, young as she is, is, without doubt, the overtopping wonder of the world'.[13]

Yet even in transforming the environment, concessions were made to it. Georgian buildings, with their urbane formality, responded to the climate by acquiring verandahs.* Apart from the mansions of grander estates, most houses in the bush were bungalows. Later on in Queensland a tropical version of the bungalow, often elevated on stilts, emerged. These adaptations created a local architectural style, but essentially they drew upon a pre-existing European colonial tradition. Both the terms 'bungalow' and 'verandah' entered the English language via India.

Just as there was plenty of room for houses to spread out horizontally, so did Australian cities. A sense of space pervaded urban as much as rural Australia. The planning of Melbourne, and even more so Adelaide, was notable for setting aside large areas for public parks and reserves; Sydney, of course, had the unique natural space of its harbour and waterways. The coming of the railway enabled Australian cities to spread even more generously over the coastal landscape.

* It is said that the first verandahs were built as a means of access to rooms, rather than to provide shade. Even so, climate was a conditioning factor in so far as a verandah rather than an internal hall was deemed appropriate.

But if the colonists were pleased with the humanised environment, whether of pastoral hill and dale or urban munificence, did this imply an aesthetic dissatisfaction with the 'state of nature'? It is not surprising that the success of colonisation should be judged by its capacity to create civilisation in the wilderness, but did this preclude an appreciation of the 'natural' environment?

The myth of the alien environment seems to have had its origin in the perceived contrariety of the new continent, which, even when a cause for amusement, helped nurture the concept of antipodal inversion. The seasons were reversed, with Christmas in the summer and Easter in the autumn. Swans were black, not white; the trees shed their bark and not their leaves; there were egg-laying mammals, scentless flowers and birds which did not sing. Such oddities, even when inaccurately perceived, were popularised, particularly in attempts to interpret the new continent to a distant British audience. Antipodal inversion became a convenient and superficial means of characterising Australia. Well might young Alice, falling down the rabbit-hole, wonder about her arrival at the 'antipathies' where people walked with their heads downwards.

Sometimes the colonists complained that the landscape was – in spite of the oddities it contained – monotonous. There was what Barron Field, a judge and amateur poet, called 'the eternal eucalyptus, with its white bark and its scanty tin-like foliage'[14]; it was a tree guilty of 'unpicturesqueness', particularly in its evergreen denial of the seasons. Often the eucalypt forests seemed 'interminable'. 'Toujours gum', protested one genteel lady traveller.[15] Later, when settlement spread across the mountains and into the interior there was monotony of a different order – of plain, scrub and desert.

The interior, however, was not – and is not – the experience of most Australians. And in spite of the accusations of monotony and the difficulties of coming to terms with evergreens, the colonists were quite capable of approving aspects of the natural landscape, particularly as early exploration revealed more diversity than first impressions had suggested. It is revealing, nevertheless, what kinds of landscape found favour with them. The savannah bushland encountered beyond the Blue Mountains was a particular cause for delight. The country was open enough for a person on horseback to gallop through it, Darwin observed, and in the lush, green valleys 'the scenery was pretty like that of a park'. Even the jaundiced Barron Field hailed it as 'the promised land of Australia, after the wilderness of the Blue Mountains'. In descriptions of such country the image of the park often recurs. For the explorer, Mitchell, a 'vale' he encountered was 'one of the most beautiful spots I ever saw': complete with murmuring stream, it has 'the appearance of a well kept park'. He declared the region which was to become the Western District of Victoria a veritable Eden, 'ready for the immediate reception of civilized man'. Theodore Scott, writing of the country around Adelaide for a British audience, praised 'the rich green plains, not covered by dense forest, but by stately trees, rising here and there from their green foundations in the same way as they do in the noble parks of England'.[16] Such landscapes were not only more accessible, in a literal sense, but also accorded with the neo-classical taste for pastoral order and simplicity. Ironically, the colonists did not appreciate the extent to which such regions had already been 'humanised' by the Aborigines, their park-like appearance owing much to the systematic use of fire.

There was also the appeal of the sublime in nature, which was another element in the neo-classical tradition. While the image of the park suggested a human scale and invited habitation, the sublime, as in the scenery of mountain and waterfall, evoked awe of nature's handiwork. Even though he disparagingly characterised the Blue Mountains as wilderness, Field admitted the views were 'very grand'; and Darwin, looking down into one of the vast, forested valleys, thought such a view was 'quite novel, and extremely magnificent'. 'Magnificent' was also the word that came to Rachel Henning's lips, twenty-five years later: an English, middle-class immigrant who viewed the colony with a critical eye, she wished that she could give her sister 'the least idea of the beauty of the scenery here'.[17] Sometimes such observations would be explicitly placed in a European context: so the explorers Oxley and Mitchell when praising spectacular scenery could both invoke the seventeenth century artist, Salvator Rosa, whose landscapes were seen as epitomising the sublime.

At the same time the growing influence of Romanticism in English culture – reflected in architecture, for example, by the new taste for Gothic – gave an added dimension to the appreciation of wild scenery. Mountains appealed to the Romantic temperament. The founders of Hobart-town, with its mountain backdrop, found the setting beautiful and romantic, while a South Australian colonist, having made the first ascent of Mt Barker, described it as 'a wild and romantic place, well worthy of being the scene of legendary love'. The explorer Eyre, attempting to cross the continent by way of the shores of the Great Australian Bight, and faced with great hardship, could nevertheless find in the line of forbidding cliffs 'grandeur and sublimity'; they had 'the singular and romantic appearance of massive battlements of masonry, supported by huge buttresses'.[18] While neo-classical taste placed great store on the 'picturesque', the very word suggesting how the landscape could be neatly translated into an image on a drawing-room wall, Romanticism demanded a more personal emotional response. Scenery needed to be imaginatively experienced, rather than appreciated in a formal sense.

Changes in European taste thus affected perceptions of the Australian environment: they also affected perceptions of the Aborigines. Primitivist thought, with its archetype of the noble savage, had influenced Cook in his description of Aboriginal life, and it is sometimes evident in the outlook of the first colonists. Just as they

3.3 'Method of Climbing Trees' is the caption to this watercolour. As art historian Bernard Smith has noted, the Port Jackson Painter did not depict Aborigines as noble savages, but he was clearly interested in their habits and pursuits. Note the wildlife in the crudely but effectively represented gum trees: a flying fox, goanna and snake.

3.4   Sir Thomas Mitchell's sketch of 'Talambé – a young native of the Bogan Tribe' – has him in classical pose in a picturesque landscape setting. This highly stylised vision is to be contrasted with the Port Jackson Painter's naïve reportage.

were curious about the flora and fauna, so too did they interest themselves in the way of life of the Aborigines. Early sketches and prints depicted them in various pursuits – canoeing, fishing, hunting, climbing trees – often suggesting a European admiration for the natives' primitive vitality. One Aborigine, Bennelong, captured especially for Governor Phillip, proved a great novelty; in 1792 Phillip took him to England, where he was presented to King George III.

Any such appreciation of the Aborigines was at best superficial, and was usually conditioned by certain assumptions about their cultural, and, ultimately, racial inferiority. It was becoming customary to grade societies according to their form of subsistence, with nomadic, non-agricultural peoples deemed the most inferior. Darwin, being treated to a spear-throwing exhibition, admired the Aborigines' skills, and remarked that 'they appeared far from being such utterly degraded beings as they have usually been represented'. But alas, they would not 'cultivate the ground, or build houses and remain stationary', nor would they even tend a flock of sheep when given to them. They thus failed the civilisation test: 'on the whole they stand some few degrees higher in the scale of civilisation than the Fuegians', which was a dire indictment.*[19] Less

* Writing of Tierra del Fuego Darwin expressed the belief that 'in this extreme part of South America, man exists in a lower state of improvement than in any other part of the world'. Although the Australian was superior to the Fuegian in acquirements, he was possibly inferior in mental capacity.

intelligent observers could dismiss the Aborigines even more easily. Prim young Louisa Clifton, arriving at a Western Australian settlement in 1841, and greeted with two Aborigines dancing, was shocked by 'this display of the degradation of humanity'. 'So thin, so hideous, so filthy; oiled and painted', they did not even look like human beings.[20]

Bennelong's case illustrates the fragility of European interest in the Aborigines. He fell ill in England and seemed 'much broken in spirit'[21]; on his return he found himself unable to adjust to either the old life or the new. He was no longer a novelty, and when he took to drinking this only confirmed the colonists in their developing contempt for the Aborigines.

So long as the penal function of New South Wales remained uppermost there was only limited official incentive for expansion, for a well-contained settlement was seen as necessary for the maintenance of law and order. As it was, the bush was often a temptation for the convicts; within the first few days several had made off into it. Escaped convicts later became the first bushrangers, outlaws who learnt to take advantage of the environment, and who proved a particular problem for the respectable citizenry of New South Wales and Van Diemen's Land.

For the early governors the main pressure for expansion was the need for the good farming land which Sydney itself lacked. Even so, Phillip had been reluctant to allow settlement of the fertile Hawkesbury River. The failure, therefore, to find a way of crossing the Blue Mountains until 1813, although technically frustrating, did not greatly concern the administrators. The relative concentration of the penal colony also helped ensure the pattern of urbanisation which has been a characteristic of Australian society. For a year or two the farming centre of Parramatta was more populous than Sydney, but soon the centralising dynamic took over.

It was the growth of sheep numbers, and the speculation about the possible development of wool as an export commodity, which stimulated the appetite for exploration. The three settlers, Blaxland, Wentworth and Lawson who led the 1813 expedition, were all landowners with an interest in finding new pastures. The Blue Mountains were hardly alpine peaks, but their cragginess had defeated earlier travellers; the 1813 explorers succeeded by following the ridges rather than the valleys. Blaxland's account, written impersonally in the third person, describes how they ascended a summit 'from whence they descried all round forest or grassland, sufficient

3.5 Sturt's Overland Expedition leaving Adelaide, 10 August 1844, by S. T. Gill: an important occasion for the eight-year old colony. Some top hats in evidence; in the foreground to the right are two bemused Aborigines.

in extent, in their opinion, to support the stock of the colony for the next thirty years'.[22]

As early as 1800 Governor King had sent some sample fleeces from the sheep of the soldier landowner, John Macarthur, for the perusal of Banks, but it was some years before significant quantities were exported to Britain. By 1820 the sheep population of New South Wales was 120,000; within a decade it had reached half a million. Once it was clear that the economics of wool production could overcome the disadvantage of distance, the hunger for new land became insatiable. An anxious government attempted to restrain the expansion by setting offical 'limits of location' comprising nineteen counties, but 'squatters' could not be prevented from simply occupying the forbidden lands with their greedy flocks.*

The explorers were the advance guard of this pastoral expansion. Whatever personal dreams lured them on – adventure, fame, self-knowledge – they were acutely aware of the hopes that were pinned on their expeditions. They were members of the educated middle class: as already noted a number were themselves pastoralists, but even more were surveyors, usually in government service. Of some 44 major explorers 24 were English, 8 Scottish (including two born in England), and 9 native born. There were also one

---

* Thus was a squatter distinguished from a landowner. Initially an illegal occupant of the land, the squatter was soon legitimised by license or lease. The term 'squatter' later came to be applied to the landholding class generally.

Irishman, one Pole and one German. The fact that not one appears to have been a Catholic may suggest that exploration was a mission with appeal to the Protestant temperament, but probably has more to do with the simple facts of British (and Irish) social structure. Most of the explorers saw their task as an imperial one: in this sense they were engaged in British, not Australian, exploration. Stuart, reaching the centre of the continent, led his party to the top of a nearby mountain where he planted the British flag, 'the emblem of civil and religious liberty', adding ominously, 'and may it be a sign to the natives that the dawn of liberty, civilisation, and Christianity is about to break upon them'. Even the German, Leichhardt, remarks how his expedition to the north began with a rousing chorus of 'God Save the Queen', 'which has inspired many a British soldier – aye, and many a Prussian too – with courage in the time of danger'.[23]

Often these intrepid travellers were not easy men to get on with. Mitchell, cranky and cantankerous, fought one of the last recorded duels in Sydney; co-leaders of expeditions fell out among themselves, and sometimes there were later squabbles about who discovered what. There was a competitive edge to exploration, and the explorer, when he published his journals, was in the business of promoting his own image. However the early explorers, who opened up the tablelands and slopes which fringe the eastern half of the continent, at least had the satisfaction of rewarding discoveries. Their aesthetic judgements of the countryside were influenced by their appraisal of the land as resource. Even as they praised a stream or range of mountains as 'noble' – it was their favourite adjective of approval – they were imagining the contented communities that would rise in the wake of their journeys.

After the 1830s exploration entered a new phase. It became obsessed with the puzzle of the interior. Where did the rivers flowing inland deposit their waters? Speculation flourished, and the idea of an inland sea became an enticing mirage. Slowly disillusion set in. Many of the rivers petered out in swampy marshes. The aridness of central Australia seemed utterly relentless. For Forrest the country was 'miserable and intolerable', for Warburton 'terrible'. Giles found the desert 'frightful'; Grey remarked on 'the general sterility of Australia'. A member of Sturt's expedition could not find the words to express the sense of desolation: 'Good heavens, did man ever see such country!' Still they stoically continued to civilise the features of the landscape with appropriate British names. Giles apologised for naming a desert spring after his Queen: 'I have no Victoria or Albert Nyanzas, no Tanganyikas, Lualabas, or Zam-

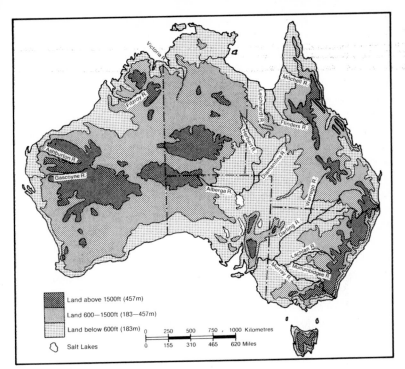

Map 4   Relief and principal rivers

bezes, like the great African travellers, to honour with Her Majesty's name, but the humble offering of a little spring in a hideous desert . . .'. Now and then their bitterness seeped through, with Mt Hopeless, Mt Destruction and Mt Disappointment. Deprived of the glory of great discoveries, they had to console themselves with deeds of heroic survival. The few who did not survive were assured a claim to memory. The Burke and Wills Expedition, which had in 1860 set off from Melbourne in a festive atmosphere for the Gulf of Carpentaria, foundered largely through Burke's incompetence. The two leaders starved to death by Coopers Creek, Wills impassively recording their decline. They could only hope, he wrote, like Mr Micawber, for something to turn up; in the meantime he offered some observations on diet and survival in 'this extraordinary continent'.[24] Leichhardt had been greeted as a national hero when his first major expedition to the north, given up for lost, reached Port Essington after more than a year in the wilderness. Three years later another expedition, in which he planned to cross the continent from east to west, disappeared. Although Burke and Wills were accorded a heroic monument in Melbourne, they tended to be recalled as part of a tale of mishap and mismanagement. Leichhardt's fate had the allure of mystery – as though in vanishing he had become part of the country itself.

The explorers had an ambivalent relationship with the Aborigines. Often they employed them and exploited their knowledge of the bush. Eyre's party included three Aboriginal boys, two of whom deserted, killing the overseer. Eyre completed his epic trek along the Bight with the remaining boy, Wylie; although Eyre had reservations about trusting him he had, ultimately, no cause for complaint. Kennedy, traversing Cape York, was speared by local Aborigines, yet died in the arms of his faithful Jackey Jackey. Gould's ornithologist, John Gilbert, who joined Leichhardt's Port Essington expedition, was killed by an Aborigine; but further on Leichhardt remarked on how 'remarkably kind and attentative' the natives were. Wills, facing the prospect of starvation, sought out the blacks 'intending to test the practicability of living with them, and to see what I could learn as to their ways and manners', but the lessons came too late.[25] The explorers were often dependent on the Aborigines, yet were vulnerable to attacks from them which seemed, from the European point of view, unaccountable. As they trekked through the unfamiliar landscape, stumbling from one tribal land to another, they had little sense of how their actions might be interpreted from an Aboriginal perspective, even though some, like Eyre, were capable of sympathetic appraisals of at least aspects of their culture.

Of course the Aborigines were right to be suspicious of the explorers, for they were the harbingers of pastoral settlement which came to monopolise the environment and left little room for their traditional way of life. The early settlers were remarkably ignorant of the effect of their activities on the Aborigines' food resources; they also failed to appreciate that when one tribe was dislodged from its land, it placed pressure on surrounding tribes. Governor Phillip had been instructed 'to endeavour by every possible means to open an intercourse with the natives, and to conciliate their affections, enjoining all our subjects to live in amity and kindness with them'.[26] But the conflicting demands which Europeans and Aborigines made on the environment precluded amity, and what the Europeans conceived of as kindness could often prove as lethal as outright hostility.

Aboriginal resistance to the European occupation of their land was often fierce, but it tended to be expressed in terms of guerilla warfare. The smallness of the Aboriginal band, and the relative infrequency of tribal meetings, meant that larger military operations on their part were generally not feasible; nevertheless Aboriginal retaliation against the incursions of the settlers ensured that the frontier had, indeed, the character of a war zone. It was an ironic but characteristic colonial device that governments should often employ Native Police to patrol the frontier. 'Troublesome' was the word the settlers used to describe the Aborigines at this time: it was a euphemism which served to draw a veil over not so much Aboriginal resistance as the savagery of the pastoral conquest. The law offered the Aborigines scant protection, and it was, in any case, an alien law. When, in 1838, a massacre of Aborigines at Myall Creek in New South Wales resulted in seven white men being hanged, many colonists were astonished and appalled. Myall Creek is remembered simply because such a prosecution of Europeans was exceptional.

At times the settlers made the pretence of negotiating with Aborigines. The most famous – and laughable – of these exercises was John Batman's 'treaty' with the natives of Port Phillip, when he claimed to purchase 'about 600,000 acres, more or less' in return for the conventional assortment of blankets, implements, looking-glasses and beads.[27] A few pastoralists made an earnest attempt to co-exist with the Aborigines, but the claims of pastoralism made this difficult. As the sheep multiplied, edging out the native animals, the Aborigines' traditional hunting was affected: yet when they killed a sheep they found themselves suddenly accused of stealing. For the European theft was a selective concept. In any case most Europeans could justify the displacement of the Aborigines in terms of their perceived uneconomic use of the land, for, as the *Port Phillip Herald* put it, 'it cannot be improper ... to reclaim their grounds from a useless waste to a state of fertility giving employment to the idle, food to the hungry, and quick sure return to the adventurist capitalist'.[28]

Where pastoralism tightened its grip on the land, destroying Aboriginal food resources and, hence, the Aboriginal economy, the whole structure of their society was threatened. Aborigines were now consigned to a dependent role, and European goodwill was demonstrated by extending them the benefits of the invading culture, in terms of blankets, clothing, provisions and, inevitably, alcohol. All were destructive. For a people used to going naked, the blanket symbolised a loss of physical resilience and a surrender to alien notions of propriety: according to an early historian of Tasmania 'among savages, the blanket has sometimes slain more than the sword'.[29] European food, particularly in its basic frontier form of flour, mutton and tea, was a poor substitute for the Aborigines' nutritious diet, whilst alcohol offered a retreat into oblivion for constitutions unused to coping with its effects. European disease was the ultimate destroyer. Although there is some doubt as to whether the European was entirely responsible for the advent of smallpox (it may also have been introduced by the Macassans from northern Australia) it is clear that a range of European diseases, including influenza, tuberculosis and venereal infections, killed many.

The tribal situation was made worse by a breakdown in Aboriginal reproduction. The European frontier was a male society, and pastoral workers, often convicts, sometimes took 'gins' (black women). Ironically, this might be with the consent of Aboriginal men, who, in a traditional context, could approve such an extension of hospitality. On the frontier this gesture was abused, with the spread of venereal disease, the disruption of tribal relationships and a decline in the Aboriginal birthrate. The mixed-race children of these liaisons had little place in Aboriginal society, and their mothers sometimes killed them.

Such were the brutal realities of a frontier where Europeans could both exterminate and exploit the Aborigines, comparatively free of even the restraints imposed by their own morality. The most extreme example was that offered by Van Diemen's Land, where the entire structure of Aboriginal society was destroyed. The Aboriginal remnants could find no place in the European economy, and were shipped off to nearby islands to wither away.*

Even though so much of traditional society was undermined by the European invasion, the Aborigines did not capitulate; rather they internalised their resistance. This was particularly evident in the fate of Christian missions. From the beginning the settlers had felt some responsibility to impress their religion on the natives. Thus in 1804, in the first few months of the settlement at Hobart, the Reverend Robert Knopwood baptised an Aboriginal child orphaned in an unprovoked assault on a Tasmanian tribal gathering; it was as though Knopwood, recognising his compatriots' guilt, was offering the gift of Christianity as recompense. The Reverend Samuel Marsden, chaplain to the convicts, missionary and pastoralist, saw the Europeans' religious and material culture as a package – one was meaningless without the other. Yet the early Christian missions made little impact, and their failure reinforced the settlers' growing

* In the sense that no full-blood Tasmanians survive, the race was extinguished, but present-day part-blood descendants proclaim their Aboriginality.

3.6 Tasmanian Aborigines at Oyster Cove in the 1860s. The European camera records them with clinical interest, in the expectation of their disappearance. It was a mere sixty years since the arrival of the white man.

belief that the Aborigines were, in a general sense, beyond redemption. Missions in the later nineteenth century were sometimes more successful in providing a haven for Aboriginal communities, but did not escape critical appraisal; in particular, the missionaries' policy of attempting to isolate children from their parents was resented by Aborigines.

The dislocation of Aboriginal society should not obscure the fact that Aborigines developed their own ways of dealing with Europeans, and that although traditional structures often disintegrated, an Aboriginal culture survived. Nor did the horrors of the frontier mean that the Aborigines were not curious about the newcomers and their civilisation, and often anxious to sample it. At times an accommodation might be reached with the whites which afforded Aborigines a measure of cultural self-respect. This was the case with their employment in the northern cattle industry, which allowed them a degree of community and, most importantly, access to their own land and its sacred sites.

From the beginning of settlement there had been a strain of

European thought which countenanced the disappearance of the Aborigines as a race. Darwin himself noted, in the Australian context, that 'the varieties of man seem to act on each other in the same way as different species of animals – the stronger always extirpating the weaker'.[30] Sometimes the Aborigines became a butt for humour, as in J. Brunton Stephens' appalling poem, 'To A Black Gin':

> Most unaesthetical of things terrestial,
> Hadst thou indeed an origin celestial?
> Thy lineaments are positively bestial![31]

At other times a paternal attitude prevailed: Australian melodrama, for example, sometimes portrayed the Aborigine as a devoted, child-like soul, with a handy talent for tracking down bushrangers. But by the late nineteenth century it was generally believed that the Aborigines were a dying race; all that was left to do was to 'smooth the dying pillow'. That the soothsayers were wrong reflects the European failure to understand the Aboriginal psyche: what seemed to them the resignation of defeat proved to be the patience of survival.

If pastoralism was identified with opening up the country for settlement, agriculture was seen as a means of sharing its spoils more equitably. In the early years wheat was grown on the coastal plains, close to the urban centres; South Australia, in particular, took advantage of the gold rushes in neighbouring Victoria and New South Wales to develop markets for its produce. Later, the coming of the railways and experimentation with wheat strains enabled the expansion of wheatfields into the inland slopes and plains. Likewise the introduction of refrigeration opened new markets for meat and dairy produce. In the complex negotiations between Europeans and environment, technology was a lever which gained concessions for the new exploiters. The colonists were usually content to import their technology, but the needs of wheat farming did stimulate a number of innovations, ranging from John Ridley's stripper (1842) to H. V. McKay's production of the combine harvester in the 1880s, while William Farrer's development of suitable wheat strains culminated in the drought-resistant 'Federation' strain of 1901.

Free Selection Acts were meant to encourage the spread of agriculture, but the squatters had no intention of meekly accepting their displacement. The ill-feeling between squatters and selectors (farmers) became part of the rural culture, and provided the setting for Ned Kelly, last of the bushrangers. Kelly and his gang evaded the police for several years in north-east Victoria partly because of bushcraft and daring, but partly because many selectors were tolerant of their exploits, seeing them as directed more at the law-and-order of the squattocracy than at themselves. Kelly also located himself in a tradition of Irish protest. When he donned his primitive armour for his last stand against the police at Glenrowan in 1880, he was already on his way to becoming a folk-lore hero, though for the 'respectable' he remained a horse thief and murderer. The train that brought the police from Melbourne and the telegraph which relayed their messages symbolised the spread of civilisation which was to consign bushranging to a colourful past. The selectors struggled on with mixed results; yet overall, the plain facts of climate, soil and distance continued to limit options, ensuring that the intensive settlement which characterised the United States would remain an illusion for Australia.

As has been remarked, the settlers tended to see their exploitation of the environment as improving it. It was understandable that immigrants would wish to establish around them familiar plants and animals, but acclimatisation also gathered an ideological impetus, and societies devoted to the cause were set up in the 1860s. The introduction of new species was seen as enriching the environment: one Victorian advocate enthused over the combination of 'a virgin country, an Italian climate, and British institutions to lend force and intelligence'.[32]

Yet there was soon the beginning of a concern about at least some of the changes being wrought to the environment. The introduction of the rabbit was a case in point. Astonishingly, early attempts to furnish the bush with rabbits met with little success, but by the time Thomas Austin, an English-born squatter of yeoman background, began to breed rabbits at his Winchelsea estate in Victoria the pastoral environment was congenial to them; his motive was sport, but he succeeded in helping unleash a plague of rabbits which swept across the continent. There were many other examples, ranging from the fox to the prickly pear, but none was to insinuate its way into Australian culture as dramatically as the rabbit. On the other hand while colonists sometimes lamented the decline of native fauna they were slow to act. In 1860 Tasmania legislated to protect black swans and some other birds, but there was often resistance to what were seen as colonial versions of English game laws. In the 1880s the founding of naturalist clubs in the cities evinced a new scientific interest in native fauna, but already some species were either extinct or endangered. The vulner-

3.7   The environmental chaos of the gold diggings, with a dishevelled landscape denuded of trees. This photograph taken at Chewton in Victoria shows the township emerging from more primitive beginnings.

able koala had to wait to the twentieth century to be accorded any protection: as late as 1927 its killing was permitted in Queensland.

Some settlers were worried about the effect of sheep and cattle on natural herbage, but of more dramatic concern was the wholesale destruction of forests. The often indiscriminate clearing of land became an Australian hallmark, and the skeletal remains of ring-barked trees an eerie reminder of the European assault. Mining was also notorious for its appetite for timber, and its mushroom communities often existed in a landscape ruthlessly denuded of trees. But by the 1860s, influenced by the American G. P. Marsh's seminal *Man and Nature*, concern was being expressed at the loss of forest resources and the possible effect on climate. The early assumptions about improvements were giving way to a more critical assessment of the European impact on the environment.

It is possible that this new element of doubt – the sense in which the environment could be seen as taking its revenge on its exploiters – contributed to the myth of the alien land which had taken formal shape by the end of the century. The experience of the explorers in

the interior, and the resistance of Aborigines to European settlement, were certainly factors. It is significant, too, that the 1890s,
during which most of the literary basis to the myth was established,
particularly through the agency of the popular weekly, the *Bulletin*,
was a time of depression and drought, when the early Arcadian
promise had turned sour.

From one perspective the function of the myth was to idealise
the men and women who confronted the environment. Here the
myth has taken different forms. One version, dubbed the Australian
legend, stresses the role of the shearers, the migratory workforce of
the Outback. The peculiar labour needs of pastoralism helped create
a kind of inter-colonial bush proletariat, recruited largely from the
convicts or their sons, the 'Currency Lads'. Convict attitudes such as
anti-authoritarianism and the 'freemasonry of felonry' were transformed by environment, it is argued, into a set of values democratic
and collectivist which are personified in the noble bushman, 'the
national culture-hero'.[33] Another version celebrates the pioneers,
usually identified as the settlers, whether pastoralist or farmer.
Whereas the Australian legend gives the environment a purifying
role, the pioneer variant casts settler and environment as adver-
saries. Assailed by flood, fire, drought and blacks, the settlers eventually 'won' the land. The pioneer tradition could also incorporate
women, while the shearer-derived legend was specifically male.
Indeed as civilisers of the wilderness women could be accorded a
special recognition: as one poet put it, 'The hearts that made the
Nation were the Women of the West'.[34]

It was understandable that such legend-making should usually
present the environment in its starkest form, the outback or never-
Never. But this was not necessarily the landscape which principally
concerned writers and artists, particularly in the early years of
settlement. Yet whatever the scenery they described or painted, the
wielders of pen and brush had to devise, or at least select, modes for
perceiving the strange environment. Antipodal inversion was one
such device, which helped create an emblematic language for the
colonial writer. It sometimes led, quite naturally, to characterising
the Bush in terms of 'weird melancholy'. The classic exposition was
given by the novelist Marcus Clarke in 1874:

In Australia alone is to be found the Grotesque, the Weird, –
the strange scribblings of Nature learning how to write. Some
see beauty in our trees without shade, our flowers without
perfume, our birds who cannot fly, and our beasts who have

not yet learned to walk on all fours. But the dweller in the wilderness acknowledges the subtle charm of this fantastic land of monstrosities. He becomes familiar with the beauty of loneliness. . . . The phantasmagoria of that wild dreamland called the Bush interprets itself, and he begins to understand why free Esau loved his heritage of desert-sand better than all the bountiful richness of Egypt.[35]

Any sense of alienation is here submerged in a Romantic relish in the 'Grotesque' and 'Weird', which owes more than a little to Edgar Allen Poe. So, too, a popular balladist could ask

Ah! who has ever journeyed on a glorious summer night
Through the weird Australian bush-land without feeling of delight?[36]

'Weirdness' could provoke delight; while even the harshest landscape was capable of being romanticised. In her hugely successful account of life on a Northern Territory station, *We of the Never Never*, Mrs Aeneas Gunn wrote of 'that elusive land with an elusive name – a land of dangers and hardships and privations yet loved as few lands are loved – a land that bewitches her people with strange spells and mysteries, until they call sweet bitter and bitter sweet'.[37] Antipodal inversion, surely, in a new guise!

It is more difficult to detect a native tradition of 'weird melancholy' in colonial painting. Partly this was because the painters were something of an international breed, adventurers who toured the world and were more likely to observe European conventions of form and taste. The early depictions of the Australian landscape were influenced by eighteenth-century notions of the picturesque, and sometimes had a propaganda purpose in presenting the colonies to a British audience. Yet the sentiment expressed in the work of an artist such as John Glover seems entirely genuine, and suggests both fascination and satisfaction with the colonial environment. By mid-century Romanticism held sway, but this often dictated a preference for majestic alpine scenery, rather than 'the never-ending plains' of the interior. Although painters were capable of exploiting gloom in the Victorian manner, it is tenuous to interpret this as reflecting alienation.

3.8   John Glover's 'The River Nile, Van Dieman's Land' [*sic.*] is dominated by its representation of gum trees as sinuous and even untidy: yet the scene retains the quality of a pastoral idyll, with Aborigines as unthreatening details.

The emergence of the so-called Heidelberg school of painters in the late 1880s – named after their association with the township which is now a suburb of Melbourne – is often seen as a nationalist beginning. Their instigator, Tom Roberts, had recently returned from Europe with an enthusiasm for painting *en plein air* (in the open air), acquired from the French and English realist schools. In their choice of subject matter Roberts and his friends were influenced on the one hand by the realist espousal of the virtues of rural life, and on the other by a local pictorial tradition of bush life in the photographs and illustrations appearing in periodicals. The landscape they painted tended to be the pastoral country or bush on the outskirts of the cities; they were also attracted to the scenery of beach and sea. There is little sense of hostility in the environment they depicted, for even the melancholy which flavours the work of McCubbin has an affectionate glow to it. Some of their paintings carried deliberate messages, such as Tom Roberts' 'Shearing The Rams', which made a powerful contribution to the elevation of the shearer as a national image. The nationalism attributed to such works represented a fusion of European fashion and local vision. Perhaps the ultimate significance of the Heidelberg painters lay in their affirmation that the landscape was not a static reality: although they were not impressionists (as they have sometimes been loosely dubbed) their landscapes were infused by a celebration of light characteristic of impressionism. The Heidelberg school's painterly infatuation with the sun reflected a new sense of what constituted the Australian environment.

It can be seen, then, that the Australian response to the environment has not been uniform. At one level the colonists took pleasure in the country they found and created. At another level they sought images which dramatised the process of colonisation and, ultimately, nation-building. Through all this they were naturally influenced not only by their own success or failure, but by the prevailing moods of the present British (and European) culture, whether the 'contemplation of order and useful arrangement' which characterised 1788, or the more turbulent Romanticism of the nineteenth century. If

3.9 (a) and (b)   Two contrasting images of rural society. On the left Tom Roberts' 'Shearing the Rams' (1889–90) concentrates on heroic labour in a context suggestive of a frontier culture. Overleaf George Lambert's 'Weighing the Fleece' (painted, a generation later, in 1921) portrays the economic reality, with the squatter assessing the proceeds. In this society there is much more of a sense of hierarchical order. The stylish squatter's daughter, equally at home in town or country, reclines casually on a bale of profitable wool.

'weird melancholy' has become a convenient focus for analysing the colonial response, it is largely because of its ambiguity: it was a comfortable Romantic device for giving the landscape emotional colour, yet it also had a more cosmic potential, suggesting a primeval desolation which was not so much hostile as indifferent to the Europeans.

Ultimately, however, such interpretations tell us as much, if not more, about the colonists as about the environment. Henry Lawson was a writer credited with a central role in developing the popular image of the bush. Lawson celebrated the bushfolk, but was determined to depict the outback as bleak and unrelenting. In one of his stories an expatriate Australian travelling on a coach in New Zealand is asked if Australia is a good country. 'Good country! . . . Why, it's only a mongrel desert, except some bits round the coast. The worst dried-up and God-forsaken country I was ever in.' Later on he declares 'It's the best country to get out of that I was ever in.'[38]

Lawson had had an unhappy bush childhood, the son of a poor selector and his disenchanted wife who longed for the city and its culture. Lawson himself gravitated towards the city, making occasional creative forays into the outback. As a writer he came to hold a grudge against a philistine society which, he felt, did not appreciate its writers; when he went to London in 1900 to seek recognition there, it was not only a conventional salute to the metropolitan culture but also an accusation against his compatriots. Lawson's personal alienation was symbolised by his alcoholism. The character in Lawson's story is very much projecting the author's own attitudes. The Australian environment was for him an inhospitable one. Lawson looked longingly to an almost innocent bush society remote from his own adult experience. Yet as a writer he was also capable of effecting a sentimental resolution to his New Zealand story. Having denigrated his own country for much of the coach trip, the expatriate gets a sudden whiff of gum leaves from some imported trees, which transforms his attitude. When a British tourist joins in with some criticism of Australia, the expatriate springs angrily to its defence. It is, as the title of the story proclaims, 'His Country – After All'.

A more general theme in the idealisation of bush society was a growing disillusion with city life. There had always been a strain in colonial culture which celebrated the urban achievements, and this reached a peak in the 1880s boom growth of 'Marvellous Melbourne'. The economic collapse of the 1890s caused widespread unemployment and poverty which undermined urban confidence.

Many of the city-based writers, who often inhabited a kind of boarding-house bohemia of the depressed inner suburbs, expressed their distaste for 'the foetid air and gritty of the dusty, dirty city', preferring instead what 'Banjo' Paterson called 'the vision splendid of the sunlit plains extended'.[39] Paterson had a rosier view of the bush environment than Lawson, but both associated the city with social malaise. The then radical *Bulletin*, which sponsored many of these writer-journalists, was an apt medium for this message: although enjoying a wide general readership it liked to think of itself as the bushman's bible.

If the idealisation of the bushman – whether shearer or settler – encouraged an image of a correspondingly harsh environment, there was a deeper level at which alienation was always a tempting possibility. Convict origins ensured that a sense of exile was fundamental to the colonial psyche (even if that exile might entail, as we shall see, a kind of liberation). Distance and isolation, both factors in the choice of Botany Bay, reinforced this condition. Whatever the satisfactions of colonial life, any experience of disappointment or disillusion could invoke again the desolation of exile, and such feelings could easily be projected onto the environment.

Such an interpretation is necessarily speculative. It is revealing, nonetheless, that much of the legend-making of the 1890s expressed a strong nostalgia for a romanticised past of dubious authenticity. Convictism was either transmuted or ignored. The idealisation of the bushworker provided a perfect escape from the convict heritage: the convict as victim was displaced by the shearer as an agent of progress and national consciousness. Reverence for pioneers, on the other hand, satisfactorily blocked out convictism altogether, focusing instead on those who settled the land.

The emergence of this mythology did not, therefore, so much reflect social reality as historical need. Not only did its romanticising of the past involve a kind of falsification, but in assuming a tradition of alienation from a harsh environment it paradoxically did a disservice to earlier colonists. There was no single environment to which the colonists responded, but rather a variety of environments, from the bays and inlets of Sydney Harbour to the deserts of central Australia. The process and pattern of settlement determined the kind of environment that most colonists found themselves in, but writers and artists made more conscious choices, in which they were as much influenced by shifts in European taste as by any sudden revelation of Australia. It is from the making of such choices that we can gain a sense of the culture, rather than from the images which resulted; for these images have since acquired a patina of cultural meaning which transforms them.

It is impossible to fully understand the colonial response to the environment without a knowledge of the kind of society the colonists built. When writers and artists came to terms with Australia they were coming to terms with themselves, whilst their perceptions of the landscape merged with their perceptions of the society which inhabited and, in a sense, created it.

4

Society

In founding the penal colony of New South Wales Britain rid itself of an immediate problem – but did not solve it. Instead the problem of crime and punishment was exported to the antipodes, and transposed to a colonial setting. Here the problem could take on a different appearance, for the colonial gaol did not return its inmates, after they had served their sentence, to the old society, but delivered them into an improvised local adaptation of it. There were always fears as to how contaminated or corrupt such a community would be, and therefore concern that traditional British institutions were not appropriate to it. Paradoxically this was to give stimulus to colonial moves for the abolition of transportation, particularly once free immigrants had become a significant element. At the same time convictism was an economic system which created powerful interests dedicated to its continuation.

To speak of the colony as a gaol is misleading insofar as it conjures up an image of walls and cells. The convicts were confined not so much by buildings but by a system which attempted, not always successfully, to regulate their employment and conduct. In the early years the government had a great need for convict labour for public works, but soon the majority of convicts were assigned to private settlers. In return for the free labour, the settlers had to feed and clothe their convict servants, thus saving the government money. If the convict misbehaved, the settler could bring the offender before a magistrate, who would usually prescribe a flogging. Unsatisfactory servants would be returned to the government. Convicts with a record of disobedience were banished to what were called the penal settlements, places such as Moreton Bay and, later on, Norfolk Island,* which were designed to be forbidding. Port

* The original colony was abandoned in 1814, following the failure to realise the promise of flax and timber industries. Its redevelopment as a penal settlement was ordered in 1824, but not achieved until the 1830s.

Arthur in Van Diemen's Land came particularly to be identified with the dark side of transportation. A British Select Committee appointed in 1837, and presided over by Molesworth, an opponent of transportation, took relish in describing the 'unmitigated wretchedness' of Port Arthur, which, situated 'on a small and sterile peninsular', was 'guarded, day and night, by soldiers, and by a line of fierce dogs'. According to the chief superintendent of convicts, the prisoners' work was 'of the most incessant and galling description the settlement can produce', while 'any disobedience of orders, turbulence or other misconduct' was 'instantaneously punished by the lash'.[1] By 1870, when Marcus Clarke began the serialised publication of the novel, *His Natural Life*, the days of transportation were long since past (though Port Arthur still had a human residue) but his portrayal of the Gothic horror of the penal settlements became a stereotype image of convictism. Even today, Port Arthur, a picturesque ruin, is capable of sending a shiver down the tourist's spine.

Port Arthur, however, was not the experience of most convicts;

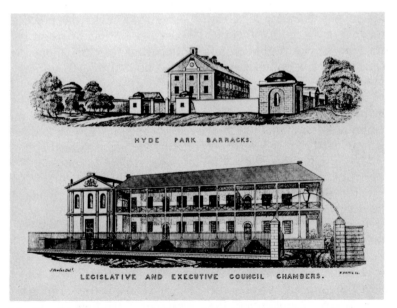

4.1   Two Francis Greenway buildings, both, appropriately enough, on Macquarie Street in Sydney: Greenway, the convict architect, was the great exponent of the colonial Georgian style. These illustrations were published in Joseph Fowles's *Sydney in 1848*.

nor were conditions at the penal settlements as universally dreadful as Clarke depicted. How the convict fared in the colony depended on a range of factors. For a man, skills were important: they were usually in demand, and therefore a convict possessed of them was advantaged. An extreme case was the architect Francis Greenway, transported for forgery, who soon after his arrival in 1814 was in private practice. Within a year or two he was designing buildings for a governor, Macquarie, who was determined to leave his mark on the colony. Other educated convicts and skilled artisans were similarly able to win privileges. Much depended, too, on the luck of assignment. It was not simply a question of good or bad masters, but of the employment involved and its physical location. The master might be the owner of a large estate, intent on following the English gentry model, and consequently treating his convicts rather as traditional servants, even dressing them in livery. Or he might be an ex-convict farmer who would eat – and drink – with his servants, though this familiarity was no guarantee of humane treatment.

It was always a problem to realise the full labour potential of convicts – Phillip had early remarked on the innate indolence of many – so carrots as well as sticks were used. A ticket-of-leave, though not changing legal status, gave the convict the practical freedom of an ordinary worker, whilst a conditional pardon restored the convict's rights but forbade departure from the colony. An absolute pardon, much less frequently conceded, was the ultimate prize.

The convicts were not altogether powerless. They had always the negative capacity to thwart their masters, by offering only the minimum of cooperation. They were servants, not slaves, and not without legal rights; indeed they often tended to assume that they had more rights than the authorities were willing to concede. Nor was it unknown for a magistrate, not from the district, to find in the convict's favour: this was particularly so when the treatment of convicts became a political issue to be manipulated by critics of the government. Transportation was a system capable of being exploited even by those who were theoretically its victims.

For female convicts, however, the choices were fewer. The only work usually available to them was as domestic servants, which placed them under greater surveillance than was the lot of many men. When they offended, they were sent to the Female Factory, where they were subject to more rigorous supervision. (After 1817 women could no longer be flogged.) Female convicts were also the victims of their reputation for being licentious and unruly, and their situation was the more easily overlooked. Yet women were not without their own resources. Given their relative fewness in the colony, their sexuality was a commodity at their disposal. Apart from the prospect of liaisons with those who exercised power, at whatever level, marriage was often seen as a deliverance from servitude. Marriage was officially encouraged, on the grounds that it would improve the morality of the colony, but for female convicts it was a means of improving their own position. Mary Haydock, for example, transported at the age of thirteen for horse-stealing, married, at seventeen, the free settler Thomas Reibey, helping him to become a successful businessman. As his widow she made her own name as a respected figure in colonial commerce. Mrs Reibey's success was unusual, but many other women profited by the marital alliance which rescued them from convict service.

Generally the convicts did not constitute a challenge to authority. In the early years the Irish were under suspicion, particularly after the 1798 rebellion in Ireland. Those fears were briefly realised in 1804 when convicts working at the Castle Hill government farm, many of them Irish, broke out and mobilised a few hundred supporters, but the ill-planned rising was promptly put down. Apart from this episode, and intermittent trouble at the Norfolk Island penal settlement where the impossibility of escape increased tension, the convict system functioned with minimal organised resistance. Settlers' concern about law and order seemed little different from that which characterises any frontier society.

A principal reason for this was that assignment dispersed the convicts, so that only in government service were there groups large enough to provide a focus for rebellion. Moreover the system deliberately played off convict against convict. Informing to the authorities was rewarded by advancing the prospect of a ticket-of-leave, while turning King's evidence gave an offender immunity. The 'freemasonary of felonry' might have operated in day to day relations with masters, but in the larger matters of survival convicts were well versed in treachery to each other. Resistance to the system was expressed either in sporadic gestures (such as rick-burning) or in escape. The system offered plenty of opportunities for the latter, but authorities were secure in the knowledge that unless the escapers turned to bushranging their return to the convict fold was but a question of time. So when despatched to a master, the convict would usually travel unescorted, carrying a pass. The servitude of convictism often did not seem so very different from that of ordinary employment, governed, as it was, by the stringent conditions of the

Masters and Servants Acts. The New South Wales Act, for example, provided for up to six months gaol for a worker found to have breached his contract with his employer.

Governors, officers and free settlers often waxed loud about the moral failings of the convicts, particularly their drunkenness and sexual proclivities; and they saw them as lacking that sense of shame which would have made the spectacle of their excesses more bearable. Yet they, the rulers, were hardly paragons. In the early years many found it easy to overcome their distaste and took convict women as mistresses. For three years after Phillip's departure in 1792 the colony was run by the officers who soon organised themselves a trade monopoly, in which rum gained such an importance as a kind of currency that it served as a nickname for the New South Wales Corps. The officers of this 'Rum Corps' catered for and profited by the thirst of their subjects. Nor did they, and their successors, lack the thirst themselves. A young surgeon arriving at Moreton Bay in 1830 remarked that 'all the officers here are desperate grog-drinkers and cigar smokers'.[2] This might, of course, have been considered almost a condition of colonial service, but a few years earlier Archdeacon Scott, returning to New South Wales, complained more generally that he saw 'the same persons, persuing the same licentious & profligate lives still in authority, setting forth all their bad examples of vice they did when I was here before'.[3]

Such a society was characterised by vexatious personal disputes, often culminating in litigation, and even duels. Bickering might be symptomatic of a small remote community, but personal animosities also became entangled with clashes of interests. A historian of Van Diemen's Land has observed that there were in that colony 'splendid opportunities for embezzlement'[4], but a system in which land and labour were so freely available to those in favour was bound to engender a more pervasive corruption. Interests quickly established proved difficult to dislodge. Successive governors tried to break the grip of the Rum Corps, yet the officers, led by John Macarthur, were so self-assured that they even took it upon themselves in 1808 to depose the unfortunate Governor Bligh when he threatened their position. Thus Bligh, the former captain of the *Bounty*, suffered a second mutiny for which he could hardly be blamed: this was indeed a Rum Rebellion.

As there emerged a class of ex-convicts, emancipists, some of whom attained wealth, if not status, and as the number of free settlers increased, social relationships became more complex. For the officers and settlers, absorbed in their efforts to establish them-

selves as a colonial gentry, it seemed essential to exclude the emancipists, even when rich and successful, from their ranks. Paradoxically, some of these emancipist merchants, like Henry Kable and
Simeon Lord, probably got their start by trading on behalf of the
officer monopolists, whose class aspirations discouraged them from
acting as retailers. They won their fortunes by determination, guile
and, in some cases, sharp practices. Nor were they reluctant to use
the law of which they themselves had been victims: both Lord and
Samuel Terry, two of the great emancipist successes, were remorse-
less litigants.

The achievement of such emancipists was in one sense an
achievement of the transportation system, but it was also an embarrassment. The free settlers, or 'exclusives' as they were sometimes
called, resisted the introduction of trial by jury, fearful that emancipists would be admitted to civil juries; they were alarmed when
Macquarie invited them to his dinner table, and appointed a few as
magistrates. The emancipists threw off any sense of social diffidence
– shame was never part of their make-up – and became a vocal
lobby. They found a leader in W. C. Wentworth, the son of a
surgeon (reputed to have emigrated to avoid conviction for highway
robbery) and a convict mother. Wentworth was an ambitious and
restless figure – he had been little more than a youth when he helped
lead the Blue Mountains expedition – who at first hoped to integrate
himself and his fortunes into the exclusives by marrying a daughter
of John Macarthur. Macarthur had been friendly enough to him, but
was unlikely to have accepted such a marriage; at about this time he
was complaining of the difficulty of marrying off his daughters who
were 'too sensitive and too well principled for this society'.[5] When
Wentworth learnt of his own origins – he had grown up not knowing that his mother, who had died when he was a child, had come to
the colony as a convict – he too appreciated the futility of his
schemes. Instead he took up the emancipist cause, identifying with
their sense of injustice.

So could the convict inheritance poison relationships and stimulate political division. Wentworth and the emancipists were cast as
liberals when they pressed for the extension of British institutions
such as trial by jury and representative government. The exclusives,
conservatively conscious of their numerical weakness, resisted, but
they too were interested in modifying the system of colonial autocracy which gave the governor such apparent power. The governor,
on the other hand, was an unfortunate buffer between a British
government which expected him to implement its policies unques-

tioningly, and a local community for whom he was a convenient scapegoat. He usually ended his term offending one or the other, quite often both.

Overshadowing all, was the future of transportation. It was ironic that much of the pressure for the ending of transportation should come from Britain, from penal reformers on the one hand and Wakefield colonisers on the other. The founding of South Australia in 1836 dramatised the incongruity of free and penal colonies coexisting on the same continent. But the criticism offered of transportation was often misinformed and inconsistent. Sometimes it was attacked for its failure to act as a deterrent, and evidence of successful emancipists could even be cited to suggest that the 'punishment' had its attractions for potential emigrants. Alternatively it was condemned for its inhumanity. The Molesworth Committee, reporting in 1838, neatly resolved this discrepancy by concluding that most people in Britain, whether criminals or administrators of justice, were 'ignorant of the real amount of suffering inflicted upon a transported felon'. Moreover the Committee argued that not only had transportation failed to reform convicts, but it had also corrupted the free, even turning some of the exclusives into 'cruel and hard-hearted slave-owners'.[6] Transportation to New South Wales ceased in 1840; it continued to Van Diemen's Land, but without assignment. Later in the 1840s the British Government attempted a modest revival, but by this time most colonists of New South Wales were convinced that the future lay with free immigration, and a quickly mobilised anti-transportation movement expressed a colonial patriotism which had all the excitement of novelty. So the process of phasing out transportation which had begun in Britain was now continued in the colony itself. As it became clear that there could be no significant moves towards colonial self-government without an end to transportation, the settlers of Van Diemen's Land, already deprived of the benefits of assignment, likewise joined the opposition. Between 1850 and 1868 the final phase of transportation saw less than 10,000 convicts (all men) sent to Western Australia, a colony which, in spite of this infusion of conscript labour, could still identify itself as 'free' in its origins.

Once the end of transportation was recognised as inevitable, the political divisions which the functioning of the system had generated underwent a transformation. Free settlers and well-to-do emancipists, concerned about the distribution of power in a society without convicts, found they had much in common. Similarly the interests of landowners and squatters began to coalesce, in the face

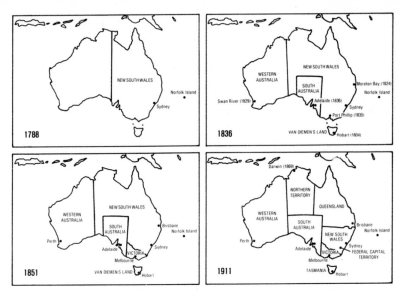

Map 5   Colonial and state boundaries, with principal settlements

of an urban middle-class led movement which, while not pressing for manhood suffrage, was beginning to make democratic demands. In this realignment Wentworth emerged as the leading conservative. With the days of gubernatorial autocracy apparently numbered, the fight was on for control of the infant state. Those who had exploited the convict system were anxious lest others should reap the benefits of self-government.

The ending of transportation encouraged a tendency to forget the embarrassments of convictism; it was almost as if there were a silent consensus to sweep the penal past under the colonial carpet. It had always been possible to turn a blind eye when the occasion demanded it. Thus Bishop Broughton, the first Anglican bishop of Australia, faced with the prospect of a great benefaction from Thomas Moore, a wealthy landowner of humble origins with an ex-convict wife, was able to overcome any qualms: 'I never thought it necessary to go back into former histories, not always a pleasant enquiry in the best of places; and *here* particularly ticklish and dangerous'. In 1855 the visiting actress, Ellen Kean, noted that the 'stain' was a topic to be avoided, and added that 'some of the respectable families are ostentatiously tolerant'.[7] Not only did it become increasingly difficult to maintain old distinctions, but later generations of families with convict ancestry were able, through self-censorship, to obliterate embarrassing memories.

In Van Diemen's Land, however, the psychology of convict society lasted much longer, and the mere adoption of the name Tasmania could not change old ways. Smaller and more isolated than New South Wales, this island community experienced less free immigration, and missed out on the growth of the goldrushes. There had been fewer successful emancipists in Tasmania, with the paradoxical result that there was less pressure for any breaking down of social barriers. In a society which was more hierarchical and paternalistic, the conservative settlers were able to retain their ascendancy for much longer, relatively unimpeded by the challenge of democracy.

But beyond these immediate and discernible effects, it becomes more difficult to assess the cultural legacy of convictism. One of the early myths of colonial society was that the native-born – the 'currency' lads and lasses, distinguished from the 'sterling' or British born – were not only, as one writer put it, 'a fine interesting race'[8], but were so partly because they had renounced their convict parents and their ways. There was certainly evidence that they were healthier than their parents: it was often noted that they were tall and lean, many of them distinguished by fair hair and blue eyes. It is not difficult to detect the environmental influences of climate and diet. Statistics also confirmed that the 'rising generation' was remarkably law-abiding. But the evidence suggests that the myth was inaccurate in depicting the virtuous 'currency' lads and lasses as alienated from their sinful parents. In the first place not all of the 'currency' generation had convict parents (and many, of course, were the children of, in this sense, 'mixed' marriages). But, more importantly, the authorities, however they judged the morality of their charges, gave them pardons and tickets-of-leave, and sometimes grants of land, and thus acknowledged that the system was, at this level, working. The colony offered greater opportunities than the society from which the convicts had come, and seemed also to be more conducive to the formation of relatively stable family relationships than the authorities would allow. That the children were 'free' and their parents ex-convict was of less consequence than the children's lack of direct knowledge of the complex and chaotic society which had shaped their parents' outlook. The contrast drawn between convict and 'currency' generations was one that gave 'respectable' colonists a convenient cause for optimism about the future and was dramatised accordingly. The possible continuities between parents and children were ignored or, at most, hinted at.

There was no one moment in which New South Wales and Van Diemen's Land ceased to be gaols and became free societies. From the very beginning transportation was integrated into the colonial economy, and the hierarchy of a convict society soon coexisted with the normal functioning of an infant capitalist system. The legal system (even without trial by jury) and the press (an independent newspaper was founded in 1824) gave the colonies some of the characteristics of a 'free' society long before representative institutions had been ceded. The antipodean gaol always existed more in the British imagination than in colonial reality.

Nevertheless the establishment of the Swan River Colony and the Wakefield-inspired colony of South Australia challenged the convict orientation of the old New South Wales–Van Diemen's Land axis. The founding of the Port Phillip District, illegally launched by land hungry settlers from Van Diemen's Land, also implied a breakaway from the system, though it was governed as part of New South Wales and had a notable input from convicts and ex-convicts.

The goldrush which began in 1851 in New South Wales and Victoria (as the Port Phillip District was now called) confirmed the end of transportation to eastern Australia. It also created a new human melting pot, as hopeful colonists flocked to the goldfields. The ensuing influx from abroad further confused population patterns. It was no longer possible – Tasmania excepted – to isolate the convict factor. In human terms the goldrush was a uniting experience, and produced a new population amalgam. This is not to say that the goldrush did not in itself create differences between the colonies: Victoria, for example, which had the richest discoveries, was most affected by the European – and Chinese – immigration. Nor is it to say that the growth of the gold years obliterated the convict legacy. The new migrants had, in social terms, to negotiate with the old. The values of convict society may have been diluted, but elements were necessarily incorporated in the new culture.

The century of migration from 1788 to 1890 saw a continuing process of cultural transplantation. Institutions and ideologies were imported from the metropolitan society and planted in the colonial environment. Some took root better than others; some grew into unexpected hybrids. The shape they took determined the social landscape of the Australian colonies.

The family – that institution considered so fundamental to European society – was hardly present in New South Wales in 1788, though children were. It was an early policy to encourage marriage, and there was some response to this, but, as has already been suggested, the convicts saw no particular virtue in the rite, apart from the immediate benefits it might confer, such as freedom for a convict woman. Yet the high rate of illegitimacy which disturbed the authorities was misleading, for many of these children were brought up in family households. Sarah Lyons, for example, transported for shoplifting, arrived at Norfolk Island in 1790, and soon thereafter met Private William Tunks, a marine. They do not appear to have married, and in Reverend Samuel Marsden's notorious female muster of 1806 she was listed as a concubine with two male illegitimate children. Yet she and Tunks cohabited to the end of his days, bringing up a family of three. Son John became a prosperous Parramatta merchant, and called one of his daughters Sarah, who in turn passed the name on to her first-born.

Nevertheless as the number of free settlers increased, and as the institutions which helped purvey bourgeois morality, such as the churches, established themselves, orthodox family values were asserted more confidently. The 'currency' generation observed the rites of marriage much more than their parents. The goldrushes, however, temporarily set back the spreading of family values. Husbands dashed off to the primitive goldfields, leaving wives and children in the cities, and sometimes this separation, theoretically for the benefit of all, became desertion. The influx of immigrants from abroad was heavily male, reinforcing the colonial sex imbalance. The sometimes rorty behaviour of the early diggers – as, for example, in their boisterous acclamation of the legendary entertainer, Lola Montez, whose notorious 'spider dance' seemed tailored for its male audience – was a cause for moral concern.

Such fears were misplaced. The great majority of immigrant diggers had conventional bourgeois ambitions: independence, home and family. Independence was to elude many, but home and family were more easily attained. For those who, in the wake of the goldrushes, took the opportunity offered by the Selection Acts to go on the land, the family was a valuable economic resource, and often a factor in determining ultimate success or failure. A large tribe of kids – not to mention a healthy wife – was a decided advantage, the extra mouths to feed being outweighed by the unpaid labour. The home also became an important ideal in urban Australia with a level of house owner-occupation high by European standards and, in the case of Melbourne, high by American standards as well. From the inauspicious beginnings of Botany Bay, the family had, within a century, become a pillar of colonial society.

4.2 Family respectability in a goldfield setting: a Coolgardie (Western Australia) interior, *circa* 1900. In this cluttered and stagey arrangement, everyone is usefully occupied at music or reading.

There were, however, distinctive features to this emerging family ethos. As is the case for all immigrant communities, families were initially truncated, lacking the extended networks which, even in industrialised Britain, remained important. Letters written home by immigrants often sought to persuade relatives to join them in Australia, and although many of these sincerely extol the attractions of colonial life, it is clear that the need felt for kith and kin was a factor. Chain migration, particularly with the Irish, did alleviate this sense of family impoverishment for some, but Australia was always to be a more daunting prospect for distant relatives than North America. Ties with neighbours, however important, particularly in the pioneer setting, could only be a poor substitute for ties of blood, and parents and children were often thrown in upon themselves. Australian families were characterised as being clannish.

Colonial children soon gained a reputation for being spoilt and undisciplined. It seems that the convict generation were not so much 'bad' parents as indulgent ones, happy for their children to run free. Cunningham, writing in the 1820s, saw the 'currency' lasses as 'children of nature', 'fond of frolicking in the water', whilst those living near the sea 'usually swim and dive like dab-chicks'; he also remarked on the frequent 'sets-to' between 'currency' urchins, attended by seconds, to be witnessed in the streets.[9] Such behaviour was, of course, encouraged by the benign environment, but by mid-nineteenth century the unruliness of children was seen as a problem. It contributed to the concern about urban larrikins, whose street rowdyism upset respectable citizens. Even so, there were some who preferred to see the unruliness of children as spirited independence, and bush children were sometimes idealised as mature beyond their years. The colonial girl in particular, a healthy tomboy who could nevertheless command the maidenly virtues, emerged as a literary and dramatic stereotype. In George Darrell's melodrama, *The Sunny South*, the heroine 'Babs, 'bred in the bush', is a strapping lass with a colourful colonial vocabulary; Mary Grant Bruce's Norah, in the Billabong children's books, offered a later, more refined version.

Sometimes the concern about children simply stemmed from a greater awareness of their presence. Babies abounded, and they were always *there*: the domestic hearth, so sentimentalised in popular Victorian literature, could in the colonies be decidedly noisy. Moreover, as Richard Twopeny noted, the baby went everywhere with its mother: 'he fills railway carriages and omnibuses, obstructs the pavement in perambulators, and is suckled *coram populo* in the Exhibition'.[10] At a middle-class level this was partly explained by the difficulty in finding servants – of which more later – so that mothers were less able to place their children in the care of others. But even upper middle-class families, with servants, had a much more free-for-all atmosphere than their English counterparts. Australia's best known children's book, Ethel Turner's *Seven Little Australians*, celebrates one such household, where in spite of a military father who believes in order and discipline, the rebellious (though, of course, loveable) children refuse to be contained by the nursery.

The demands on mothers were great. Not only did they have the responsibility for child rearing, but often two decades or more of repetitive pregnancies. Yet it has been suggested that within marriage Australian women enjoyed a relatively high status, particularly when a family enterprise such as a farm was concerned. According to the actress, Nellie Stewart, there was no country 'in which the sexes meet on so healthy a plane of frank comradeship'.[11] Certainly the sex imbalance which existed through most of the colonial period gave women a kind of psychological bargaining position when it came to marrying. Trollope, visiting the colonies in 1871–72, remarked how easily his cook was able to make an advantageous marriage. In spite of being so locked into home and child-rearing women gained political rights in Australia much earlier than in Britain, South Australia leading the way with female suffrage in 1894; though this clearly also had something to do with the more politically democratic climate of the colonies.

It may at first seem surprising that there was in the eastern colonies, Tasmania excepted, such a rapid transition from autocracy to democracy – or at least that limited form of democracy based on manhood suffrage which had been introduced by 1858. The agitation for representative institutions before the goldrush included a radical component, nourished particularly by free immigrants, who brought with them a range of British influences including trade unionism and Chartism. The diggers of the 1850s, however, brought a sudden infusion of ideas and expectations. Although they were, in many ways, a transitory population, moving from place to place as new 'rushes' were publicised, and not necessarily expecting to remain in the colonies, they nevertheless formed articulate and politically conscious communities, particularly once the decline of alluvial mining had set in. As early as 1853 the diggers of Bendigo were vocal about their grievances (especially the gold licence and its administration), and soon a wider democratic platform was being invoked to challenge the established colonial interests. On 30 November 1854 angry miners at Ballarat, whose leaders were an international crew of English, Irish, European and American diggers, built a stockade and prepared to defend it. It was a gesture of defiance, and not a revolutionary assault on the government, but the authorities foolishly decided to attack, and in the ensuing brief affray some thirty diggers and five soldiers were killed. Eureka quickly acquired an aura of popular legend – juries would not convict the rebels – and the political implications of such discontent were soon appreciated. Although some conservatives were alarmed at the perceived threat to the old society of landowners, squatters and allied mercantile interests, the democratic concessions offered were a tactical compromise. The Chinese, portrayed as the racial villains of the goldrush, were also a handy scapegoat, and legislation aimed at them to some extent placated the diggers.

Although the colonial parliaments were miniature Westminsters, not all British political institutions were easily transplanted. The party system, so often considered an integral part of the British parliamentary tradition, did not develop until towards the end of the century; only in Victoria, where the goldrushes had caused such ferment, did something resembling liberal and conservative parties take early shape, and then only intermittently. Generally a faction system predominated, with a complex interaction of personalities, issues and localism. In New South Wales Sir Henry Parkes symbolised the nature of the system. A poor but ambitious ivory turner from Birmingham, Parkes emigrated with his wife in 1839 and soon became enmeshed in journalism and radical politics. In his parliamentary career Parkes saw himself as a British free-trade liberal, whose heroes were Cobden, Gladstone and Carlyle. No one could have been more vocal in upholding British parliamentary values, yet no one was better able to operate and exploit the faction system which was the product of the local situation.

It was not that the colonies lacked divisive political issues. The attempts to break the squatters' grip on the land to pave the way for a farming yeomanry caused much strife, and the debate about tariff policy and taxation likewise roused passions, particularly in Victoria which, in an attempt to create industries and jobs, set itself on a protectionist path. But although some saw politics as a struggle between the 'classes' and the 'masses' – which often meant between upper and lower houses – in the popular assemblies alliances of interests shifted too frequently to be cemented in formal parties. The very flux of colonial life, and the competing local interests which sought their share of roads, bridges and, most importantly, railways, militated against party order.

Moreover the period from 1851 to 1890 was characterised, dispute over particular issues notwithstanding, by an underlying social optimism which encouraged the politics of growth rather than division. It might seem that convictism was too easily forgotten, but in enthusiastically taking up fashionable nineteenth century ideas of moral improvement the colonists were recognising that they had particular application to a society with such an inheritance. As early as 1827 a Van Diemen's Land Mechanics' Institute had been established, and the 1850s saw a renewed growth of such institutes dedicated to mutual improvement and the diffusion of useful knowledge. In the 1840s the movement to found a Sydney University began, and it took its first students in 1852. With astonishing and competitive speed Melbourne followed suit, it being argued that the institution of a university for the education of Victoria's youth would 'go far to redeem their adopted country from the social and moral evils with which she is threatened'.[12]

Universities, of course, were for the elite, and even mechanics' institutes, in spite of original intentions, soon became part of the middle-class landscape of urban Australia. While being promoted as appropriate to the democratic colonial environment, the institutes could still acknowledge the inherited structures of class. So the mayor of Geelong could proclaim the social benefits:

> Let them put aside the old fashioned notions of aristocracy, let the people mingle together for their mutual improvement. People of all classes might meet together and deport themselves like ladies and gentlemen and yet each maintain their respective positions in society.[13]

However if they were serious about their mission in a social sense, the improvers had ultimately to look to public education. Given that the hope of the colony lay in the 'rising generation', it was understandable that the importance of education in the convict settlements should be stressed. In both New South Wales and Van Diemen's Land the government helped set up schools, sometimes paying the wages of teachers who were, ironically enough, often convicts or ex-convicts. However in the British context any belief that *all* had a right to education was still, in these early years, deemed not so much controversial as preposterous. Nor did one have to be an upholder of the churches' monopoly of education to be suspicious of a state role, though in the convict colonies circumstances encouraged a dependence on state initiatives. It is therefore not so surprising that as late as 1844 more than half the children of New South Wales were receiving no education. By this time the churches had their schools, and attempts to establish 'national' schools foundered on objections by Anglicans and Catholics to the provision made (or lack of it) for religious instruction.

The goldrush stimulated the demand for education at several levels. The image of a society consumed by disorder and greed encouraged anew the promotion of education as an agent of improvement. But the gold immigrants themselves, generally more literate than their predecessors, also wanted education for their children. The granting of manhood suffrage introduced a dimension of practical politics, summed up in the jibe attributed to Robert Lowe, 'We must educate our masters'.[14] Initially church and state schools coexisted, both supported by government funds. But as the liberals gathered confidence in advocating the national virtues of 'free, compulsory and secular' education, the debate focused not only on the nexus between Church and State, but on the relationships between the churches themselves. In the end state aid to the

4.3 The importance of the school in a new community: this picture was taken at an outfield near the goldmining town of Gulgong in New South Wales in 1872, a time when the provision of education was a major political issue. The photographer, Beaufoy Merlin, worked in the field, formally recording entire townships for the benefit of their residents – families outside their homes, tradesmen in front of their shops etc. Merlin's patron, Bernard Holtermann, was interested in the use of photography to promote emigration to Australia.

churches and their schools was withdrawn; South Australia, with its strong voluntaryist tradition, had led the way in 1851, while Western Australia, then the smallest of the colonies, was the last to make the break in 1895. The colonies were left with a tripartite system of education: private (sometimes, in the English manner, called 'public') schools run, usually, by the Anglican and Protestant churches for the children of the well-to-do; a completely separate and self-contained system of Catholic schools for the children of the Irish-derived community; and the new state system, seen by its promoters as being for 'the people', but in fact for those not catered for by other schools.

This outcome can only be understood in terms of the unique denominational balance of Australian society. In the beginning the Church of England had been attached to the state: it provided chaplains who were under the authority of the governor. No one bothered to spell out whether the Church was 'established' in the

English sense, though this tended to be assumed, not least by the Church itself. Other churches were ignored. Catholics, for example, were without official chaplains for thirty years; but the early fear of Irish sedition, to which Romish priests were seen as contributing, was eventually overtaken by an acceptance that any religion, even Catholicism, should be exploited in controlling the convicts. Furthermore, as convictism receded, and as a population pattern emerged in which Anglicans, even in a nominal sense, did not form a majority, governors found themselves compelled to deal with the different denominations on something like an equal basis.

Sometimes pioneering conditions encouraged a sort of informal ecumenism. For the first few years in Adelaide Presbyterians were content to join the Anglicans for worship; Colonel Light, the surveyor who planned Adelaide, even envisaged a cathedral for the use of all denominations. But as priests, ministers and preachers arrived, and as the churches established their colonial infrastructure, denominational boundaries firmed up. It was a time, too, of dispute within the churches. Rome, to appease the British, had appointed English Benedictines to nurture the faith in Australia, and this naturally enough provoked a struggle to remake the Church in an Irish image. The Presbyterians, among whom the radical J. D. Lang was a disturbing presence, fell out among themselves, even before the Scottish 'Disruption' emigrated to the colonies. The fragmentation of Wesleyanism into several Methodist sects came with their adherents, while the contest between evangelical and tractarian (Anglo-Catholic) movements for the soul of Anglicanism was likewise imported.

Nevertheless in spite of these inner tensions, and in spite of what might have seemed unpromising human material in the convict colonies, the churches were soon integrated into colonial society. Chapels, churches and modest cathedrals were built, and proudly pictured in colonial guides; romantic Gothic and occasionally Romanesque styles became fashionable even with 'nonconformists' (an inherited label which lacked meaning in the colonies). Clergy penetrated the bush, bringing the comforts of the sacraments and the Word to a society which, while it may have been able to cope without them, nevertheless respected these symbols of its culture. Institutions as various as orphanages, bible classes and Sunday schools (these latter particularly important in terms of improving the 'rising generation') all represented aspects of the churches' mission; while the modern temperance movement, with its democratic American origins, had a special reforming role in a society which, it could be said, had been baptised in grog. Although regular church-goers were never to be a majority, church attendances grew steadily through the century, though tapering off towards the end.

The churches, then, pursued improvement in their own way, but they also pursued each other. All the other denominations had reason to dispute Anglican claims to pre-eminence, but Anglicans and Protestants showed a growing concern about Catholic expansionism. The Anglican Bishop Broughton was himself a High Churchman and sympathetic to the tractarians, but he was also an anti-Catholic who, in the wake of the British Catholic Emancipation of 1829, was obsessed with Rome's designs on England. That his own appointment had been stimulated by a Colonial Office decision to let a Roman Catholic bishop into New South Wales increased his sense of the colony being an arena for this religious war. Later the creation of a new Roman hierarchy in England, the Syllabus of Errors and the promulgation of Papal Infallibility all reinforced colonial anti-Catholic sentiment. When, in the course of the colonies' first royal tour in 1868, a neurotic Irishman took a potshot at Prince Alfred, Duke of Edinburgh, the identification of Catholicism with sedition was, for many, confirmed.

The liberal crusade for education for all now became inextricably entangled with sectarian spite. The stridency of Catholic opposition to 'Godless' state education alerted Protestants to the realisation that withdrawal of state aid would harm Rome more than them. Whilst Anglicans were divided on the issue, they too recognised the sectarian benefits. The triumph of secularism was not, therefore, necessarily an indication that 'moral enlightenment' reigned in the colonies, but rather that the tense religious balance made secular solutions the path of least resistance for politicians. Some Protestants hoped that the Catholic community would now be split between those who would have to send their children to state schools and those left with an impoverished Catholic system. In fact education became the Catholic obsession, as funds were raised to build new schools, and the Irish-Australian community turned inwards more than ever. Social prejudice against Catholics was reinforced. While a few Catholics were successful in the professions and in trade (pubs were an understandable favourite), and while the degree of their acceptance varied from colony to colony, most Catholics were confined to working-class or farming occupations, with the public service offering white-collar respectability for some. Sectarianism had always been present in colonial society, as in Britain, but the education settlement institutionalised and embedded it deep in the childhood experience of all Australians.

Thus the way in which the Anglo-Protestant majority and Irish Catholic minority dealt with each other, at all sorts of levels, became part of the colonial culture. Marriage, for example: in the convict years when the churches, Catholic included, had believed that any marriage was better than an illicit union, mixed marriages had been common, but as the Catholic Church became both more aggressive in dogma, and at the same time more sensitive to the Australian Irish community's social vulnerability, mixed marriages were actively discouraged, if not forbidden. Yet they still took place, and posed difficult questions of acceptance or rejection for the families concerned. In work and recreation Protestants and Catholics met and intermingled, yet all the time were increasingly aware of what could be called the etiquette of sectarianism. Religious (and cultural) dispute discreetly manifested itself in the debate on issues such as education and Irish Home Rule, in the gossipy propaganda of electioneering at the local level, or in the internal factionalism of the public service: otherwise for much of the time it was possible to pretend that it did not exist.

The workplace gave rise to its own institutions. An immediate impact of the goldrushes was to create a shortage of labour, and thus an economic climate conducive to the formation of trade unions. High wages attracted many immigrant artisans away from mining, and, infected by the goldfields ethos, they joined together to exploit their market advantage. The eight-hour day was an early success for building tradesmen, who were careful, nevertheless, to draw on the rhetoric of improvement for their cause: the stonemasons, for example, argued that shorter hours would not only be beneficial for the trade, but would 'also tend to improve our social and moral condition'.[15] Eight Hours Day, which celebrated this initial success of craft trade unionism, was to become the symbolic festival of colonial labour.

The founders of trade unions and friendly societies usually drew on British experience. In the case of the Amalgamated Society of Engineers the immigrants simply formed a colonial branch of an imperial union. By the 1870s miners, both of gold and coal, were beginning to organise, and the Amalgamated Miners' Association emerged as one of the first big intercolonial unions. Perhaps most surprising of all was the unionising of the migratory shearers in the later 1880s in what was to become the powerful Australian Workers'

Union. Meanwhile in the cities the growth of trade unionism was reflected in the linking up of individual unions in trades and labour councils. Even though the majority of workers remained outside trade unions the mood of labour leaders was confident. In 1889 the strike of the London dockers provided the occasion for an expression of the colonial labour success story, when the Australian colonies sent about £37,000 to support the strikers, whose cause had won widespread sympathy.

The professions also acquired their organisations. Lawyers and doctors could hope for a higher social status in a fluid society which lacked a traditional aristocracy, but their associations were much concerned with reinforcing their position, particularly in terms of controlling entry. Sometimes they fell out among themselves: competition for hospital honorary appointments caused medical faction fighting, while solicitors and barristers were at loggerheads when the former sought the amalgamation of the profession. Other professionals such as architects, accountants and dentists sought, through their associations, the status and control mechanisms which the lawyers and doctors had. School teachers were organising from the 1870s, partly in response to the creation of new centralised education departments to run the state system. Their associations served some of the functions of a trade union, for the teachers were employees, but also strove to attain the dignity and standards of a profession, though, given the primitive training they received, with less success. The rise of the professions and their associations was a universal aspect of nineteenth century bourgeois society, but in the context of the colonies, where the pecking order was much more negotiable, became crucial. The professional classes grasped the opportunity to establish themselves as a cultural elite, particularly in urban society, while their associations, all the more powerful for being less noticeable, exceeded in effectiveness the trade unions of the workers.

Business lobby groups such as chambers of commerce and manufactures, and associations of particular employers such as coalmine and steamship owners, grew in response to the need to make representations to governments and to deal with trade unions, but only in the the late 1880s were moves made to organise employers more generally. Businessmen, of course, had, along with squatters and professionals, a range of other associations which meshed into their working lives, gentlemen's clubs perhaps being the most significant. And Freemasonry, with a reputation for tolerance which included Jews, even if it in practice excluded Catholics,

4.4 The handsome, classical edifice of Melbourne's Oriental Bank, built in 1857. The pristine grandeur of the temple-like facade contrasts with the primitive state of the street.

was an institution particularly suited to the colonial need for establishing networks of influence.

In trade unions, clubs and lodges the concerns of work and leisure often intertwined. Similarly the societies and institutions dedicated to improvement also catered for the appetite for amusement. Lectures and political addresses – even sermons – were in this sense performances, and the oratorical skills of politicians and clergymen were respected, even when their messages were not. Libraries and galleries were to uplift, but they were also urban landmarks and attractions. On the other hand entertainments such as cycloramas and waxworks, which appealed to the Victorian taste for visual excitement, were often marketed in terms of their instructive value.

The local worthies who strove to civilise their colonial surroundings clung to important symbols of English culture. Thus Redmond Barry, the Anglo-Irish lawyer who did much to found Melbourne's Public Library, felt that it should have on its shelves every work

4.5　In a rapidly changing society photography was an important technological innovation. A rather raffish collection of town characters gathered in front of the studio: the photographer, Beaufoy Merlin, standing at the doorway, hands in pocket, is appropriately more bohemian in appearance.

referred to by Gibbon. The relatively literate colonists of the post-gold era soon gained a reputation for being readers, but the books they read were, naturally enough, mostly imported. Special cheaper colonial editions of books catered for the empire market, of which Australia formed the most lucrative part. It was a cause for concern, however, that the novel – still a frivolous form of literature for many serious persons – was so popular, though the great Victorian exponents of the form were beginning to be acceptable. Dickens was a colonial favourite.

Newspapers were also much devoured, and any town of even modest size came to boast at least one. The new technology in printing, paper-making and communications which made possible, in the second half of the nineteenth century, the rise of the popular (often penny) press gave the city newspapers the opportunity to extend their territorial influence. Based on English models, these papers conveyed much British content to their readers ranging from news to serialised fiction, but they also became organs of colonial influence. Melbourne's *Age*, owned by the evangelising protectionist Scotsman, David Syme, gained for some years a legendary power in Victorian politics which owed much to the extraordinary 90,000 circulation the paper is reputed to have enjoyed by the 1890s.

The strength of the British connexion and the smallness of the local market often made for a tenuous existence for colonial writers. Patronage existed but usually at a low-key level of minor encouragement, or perhaps helping out a needy writer in terms of employment; Parkes, for instance, himself an ardent if untalented rhymester, saw to it that the poet Henry Kendall was given a government job. Local publishers were few, and the authors of colonial novels usually sent their manuscripts off to London. Writing was sometimes a spare-time activity for the reasonably well-to-do or for women who were able to use their marriage as a base; it could also be a cause for struggle and anguish. The writers' perception of colonial society as unresponsive or philistine sometimes compounded more personal problems. The poet Charles Harpur wrote an embittered epitaph for himself about the 'sham age' in which he lived[16]; Kendall and Clarke drank themselves into early graves; Adam Lindsay Gordon, later to be hailed as the 'National Poet' and accorded a bust in Westminster Abbey, simply got up one morning, went out on the beach and shot himself.

Painters had the reassurance of a more specialised market, for it was not long before successful colonists wanted their houses – and themselves – painted. But painting was also less specifically British in a cultural sense, and merely to recite the names of some of the leading painters – von Guérard, Chevalier, Becker, Buvelot, Nerli, Loureiro – suggests the more cosmopolitan context. By the same token many of them were less committed to the colonies and either returned home or moved on to new adventures.

Whilst in music there was a certain deference to German culture – *liedertafels* were formed and German bands were popular – taste tended to follow British example. The Romantic appetite was well catered for by the swelling sounds of choral and organ music, and it has been suggested that the secular choir, an organisation of democratic character which usually appointed its own conductor, was well suited to the colonial temperament. Opera enjoyed a peak of success in the 1860s and 1870s when the company of W. S. Lyster introduced a large repertoire to an often enthusiastic and by no means elite audience.

The leading actor-managers and entrepreneurs came usually

from Britain, sometimes, as in the case of J. C. Williamson, from the USA. They brought with them the traditional repertoire which immigrants were used to, ranging from Shakespeare to pantomime. It was reassuring for many in 1855 when the Irish tragedian, Gustavus Vaughan Brooke, trod the colonial boards: as one critic said of his *Othello*, 'it was a performance such as on leaving our English home we never again expected to witness'. Some like Brooke and Charles and Ellen Kean (who thought it 'a country for artisans not artists')[17] hoped that their tours would restore financial fortunes; others stayed on and became part of the colonial scene.

For some people theatres were raffish places, associated with liquor and painted women. But the leaders of the profession strove hard, in Australia as in England, to establish the respectability of theatre, and many of their dramatic vehicles trod a careful path between popularity and moral sentiment. Pantomime – in spite of the dubious presence of a leggy 'principal boy' and chorus – was family entertainment, with spectacular effects and transformations, whilst melodrama combined sensation and blood-curdle with a cosmic but simple morality. Both pantomime and melodrama were resourcefully adapted to colonial conditions. It was of the essence of English panto that it offered a revue-like commentary on contemporary events, so this compelled some adaptation, but sometimes the colonial creators transposed traditional stories to a local setting. Gulliver, for example, identifies his unfamiliar antipodean surroundings with the aid of very familiar pantomime punning:

No trace of man I can discover yet;
Nothing but trails of horses can I get.
Man's impress in this region seems a failure –
This country must, I think, be Cook's Horse-trail-yer.[18]

Likewise the clichés of melodramatic plotting were placed in a colourful colonial panorama, with a squatter or digger hero, a hearty native-born heroine, a comic 'new chum' and other local stereotypes. Sometimes the bushranger was exploited as a symbol of evil, but colonial adapters found it hard to part with the suave cloak-and-daggery of the conventional villain. These productions were not self-conscious exercises in national drama, but ephemeral entertainments targeted at a popular audience.

A temperate climate was a natural inducement to outdoor leisure activities, but it was the gathering pace of urbanisation which provided the incentive for the development of spectator sport. The gradual introduction of the Saturday half-holiday was a response to the demand for leisure opportunities, but in turn helped create the demand for spectator sport. The early colonists had brought with them traditional British leisure pursuits. The British love of horses, for example, was easily accommodated in the colonial setting, even if it meant, as in the early years at Fremantle, racing horses along the beach; to this was added a colonial passion for gambling which derived at least in part from the fatalism of the convict temperament. But racing as a mass entertainment came later, an event of symbolic importance being the running of the first Melbourne Cup in 1861. A handicap race, it soon acquired a local, and then, more surprisingly, a national popularity. By 1870 there was a crowd of 30,000 attending, and the day itself (at this time a Thursday) was already becoming something of a bank holiday in Melbourne.

Cricket, too, already had a history when the British made their settlement in 1788; indeed, in that very year the Marylebone Cricket Club had set out rules for the game. However as with other sports there was still much variation in the way the game was played, and codification awaited the development of regular and organised competitions. When the first English team came out in 1862 – their tour was promoted by two colonial entrepreneurs – the visitors' eleven would usually play 22 colonists, judged an appropriate handicap. There was enormous public interest, even though the playing relationship between English and colonial resembled that between teacher and student. The first Australian tour of England was made by an Aboriginal team, but although the players were proficient it seemed to be sponsored more for its antipodean oddity. It was not until the 1880s that the rhythm of reciprocal tours was established, and the successful Australian team of 1882 returned from England with, for the first time, the 'ashes' of English cricket. The relationship of friendly but intense imperial rivalry had been set.

It was in football, however, that the most interesting adaptations occurred. In the winter of 1858 a well-known cricketer, T. W. Wills, wrote a jovial letter to a Melbourne journal referring to 'the state of torpor' now enveloping his fellow cricketers, and suggesting the formation of 'a foot-ball club' which would, among other things, 'keep those who were inclined to become stout from having their joints encased in useless superabundant flesh'.[19] What emerged from this call was an enjoyable game between two of Melbourne's new 'public' schools, Scotch College and Church of England Grammar. At this time there were no codified rules for football in England, but Wills, who, although native-born, had been sent to school at Rugby, drew on that experience. However, Wills thought that the Rugby

4.6 (a) and (b)   Two images of the main street. [On the left] Fremantle's High Street, relatively narrow with its imposing verandahs, suggests an intensive urban environment. Much of Fremantle has survived and has been recently restored as a tourist precinct. The main street [on the right], of an unidentified town in northern Queensland, seems to disappear in a nothingness of bush. A solitary figure is making the journey from one side to the other.

game was not entirely suited to the hard Australian grounds, and even from the beginning there seemed to be a conscious preference for a game which, although 'manly', was fast and not unduly rough. So over the next decade Melbourne football evolved its own distinctive rules, and its crowd appeal was early appreciated: in 1863 it was remarked that spectators 'understood it better than cricket; it is more exciting'. One English visitor, while noting a lack of science, admitted that it was 'the fastest game I have ever seen'.[20] Soon the game which had begun as a public school diversion became the principal winter entertainment of suburban Melbourne. When the Heidelberg painter, Streeton, put one such Saturday afternoon on canvas in the late 1880s he called it 'The National Game'. As a Victorian he was exaggerating, for New South Wales and Queensland remained impervious to its appeal, a fact which his compatriots have attributed to a perversity born of colonial rivalry. The more likely explanation is that the stirring of interest in football in Sydney, which had not experienced the goldrush boom of Melbourne, occurred later, when rugby was already codified and, therefore, 'available'. Often the ties between 'Home' (as Britain was called) and colony could be stronger than between, say, Victoria and New South Wales.

The Australian colonies – and particularly Victoria – were in the forefront of the development of spectator sport, and the early crowds attracted to sporting fixtures were high by world standards. It was not simply climate and urbanisation, however, but the dispersed character of Australian cities, with their generous provision of parks and grounds, which so encouraged sport. As a result this subtle fusion of the pursuits of pleasure and excellence became a significant expression of the colonial culture. Sport could nominate heroes – and later on heroines – who could command uncontroversial respect in a society still uncertain, even divided, about its origins and history.

The growth of the cities had been a remarkable feature of the prosperity of the period 1851–90. To contemporaries it often seemed paradoxical, even unhealthy, that an economy dependent on primary product exports, whether mining, pastoral or agricultural, should countenance such a high degree of urbanisation. Mining, of course, itself created urban communities often characterised by intense civic pride even when conditioned by transience; it was also the nature of pastoralism, with large holdings and only intermittent labour needs, which helped reinforce the urbanising process. Agriculture was the main hope for closer settlement but the selection acts met with only limited success. Farming, as has been remarked, so often depended on the family economy, but was then unable to provide a living for all the children when they came to marry. In spite of the export importance of the rural industries, much of the economic growth of this period was in the capital cities. Government and business were heavily centralised in these cities, and only

4.7   These gold-diggers have travelled from Charters Towers in northern
Queensland to Kalgoorlie in Western Australia *circa* 1895, but not,
presumably, on their bicycles. The recently introduced modern bicycle was
understandably popular in the spread-out urban communities of colonial
Australia.

in Queensland and Tasmania was there a measure of decentralisa-
tion. By the end of the century 35 per cent of colonists lived in six
capital cities, and this figure, based on boundaries which often
lagged behind the reality, is probably an underestimate.

The gathering impetus of urbanisation points to another significant feature of this period with cultural implications, namely, the
geographical mobility of much of the population. Immigrants rarely
found their niche the first time; moving was part of the settling
process. Cities of gold mushroomed overnight, some to wither
away again into ghost towns. Diggers sometimes travelled great
distances. The Kalgoorlie rushes of the 1890s brought thousands of
't'other-siders' (as migrants from the east were called) to sleepy
Western Australia; there were even miners who came from Charters
Towers in northern Queensland, circuiting half the continent. Seasonal work, such as shearing, created another sort of migratory
population; in the bush families were used to being separated. The
economic fluctuations of colonies and regions caused complex patterns of migration, and colonists, in the quest for betterment, developed a disregard for distance.

Such a shifting population promoted a degree of cultural integration, but it did not submerge regional identity. Those on the
move were least likely to influence civic institutions, while it was the

older, long-established citizens who usually monopolised positions of authority. It was as if there were two communities, migrants and settlers, whose interests and outlooks did not always coincide. So it was possible that in spite of such movements of population around the continent the six colonies, as political and economic entities, could remain remarkably isolated from each other. When, in 1881, Melbourne and Sydney were linked by rail for the first time, the ceremony at the border symbolised the power of parochialism. The two premiers, Berry and Parkes, were both successful British emigrants, yet seized the occasion to promote the provincial interests of their adopted colonies. Nor could the ceremony disguise the fact that the different rail gauges of Victoria and New South Wales meant that for the next eighty years travellers would have to change at the border – a symbolic acknowledgment of colonial separatism.

Social mobility was the colonial boast, but was in fact problematic. There were certainly success stories, particularly in the early days. George Coppin, for example, was an actor turned entrepreneur who, from the 1840s on, won and lost several fortunes. He also won election to Victoria's elitist Legislative Council, cheekily putting down his occupation as 'comedian'. Coppin, a loyal Freemason, was, according to Ellen Kean, honourable and upright but – and here was the colonial rub – 'a common man'. In one sense the Legislative Councils of the colonies were full of 'self-made men' of the old generation, and it was easy for an English upper-middle-class socialist like Beatrice Webb to characterise Coppin's colleagues as 'a mean undignified set of little property owners, with illiterate speech and ugly manners', just as an earlier radical, George Higinbotham, had called them 'the wealthy lower orders'.[21]

In their first experience of the colonies immigrants often felt that their expectations were justified. 'We are sure of making a comfortable independence for ourselves and being able to put our children in the way of doing so too', wrote Penelope Selby in 1840; 'I never saw my way so clear to Independence as I do now,' affirmed Francis Mapleson in 1854. Yet many were to face at least partial disillusion. As one Irishman observed in 1884 the squatters were still powerful 'so the[y] make the laws to suit themselves like the landlords of Ireland'.[22] Even in the years of prosperity while many immigrants may have found themselves relatively 'comfortable' they were denied the 'independence' emigration seemed to promise. The rise of trade unionism was in itself a recognition that the colonies were, in an economic sense, not so much a new world as a capitalist extension of the old.

4.8   George Coppin, comedian and colonial success story, here in Masonic regalia. No doubt his Masonic connexions were useful to him in his career.

The myth of social mobility also ignored a sizeable minority who were the victims of the colonial enterprise. Aborigines, it went without saying, were not part of the colonists' society, but rather a legacy of the conquered environment. Although a few Chinese were successful as merchants, and others made a competence in market gardens, laundries and furniture making, 'Asiatics' were in effect socially quarantined. Indeed this pattern had been established on the goldfields when they were herded into 'Protectorates'.

But there were others, too, who did not share in the feast. The new manufacturing industries often exploited female labour, and by the 1880s 'sweating' was a problem. Women's 'mobility' was constrained by marriage, children and the very wage discrimination which made their employment attractive to manufacturers. They were also virtually ignored by the trade union movement. Even at times of peak prosperity there were always stubborn pockets of poverty. Furthermore, the myth of social mobility in focusing on the self-made men of the market place failed to acknowledge that in an era marked by the rise of the professions, educational opportunity was crucial. There was at this time almost no provision for secondary education in the state system; indeed, the main interest in educational reform was in the technical sphere, with an emphasis on teaching the sons of the working class appropriate skills.

Yet in spite of the gap between myth and reality, the expectation of mobility, even of a marginal nature, conditioned attitudes to wealth and authority. Colonial manners eschewed servility, and even deference was questioned. It was early remarked that the native-born disliked domestic service, which inherited an association with convict status. It remained largely a female preserve, and the colonial opportunities for marriage further whittled away the labour supply. No matter how much the middle class complained, and sponsored the immigration of single women (particularly Irish), the 'problem' seemed insoluble. Later in the century it was evident that women preferred to work in factories, which, no matter how much exploiting them, were at least sociable places, with their own working-class culture, while to be in domestic service usually meant loneliness (most such households only ran to one servant) in an alien social environment.

Elsewhere colonial society devised subtle mechanisms for accommodating master-servant relationships. Manual labour, with its pioneer heritage, commanded respect, as much from self-made men as workers. Hence even when industrial war raged between squatters and shearers, the Tom Roberts heroic image of 'Shearing the Rams' was still broadly acceptable. It was convenient, in the colonial environment of growth, for both employers and workers to profess that they met as equals, and the workplace developed social rituals quite different from those that operated, say, in the home. It was possible, therefore, for the great majority of colonists to ignore the deprived and disadvantaged and to congratulate themselves that they had truly created 'a workingman's paradise'.

In 1890 a month-long maritime strike, in which the cocksure unions were outmanoeuvred and defeated by a quickly mobilised alliance of employers, signalled the end of an era. Strikes in the shearing and mining industries followed and again the unions were humiliated. The economic climate was changing. The collapse of Melbourne's land boom in 1888 heralded a recession; British investors began to lose confidence in the colonies; and 1893 saw an alarming succession of bank crashes. The depression which had materialised affected all

4.9   George Niné, an Islander labourer, who by 1897 is said to have owned a property. The photograph suggests that he owed something to the Salvation Army which had established a significant colonial presence.

colonies except Western Australia, now experiencing its own gold rush, but Victoria, which had been most infected with the boom mentality, suffered the worst.

This reversal of economic fortunes was much more than a hiccup in a saga of growth. It profoundly shook not only economic but cultural confidence in the broader sense. On the one hand the evaporation of British investment reminded colonists of their dependence on imperial approval. On the other hand unemployment and poverty on a scale unacceptable in a 'workingman's paradise' induced soul-searching and guilt. 'Our prosperity . . . has been our ruin: we became intoxicated by it: it has materialised our lives', bemoaned the Anglican bishop of Brisbane.[23] Moreover, the colonial dream of independence, already fragile, seemed to have been finally shattered. Even some of those who had appeared to control their own destinies, like the squatters, were revealed as being in hock to the land and finance companies.

Economic collapse exposed fissures in colonial society which earlier prosperity had papered over. The railway-assisted growth of middle-class suburbia in Sydney and Melbourne had increasingly left the inner suburbs to become working-class territory, now characterised as slums; in Brisbane and Adelaide there were signs of a similar dichotomy developing. A new bitterness was evident in strikes, sometimes with confrontations – as in the Queensland bush in 1891 and the mining town, Broken Hill, in 1892 – with a whiff of civil war to them. Pastoralists and mine owners invoked the law which arrested and gaoled union leaders. As the trade union movement lost ground industrially, infant labor parties entered the colonial parliaments. In the 1880s trade union leaders had talked about 'direct representation', but now they were motivated to act. The faction system was giving way to party politics, and in this transition the labor party was to play a crucial role. The shifts and movements of colonial society were stabilising into relatively permanent social structures.

Radicals were as much disoriented by the depression as conservatives, but they drew some comfort from the middle-class crisis of conscience. While the *Bulletin*, generally sympathetic to the labour movement, published the odd ballad by Lawson and others with a revolutionary flavour, its idealisation of the bush was a more serious attempt to forge a healing but progressive ethos. The Heidelberg painters struggled to make a living – many evacuated shell-shocked Melbourne for Sydney which at least seemed sunnier – but found reassurance in a sense of cultural mission. Roberts saw it as an important time for painters simply because 'they were getting the last touch of the old colonial days'.[24] In a population in which the native-born now predominated, it was significant that many of the new writers and painters were similarly creatures of the colonial environment.

Yet any pursuit of nationalist themes seemed conditioned by the new pessimism abroad. Particularly was this evident in racial fears. Since the end of transportation there had been an employer lobby which sought the introduction of cheap non-European labour. Attempts were made to ship in Chinese and Indian 'coolies', but from the 1860s attention focused on the Queensland recruitment of indentured labour from the Pacific Islands, 'kanakas' as they were called, particularly for the sugar industry. Such schemes were propped up by a new conviction that the tropical climate was unsuited to the white man, and therefore that white labour could not be relied upon to develop northern Queensland. As has been remarked, this had not worried the early European settlers of the region, but it was more than a local artifice of greedy employers. The new stress on race and environment was evident, for example, in Charles Dilke's *Greater Britain*, in which he depicted the tropics as alien to the white man, even condemning the soft-fleshed banana as a symptom of tropical sloth.

Trade union and liberal opposition to the introduction of Asian or Melanesian labour drew on humanitarian concern about the connotations of slavery, particularly when recruitment was more akin to kidnapping. But more generally it reflected an increasingly strident obsession that the continent should be kept racially pure: beneath its banner, 'Australia for the white man', the *Bulletin* promoted a relentless and vicious brand of jocular racism. This obsession not only consigned the Aborigines to either extinction or irrelevance, but also hounded the local Chinese community. At a time when Chinese numbers were actually declining, hostility to them intensified. Western Australia, for example, legislated to prevent Chinese from settling on its new goldfields. Yet this racial paranoia must also be seen in a broader European context. Imperialism was predicated on notions of racial hierarchy, but even while the European nations scrambled for what was left of Africa, fears were surfacing about the future balance of races. The new racial pessimism was expressed locally in Charles Pearson's *National Life and Character* published – in Britain of course – in 1893. Pearson, an English-born liberal intellectual who had made a great contribution to colonial education and politics, saw the future of Europeans as threatened by the multiplying numbers of the black, brown and yellow races. As a slogan 'Australia for the white man', for all its bravado, reflected a real sense of racial vulnerability, heightened by geographical isolation.

This was part of the context of the federal movement which took shape in the 1890s. A concern about immigration and defence fused with a new belief that federation might improve economic prospects, at least in commanding greater respect on the British money market. Political leaders took up the federal cause with varying degrees of enthusiasm, but the written constitution which emerged was essentially a pragmatic compromise between competing provincial interests. So in Queensland the separatist north wanted federation to reduce its dependence on its distant capital, Brisbane, whilst in Western Australia the 't'othersiders' of the goldfields were advocates partly out of resentment towards the old western Australians who governed them. The strongest resistance to federation was centred in free-trade New South Wales which felt it had least to gain. Although some of its leaders, like Barton and Deakin, saw federalism as a mission, the movement as a whole lacked zest and originality. Federation seemed a reasonable, and perhaps inevitable, outcome for the colonies, rather than a cause worth fighting for. British approval removed even that potential barrier. So when on 1 January 1901 the new Commonwealth was proclaimed in a Sydney park, the good-humoured festivities seemed lacking in patriotic fervour.

It might seem appropriate, even admirable, that Australia should escape the lurid excesses of patriotism, but it raises questions about the kind of society the colonists had created and the loyalties it fostered. The early history of the colonies had been bound up with notions of exile or escape from Britain. Yet the Australian settlements were, or quickly became, an economic frontier for British capitalism in expansionary mood. When Britain conceded self-government it was in the secure knowledge that economic ties were strong enough to sustain the colonial relationship. The complex interactions of race, religion and class which had created a colonial culture had been conditioned by this imperial context. The year 1901 marked little more than the formal birth of the Commonwealth: in one sense 'Australia' already existed, while in that other patriotic sense it would remain curiously problematic. But federation did summon the colonies into a twentieth century in which European events would impinge on them more than ever.

Part 3

The culture: 1901–1939

5

Loyalties

The Boer War began in 1899 just as the colonies were poised to federate: as an imperial experience it was well timed to expose the ambiguities of Australian loyalty. With Britain being portrayed as an imperial bully in Europe, the confrontation with the stubborn Boers was early seen as a test for the Empire. Colonial Secretary Joseph Chamberlain therefore confidentially encouraged the colonies to be forthcoming with offers of support. The governments of the Australian colonies dutifully obliged, many leaders assuming that they could not question British policy; as the premier of Victoria confessed, it was 'difficult for us to say what the merits of this question are, because we are a long way off'. Soon public enthusiasm for the war had been drummed up, contingents despatched; the relief of Mafeking was the occasion for widespread rapture in the streets. Federation converted the war in South Africa into a potentially Australian cause. It seemed to many symbolic that the Commonwealth should be born in this moment of imperial truth. According to one politician, 'the moment the first drop of Australian blood was drawn and the first Australian life lost in South Africa, that moment Australia merged into an integral part of the Empire'.[1]

Yet the rituals of public patriotism disguised small but significant opposition together with elements of discreet apathy. Some radicals and a few Labor members questioned the morality of the British cause, and wondered aloud why the colonies should be expected to contribute to a war about which they had not been consulted. Such criticisms distressed the loyalists, but were at least debated; however they became cause for grave suspicion if voiced by representatives of the Irish Australian community. When Catholic newspapers impugned the war, it mattered little that Catholics nevertheless appeared to be well represented among those volunteering for service. Colonial convention required that the suspicion of Irish disloyalty had to be expressed by inference, and many of the patriotic demonstrations were not so much spontaneous outbursts of imperial loyalty as accusations directed at the silence of the minority. While there is no doubt that the commitment to South Africa commanded the support of a substantial majority, the degree of enthusiasm is more debatable. The *Bulletin* took the unpopular course of opposing the war, yet its circulation did not appear to suffer unduly.

More than 16,000 men went to South Africa, compared to about 6,000 Canadians; the commitment, although small, was more than token. It was enough to give many Australians an agreeable feeling that their country was an active partner in the imperial enterprise. Yet the Australian participation in the war itself exposed a thread of anti-British sentiment. There was British praise for the military performance of the colonials until in 1901 the 5th Victorian Mounted Rifles suffered a bad defeat at Wilmansruist, and their British general was said to have described them as 'white livered curs'.[2] Mutinous mutterings amongst the Victorians led to three soldiers being court-martialled and sentenced to death, though Kitchener commuted the sentences to prison terms. Then in 1902 two Australian lieutenants were executed following court martial convictions for the murder of Boer prisoners and a German missionary. In both cases the Australian government and public were not informed until after the event. Colonial sensitivity about the Wilmansruist defeat gave way to some resentment towards the British military machine. Yet although the Commonwealth government nervously asked questions (which do not appear to have been answered) the three survivors, whose convictions were later quashed, allegedly for legal reasons, proved something of an embarrassment on their return to Australia. In the midst of colonial expressions of imperial enthusiasm they were unhappy reminders of an episode which many preferred to forget.

Nevertheless the South African war encouraged a perception of the distinctive qualities of the Australian soldier – what Lord Roberts had called colonial 'individuality', his bush skills, resourcefulness and lack of military formality. It also encouraged a certain respect for the Boers, dour settlers in a landscape not dissimilar to Australia's. There was a disparity between the official rhetoric of the war and the soldiers' own experience of it. 'Why did we ever come?' asked one disillusioned corporal. 'Where is all the "pomp and circumstance of war"? . . . Where's anything but dirt, and discomfort, and starvation, and nigger-driving? Who wants to participate in a shabby war like this?'[3] For the infant Commonwealth the South

African experience rehearsed the questions of loyalty and war which were to be posed so dramatically in 1914–18.

In the second half of the nineteenth century there had been an element of republicanism in the colonies. As early as 1850 J. D. Lang had urged a republic, and there had been a hint of such sentiment at Eureka. The tendency to see the United States as a model had encouraged the notion that a republic was at least a possible future. British republicanism which surfaced during the years of Queen Victoria's extended mourning for her consort no doubt had an effect too, but the *Bulletin*, which espoused a republic, continued to blow raspberries at Royalty even through the years of her resurgence. Yet in the new century republicanism, which had never been a purposeful movement, withered away entirely. Perhaps federation made it seem irrelevant; perhaps the death of Queen Victoria and the succession to the throne of the jaunty Edward VII encouraged a more relaxed acceptance of the monarchy; but overall it would seem that rising imperial enthusiasm in Britain was transmitted to Australia, stifling any residual republicanism in the process. The *Bulletin* was hostile to the first celebration of Empire Day (which it called Vampire Day) in 1905, but thereafter it increasingly retreated into silence.

Empire Day was part of the marketing of the new imperialism. Stemming from Canada in the late 1890s, the idea was taken up by the British Empire League, an Australian branch of which had been established in 1901 to promote the Boer War cause. In 1905 the observance of Empire Day on 24 May (Queen Victoria's birthday) was officially recognised, although the League did not succeed in having it made a public holiday. From the beginning the emphasis was on inducting school children to imperial citizenship. There was an 'Empire Catechism' of facts and figures, and on the day, as the Victorian School Paper put it, 'the children of Great Britain and Greater Britain (the "Dominions beyond the Seas") will be reminded of the empire in which every one of them has a share'.[4] It was the era, too, of the Boy Scout movement, founded by Lord Baden Powell, the hero of Mafeking: its relaxed militarism and outdoors emphasis seemed suited to Australian conditions.

Catholic schools generally declined to take up Empire Day. Cardinal Moran of Sydney thought it 'out of place', and instead converted 24 May to 'Australia Day'. When St Mary's Cathedral marked the occasion by flying the flags of Ireland and Australia, the loyalist *Sydney Morning Herald* frostily headlined its report, 'NO UNION JACK IS FLOWN'.[5] The affair highlighted the ambiguity of Catholic promotion of Australian sentiment, as it was often a tactical means of avoiding the rhetoric of imperial loyalty. Yet in the years before the Great War even Catholic suspicion of the Empire waned, particularly as hopes for Irish Home Rule increased. In 1905 the Commonwealth parliament had carried resolutions urging Britain to grant Ireland the self-government which the dominions already enjoyed.

The diffusion of imperialist ideology was complemented by a growing sense of national vulnerability which stimulated consideration of defence needs. Partly this reflected the intensifying imperial rivalries of Europe – hence the 1909 dreadnought scare, when raucous concern that Britain was falling behind Germany in naval strength reverberated throughout the empire – but partly it stemmed from regional sensitivity, particularly in the wake of Japan's 1905 defeat of Russia. It was in this context that the Labor Party joined those advocating compulsory military training, at a time when conscription was not favoured in Britain or the USA, though it existed, of course, in much of Europe. Labor, with a traditional radical suspicion of a standing army, saw compulsory military training as the basis of a democratic 'people's army'. In 1911 a Labor government presided over the introduction of compulsory cadet training for boys and youths between twelve and seventeen. Alfred Deakin, the Liberal leader who also supported what came to be called 'boy conscription', hoped that enthusiasm for the training would 'to some extent, take the place of those sports on which our young people look and speculate every Saturday without otherwise participating in'.[6]

This new emphasis on defence could be promoted, as it was by Labor, in nationalist terms, but it assumed an imperial framework, and was increasingly infused with the sentiment attaching to that. So the English journalist, John Foster Fraser, wrote in 1910 that 'you drop from Imperialism to something like parochialism in Australia, with little of the real national spirit intervening – though it exists and must increase'.[7] Federation had not abolished old colonial loyalties, but merely provided new structures within which they could compete.

The main focus for 'real national spirit' was that sense of race summed up by 'White Australia': as the radical H. B. Higgins put it, 'if Australia has any national question this is it'. When, in the early days of the federal movement, Parkes had invoked 'the crimson thread of kinship', it was the British heritage which he saw as uniting the colonies. In 1902 nearly all Australians would have agreed with Deakin in seeing 'unity of race' as 'an absolute essential

5.1   A *Bulletin* 1901 comment on White Australia. A black-infested, errant Queensland is about to be cleaned up by Australia's first Prime Minister, Edmund Barton. The original caption has Barton saying to Queensland 'You dirty boy!'

to the unity of Australia'. While some tactfully argued that it was the low living standards of non-white races which were objected to, 'the possibility and probability of racial contamination' (as Labor leader, Watson, put it) became the dominant concern. White Australia meant not only an immigration policy which excluded non-whites, but a corresponding policy of, in Deakin's words, 'the deportation or reduction of the number of aliens now in our midst'.[8] Although the term 'White Australia' was never officially endorsed in the legislation, the strength of the sentiment ensured that it was one of the first issues addressed by the new Commonwealth parliament.

In one sense racism itself was part of the British heritage, but there is no doubt that the advocacy of White Australia revealed a new and nasty stridency. Yet it was a cause which could evoke emotional commitment and even idealism. As the international climate became more unstable, and as Australia as an isolated European outpost seemed more vulnerable, a White Australia acquired the aura of an antipodean sanctuary. British insecurity at this time was reflected in fantasies of invasion; Australians had similar fantasies, except that they were racial nightmares as well. In 1909 Randolph Bedford's *White Australia*, billed as 'a powerful patriotic play', adapted the conventions of melodrama to an extravagant tale of Japanese espionage and invasion.[9] Bedford pointed an accusing finger at the degeneracy in our midst, represented by Cedric, the traitorous nephew of a Northern Territory squatter, and Pawpaw Sal, a white woman who had apparently succumbed to the tropics. The drama climaxed with the destruction of the Japanese fleet in Sydney Harbour by the assault of an airship designed by the squatter hero. For its audience the improbabilities lay more in the mechanics of the plot than in the prospect of Japanese invasion.

Whilst the fear of China had been one of Asian 'hordes' submerging an Anglo-Celtic culture by sheer force of numbers, the Japanese threat was perceived as a military one, all the more immediate for Japan having recently graduated as a world power on a par with the European nations. Would not Japan imitate Europe in imperial pretensions as well? Instead of whites colonising other races, there was now the nightmare possibility of the process being reversed. It was a matter of acute embarrassment that Japan was an ally of Britain's. In instituting the White Australia immigration policy it had been necessary, out of imperial tact, to follow the Natal practice of using an arbitrary dictation test, to maintain the pretence that race was not at issue. At the outset of the Great War the sleazy *Truth* lamented:

> The war drums beat! The scene is changed! The brown man is a
>   brother!
> Alas, for dear Australia White! The Japs are pals of Mother![10]

Australians did not need to be told that it was better to have Japan as an ally than a foe. The real, if implied, complaint was that Britain was abdicating its imperial responsibilities in the Pacific. From this point of view the Japanese alliance did not strengthen the Empire so much as expose its weakness.

The coming of the war of necessity pushed such doubts into the background: the Empire now was everything. Unease about Australia's own position gave way to what the Governor-General, Munro Ferguson, called 'indescribable enthusiasm' for the British cause in Europe, and by the end of 1914, more than 50,000 men had enlisted. Even in union towns like Broken Hill and Kalgoorlie there was a rush to be part of the great adventure – for that was how it seemed to a generation which had grown up with no experience of war other than the uneven encounter in South Africa. And after all it was a Labor leader, Andrew Fisher, the Scottish-born miner soon to be prime minister, who promised that Australia would defend Britain 'to our last man and our last shilling'.[11] Enlistment could, of course, be encouraged by more pragmatic considerations, such as the prospect of a free trip abroad. A close examination might have also revealed that there were pacifists and socialists who did not share the excitement, and that sometimes unemployment, as in Broken Hill, could be a spur to enlistment. But in 1914 and early 1915 the festive atmosphere disguised such undercurrents.

The Australians' first experience of the War at Gallipoli in 1915 brought to an end this prelude of innocence, but it also was to provide the basis for the mythology of Anzac. There is no need here to tell the story of Gallipoli, from the dawn landing of 25 April to the successful evacuation of December which helped subsume the humiliation of defeat: but it is important to appreciate the subtle mixture of ingredients which gave the myth its character. Even before the Australians landed, the event was guaranteed national significance. This was not only Australia's entry into the Great War but history as well: South Africa could now only be regarded as a rehearsal. And because Australia was offering its best – for the first eager recruits were recognised as being physically fine specimens – it offered a splendid opportunity to present a flattering portrait of the Australian as a national type. The British generously cooperated in this venture. The dramatic account of the landing by the London *Daily Telegraph* correspondent, Ellis Ashmead Bartlett, claimed that there had been 'no finer feat in this war'. Bartlett's tour of Australia and New Zealand in early 1916 consolidated his role as a publicist of Gallipoli. One of the most striking accolades was that given by the poet, John Masefield, who praised the Anzacs, 'those smiling and glorious young giants', for their 'physical beauty and nobility of bearing'.[12] Such tributes facilitated the more deliberate myth-making in Australia itself.

Gallipoli offered one giant problem – it was not only a defeat, but, in the end, an irrelevant sideshow. This, however, allowed for a subtle anti-Britishness to intrude itself into the saga. The defeat could not be laid at the feet of the heroic Anzacs: the failure of Gallipoli was a failure of British strategy.* Hidden in the Anzac myth

---

* This, too, had been Ashmead Bartlett's message, delivered in the United States, though he was warned off repeating it by authorities in Australia and New Zealand.

is a feeling that the Anzacs had been sent on a fool's errand. But the sense in which Gallipoli was a sideshow also had the effect of giving the Anzacs a slightly proprietorial attitude to the campaign, ignoring the fact that British soldiers were in the majority.

That Gallipoli had a special significance for both Australia and New Zealand created a further historical dilemma. The very word 'Anzac' fused the military identities of the two countries: how, then, could the myth be subdivided? New Zealand had had close ties with the eastern colonies in the nineteenth century, and in the early 1890s appeared a more likely participant in federation than Western Australia. In the event, the difficulties in uniting the Australian colonies proved great enough without attempting to include New Zealand, which went its own way. In spite of Australia and New Zealand sharing much in heritage and experience, the artificial creation of separate national identities in 1901 was a starting point for cultural divergence. Anzac was an uneasy reminder that the two countries could, nevertheless, not escape being involved in each other's destiny.

The theme, ultimately, of the Gallipoli legend is tragic: the death of innocence, and heroic sacrifice in the midst of stupidity. When C. E. W. Bean, later the official war historian, and another correspondent were discussing the evacuation they had just witnessed, Bean's colleague complained that the problem, 'from a journalistic point of view', was that there was no battle. Bean disagreed, saying that battle stories were 'almost commonplace nowadays' and that 'the spectacle of our whole position gradually left bare' was just as good.[13] The Gallipoli myth which Bean was to play a major part in constructing was no ordinary tale of battle bravery: the almost ghostly image of the evacuation gave the event a dramatic unity, offsetting the heroics of the landing against the skill and cunning exercised in defeat. It was the ultimate achievement of the myth that in spite of its inner ambiguities it could nevertheless be firmly committed to the imperial cause.

The myth that evolved from Gallipoli was, like all national myths, designed to be unifying. But even while its foundations were being laid, the war, on another plane, was proving a divisive experience. After the retirement of Fisher in October 1915, the Labor government was led by W. M. (Billy) Hughes who was ardently committed to the war. In 1916, Hughes, London-born of Welsh parents, visited England where his fervour and energy made an impression; he returned, convinced that Australia would have to countenance conscription to sustain its commitment. The issue provided an immediate focus for gathering trade union discontent which had been stimulated by inflation and unemployment. Hughes sought to by-pass dissent in his own party by putting the conscription proposal to a referendum, assuming that simple patriotism would ensure its endorsement.

The Labor Party split, Hughes eventually leading his supporters into a new anti-labor amalgam, the National Party. But opposition to conscription was not limited to the trade union movement and pacifists. Some farmers, pragmatists as ever, saw conscription as a threat to their labour supply at harvest time, while an emotive campaign was launched to persuade women to reject the 'blood vote'. The whole issue then became coloured with sectarian bias when, in the wake of the British reprisals against the leaders of the Dublin Easter Rising in 1916, the Irish question resurfaced. Catholics found in Melbourne's Archbishop Mannix, who had arrived fresh from Ireland in 1913, a leader eager to revitalise their historic commitment to Erin. Most Catholic clergy preferred to stay out of the conscription debate; a few, like the archbishops of Perth and Brisbane, were advocates. But Mannix, although he offended some Catholics, particularly the well-to-do who saw him as wilfully reactivating sectarianism, served as a focal point for Irish suspicion of British motives. Protestant activists, who generally supported conscription, saw Mannix as a traitor; Hughes himself believed that Mannix was a Sinn Feiner, and seriously considered moves to deport him. That the first referendum, against all expectations, was closely defeated exacerbated tensions. At the 1917 elections Hughes, to help secure his return to office, promised not to introduce conscription without another referendum; so, later in the year, the community was forced to go through the whole divisive experience again. This time the proposal was defeated more decisively.

Imperial loyalists were shattered by these twin defeats, and felt humiliated in the eyes of the land they called 'Home'. The targets for their bitterness were the trade union movement and the Catholic Church, the former identified with Bolshevism, the latter with Sinn Fein. These two disruptive forces merged into a composite revolutionary ogre dedicated to undermining the Empire; that the departure of Hughes and his supporters from the Labor Party left Catholics in a strengthened position in Labor politics gave some plausibility to the perceived alliance. When, in the 1918 St Patrick's Day procession, Archbishop Mannix doffed his biretta for a banner inscribed 'To the Martyrs of Easter Week' but failed to do so for a band playing 'God Save the King', the loyalists were outraged. As the Great War ended and Ireland sank into chaos, there were bizarre Australian echoes as stories circulated of arms being secretly stock-piled in convents; loyalist organisations mushroomed, some with a paramilitary flavour. So the soldiers who had left a country apparently united in enthusiastic support for the war returned to a society racked by disillusion and division. Some had been away from home for four years or more; having survived the horror of the trenches they now faced a difficult adjustment to the realities of survival at home. There were diggers who rioted at the sight of a red flag, seizing on Bolshevism as a betrayal of their cause; sometimes the restless discontent was evidenced by less specific rowdyism, which fixed on symbols of civilian authority, such as those other wearers of uniforms, the police, as their immediate oppressors.

It was in this context of dislocation – and the wider context of fears of racial degeneration* – that the myth and ritual of Anzac were developed. In 1916 the landing at Anzac Cove was commemorated at church services throughout Australia, though the occasion was also linked to fund raising and recruitment. In contrast, soldiers in Egypt marked the anniversary in a much more relaxed manner. Monash, later to be corps commander and Australia's outstanding general, records how he 'turned out' his whole brigade at 6.45 a.m. for a 'short but very dignified Service' after which the day was spent at sport, culminating in 'a great Aquatic Carnival' in the Canal, with 'one teeming mass of naked humanity – at times there were over 15,000 men in the water'. There were also unscheduled 'comic items' including 'a skit on the memorable landing', something that would have been unthinkable in later years.[14]

With the coming of peace commemoration took on a new signi-ficance, for Anzac now had to serve as an expression of the whole experience of Australia at war. The commitment, the absence of conscription notwithstanding, had been immense; out of a total population of about five million, some 417,000 enlisted and 330,000 actually sailed off to battle; more than 59,000 were killed and about 174,000 wounded. The casualty rate was a very high 68.5 per cent, compared to Britain's 52.5 per cent. While occasions such as Armistice Day would have their due importance, Anzac alone could provide a national focus for such a sacrifice. Yet there was no immediate agreement as to what form the commemoration should take. There was often tension between civic authorities who assumed that they had jurisdiction and the organisations of ex-servicemen which saw

* See Chapter 7.

Anzac Day as 'theirs'. Gradually over the next decade the elements came together, though in each State the amalgam would vary slightly. Commemoration would take place on the exact day, in spite of church resistance when it fell on a Sunday; Anzac Day would thus be distinguished from frivolous public holidays, of which employers complained there were too many, taken on a Monday. The march would bring all the diggers together, even if Catholics hived off for a separate service afterwards. The main service would be Protestant in tone but deliberately avoid any specific Christian references. The dawn service, inspired by the hour of the Anzac landing, also would become part of the day's cycle, and provide a religious experience even more devoid of Christian content. Anglican and Protestant clergy sometimes resisted this trend, but had increasingly to go along with the kind of ceremonies which the Returned Servicemen's League, as it came to be called, deemed appropriate. It was as if the ex-servicemen leaders wanted Anzac to have a kind of religious autonomy, which would ensure that it would not be swallowed up by conventional Protestant pietism. It would also become accepted that while the morning would be dedicated to the solemnities, a certain amount of old-soldierly abandon was permissible in the afternoon. Police would turn a blind eye to the illegal schools of two-up (a simple form of gambling using pennies) which sprang up in the streets.

By the mid 1920s this pattern of observance was taking shape, but it was already clear that Anzac required its own monuments. There were often proposals for 'useful' memorials – club houses for returned servicemen, or, as was suggested in Melbourne, a city improvement in the form of an Anzac Square. But the digger lobby generally came to the view that the commemoration of Anzac would be demeaned by such utilitarian considerations, just as anything triumphal in character was also unsuitable. The results were often monumental and often curious. In Melbourne there arose a massive Shrine of Remembrance, a 'visible manifestation of the people's grief', which, inspired by the Mausoleum of Halicarnassus, resembles a pyramid crossed with a Greek temple. The inscription on the west wall, which commences 'LET ALL MEN KNOW THAT THIS IS HOLY GROUND', was written by Monash himself. Sydney chose not a Shrine but a Memorial, similarly proportioned, but contemporary art-deco in style. Entering the Hall of Memory one looks down into the Well of Contemplation, dominated by a sculpture of Sacrifice, a surprisingly erotic nude male figure borne on a shield by three women. According to its architect the Memorial was designed

5.2   The Melbourne Shrine of Remembrance, photographed at its
dedication in 1934, which was witnessed by a crowd estimated at 300,000.

'to outlast any drab depression which might arise out of personal
grief for the fallen'.[15] Canberra, the national capital from 1927,
eventually followed with the Australian War Memorial, with a
garden court, complete with a Pool of Reflection, leading into
another Hall of Memory. Its three windows contain fifteen figures
in uniform, a nurse being the only female. Each figure represents
one of the qualities of Australian servicemen and women, ranging
from candour, curiosity and independence to comradeship, patriotism and chivalry. The nurse, of course, is devotion, and has as a
symbol of charity the pelican feeding her young from her bleeding
breast. The importance of the Memorial is emphasised by its position on a direct axis facing the old (and new) Parliament House. But
just as significant as these major monuments were the memorials
erected in the main streets or parks of cities, towns and villages
across the country – sometimes just a simple obelisk recording the
names of the fallen, but often presided over by the symbolic digger,
depicted not as a larger-than-life hero going into battle but as a very
human survivor reflecting on the meaning of it all.

These developing patterns of ritualised remembrance were complemented by a growing body of myth about the Australian ethos, particularly as epitomised in the digger. The digger was capable of serving as a symbol of Australia itself. Before the War *Bulletin* cartoonists had often depicted Australia as a cheeky but rather spoilt child: now he could be discarded in favour of the mature, even world-weary, digger. The fleshing out of the digger as a national type owed much to the remarkable *Official War History* edited by C. E. W. Bean. The first of its twelve volumes, *The Story of Anzac: The First Phase*, was published in 1921; the last appeared in 1941 when the world was at war again. Bean, an English-born journalist who had already developed before the war an admiration for what he perceived as bush values, wanted to produce a people's history, written, as much as possible, from the viewpoint of the ordinary soldier. To a large extent the *History*, its index packed with the names of soldiers of all ranks (though officers of the lower echelon predominated), achieved this purpose, but Bean's generalisations about the digger were flavoured by nationalist romanticism. For Bean the essential qualities of the digger – his resourcefulness, independence and egalitarianism – derived from the bush. In the face of the plain facts of urbanisation he offered little evidence to support his thesis, beyond such assertions as that 'the bushman is the hero of the Australian boy'.[16]

The popular verse of C. J. Dennis, which enjoyed a great vogue amongst the diggers themselves, offered a different perspective. Dennis's first great success, *The Sentimental Bloke*, affectionately satirised the urban larrikin sub-culture, but in its sequel, *The Moods of Ginger Mick*, the war has a transforming impact. The Bloke's mate, Ginger Mick, goes off to war lured by 'the call of stoush' (fighting), but becomes a hero, even 'a gallant gentleman', and dies at Gallipoli. The *Bulletin*, which was also a convert of the war to the imperial cause, hailed *Ginger Mick* as 'a finely patriotic book, a uniquely Australian book'.[17] Dennis paid lip service to the rural dream – both the Bloke, and, later on, the returning *Digger Smith* seek independence on the land – but his characters were essentially urban. His larrikins were creatures of a middle-class imagination, and his sense of the vernacular inaccurate, but as urban fantasy Dennis's works amused and entertained. Moreover, in conveying a mood and humour which many identified as Australian, they suggested that Bean's invocation of the bush was not necessary to the new ethos.

Some have argued that the Anzac mythmakers took over a native, radical ethos and effectively harnessed it to a conservative

5.3   Ginger Mick before and after: [on the left] looking very disgruntled as he pauses 'loadin' up 'is truck' at the 'markit' to 'blarst the flamin' war!'; [on the right] transformed into a daredevil fighting soldier, one of 'the Southern Breed' who 'could play the game for keeps'.

purpose. But, as we have seen, the nineteenth century ideology of the bush was not necessarily radical; the Billabong children's books of Mary Grant Bruce had already offered popular evidence of a conservative celebration of the bush. Nevertheless it is true that Bean, Dennis and the many others who helped assemble 'the digger' drew eclectically on the traditions to hand, whether rural or urban, and dedicated the new hero to the imperial cause. In a sense they had no choice: if the war was not justified in imperial terms then it had, for distant Australia, no meaning at all. So in spite of its anti-English undertones the ethos could only be 'Australian' insofar as it was also 'British'. Hence it was appropriate that the Duke of Gloucester should dedicate Melbourne's Shrine on Armistice Day 1934 and that Kipling should mark the occasion with an ode which told how the soldiers returned to

> The kindly cities and plains where they were bred –
> Having revealed their Nation in Earth's sight.[18]

Although Anzac had, by the late 1920s, become a powerful focus for patriotic sentiment, as a *national* myth it contained the seeds of its own decline. There were few, in those early years, who

would not have gone along with the portrayal of the democratic digger, particularly in his implied superiority to his British brother. But the rituals and monuments of Anzac had full meaning only for the diggers themselves: while an attempt was made to reach out to women (as in the nurse's devotion, and the three women bearing Sacrifice) they were summoned to the ceremonies not as participants but as a respectful chorus. The monuments, carved with the names of foreign battlefields, told of an experience which was, literally, remote from those who had not fought. Indeed, that the young diggers made a pilgrimage to old Europe – for 60,000 a pilgrimage of death – was part of the essence of the Australian war. The diggers, as volunteers, were an elect, and Anzac was something that they shared, and in many cases, felt a need to go on sharing. But how could those who had, for whatever reason, not volunteered to serve, partake of it? The divisions of the war could not be obliterated by shrines and memorials. When the Melbourne *Argus*, reporting the dedication of the Shrine, headlined that 'ALL CLASSES PAY TRIBUTE TO SELF-SACRIFICE' it was a claim that implied the fear that there might not be unanimity.[19]

Anzac was also a generational experience. Schools inculcated children in the solemnity of the occasion, but the rhetoric which stressed what 'we' owed to 'them' widened rather than narrowed the gap. Donald Horne writes of his childhood in the 1930s:

In the bottom right-hand drawer of his side of the dressing-
table Dad kept the symbols of his most important beliefs.
When there was no one in the house I sometimes took them
out and wondered at them. There was his Masonic apron, his
Bible, his war medals, a bedouin's knife he had brought back
from the Palestine campaign, an army revolver, his spurs. One
day I put on the Masonic apron and the medals. Holding the
revolver in my hand, with the bedouin's knife at my waist and
the spurs on my feet, I looked at myself in the mirror and saw
an Australian.[20]

But an Australian, necessarily, of that generation: Horne's theatrical
image suggests how the child could never be the father, except in
mirror pastiche. Horne's own experience of war would be a rather
different one. While the Second World War would renew and even
expand the appeal of Anzac, it would also serve to dilute it.

The extent to which Anzac became the preserve of the RSL
pointed to a further limitation on its national potential. In the years
between the wars the RSL became a powerful lobby group, but for
most of the period it could not claim to represent the majority of
diggers. In the mid 1920s, when the Anzac rituals were being established, its membership hovered around the 25,000 mark, though by
the outbreak of the Second World War it had expanded to 82,000.
There were always many diggers who preferred not to identify
themselves as such, and who therefore did not join the League, or
did not march.

Anzac was a powerful emotional and religious expression for
many, but primarily for a proportion of the diggers themselves; in
spite of its public rhetoric, it could not encompass all Australians.
Yet Anzac emerged in the 1920s largely unchallenged by its potential critics. (Most of the controversy concerned the mode of commemoration, and was engaged in by its professed supporters.)
There was, it would seem, a question of tact and respect involved.
Few of those who had resented the jingoism of the war years would
now deny the diggers 'their' day. Those who did not bow their
heads before the shrines and memorials nevertheless accepted that
for others they were 'holy ground'. This was one of the silent
accommodations reached by post-war Australian society, which
gave the impression of a greater unity than in fact existed. The old divisions would be expressed in other ways and through other avenues.

This sense of Anzac being important, yet somehow segregated
from real life, perhaps helps explain the curious neglect of the war

by writers of the 1920s and 1930s. Apart from a little verse, which only in a few cases rises above the banal, and one or two novels, the principal literary monument was Bean's emerging *History*, the volumes of which, in their distinctive maroon binding, were to occupy a place of importance on many an Australian bookshelf. Although from 1916 official war artists, of whom George Lambert was perhaps the most significant, dutifully put the war on canvas, the gathering of most of their work in the War Memorial in Canberra reinforced its separation from the cultural mainstream.

There was a tendency, too, in looking back to identify the horrors of the war with the decadence of Europe. For Vance Palmer, who had enlisted in 1918,

> Europe is very old,
> It has known wars and death,
> The live past stirs within the mould,
> Yet chill cometh its breath.

Palmer turns his back on a Europe which, although 'pensive, subtle, profound' is a captive of its past:

> I will go south and south,
> There Life has scarce begun.[21]

The suspicion of the disruption and disjunction which seemed rife in Europe – particularly in the various 'isms' of art with their bizarre extremes – stifled artistic innovation in Australia, but it also encouraged a modest re-assertion of bush values. Although the Heidelberg vision had met with some official resistance – the Victorian Gallery did not buy its first Tom Roberts until 1920 – it was now in the process of being institutionalised in the popular imagination. The sometimes sentimental landscapes of Elioth Gruner and the stately gumtrees of Hans Heysen became accepted national images. Heysen, who was six when his family had arrived in South Australia from Germany, suffered some anti-Hun prejudice during the war, but was nevertheless patronised by governors and, even more significantly, by Dame Nellie Melba, now a *grande dame* of the local scene. Heysen saw the gumtree as 'a poet's tree, a painter's tree'[22], and some of his paintings were almost portraits of trees, depicting gnarled, massive trunks, with flaking skin of crumpled bark.

This painterly elevation of the gumtree as *the* symbol of the bush was complemented by a growing interest in Australian flora and fauna generally. While evident in the late nineteenth century, this

5.4   Dame Nellie Melba photographed at her home, Coombe Cottage, near Melbourne, not long before her death in 1931. Melba claimed that she raised £100,000 for the war effort, and in recognition of her work was awarded the DBE in 1918. At the time it was announced, Melba was in America, in her private railcar. Her secretary, going to Melba to congratulate her, found her prancing naked around the room, gleefully chortling 'I'm a Dame! I'm a Dame!'

interest now took more concerted forms. In the early 1900s there was a movement to promote the wattle as a national flower – in its golden innocence it was said to stand for 'home, country, kindred, sunshine, and love' – and a sprig was incorporated in the Australian coat of arms in 1912.[23] After the war home gardening took more systematic notice of native flora, and wildflower shows became popular. In children's literature the gumnut babies of May Gibbs and Dorothy Wall's mischievous young larrikin of a koala, Blinky Bill, reflected and themselves contributed to the new environmental awareness.

There was also a revived market for books about the frontier, which now meant either the centre or the north, thus focusing on the Northern Territory, Queensland and Papua-New Guinea.

Usually documentary in style, and often influenced by the *National Geographic* tradition, these books evinced admiration for pioneers, a fascination with environmental extremes such as desert and jungle, a neo-anthropological interest in Aborigines, and often an ideological commitment to developmental policies. Amongst the landscape writers, as they have been called, Ion Idriess was one of the most successful, becoming, by the late 1930s, a proven best seller. His subjects ranged from the myth of the lost gold reef (*Lasseter's Last Ride*), to the Flying Doctor (*Flynn of the Inland*) and the Aborigines or 'stone-age man' (*Over The Range*). He also published a much praised account of the Australian Light Horsemen at Gallipoli (*The Desert Column*), and what was almost an expedition manual for the Depression unemployed, *Prospecting for Gold*. Like many other such writers he was an ardent proponent of great water diversion schemes which partook of technological fantasy. Idriess sometimes took liberties with his facts, and his popular success galled some, though not all, more serious writers, but he had cleverly helped locate and exploit a popular curiosity about the 'real' Australia – that is, the Australia where few Australians actually lived, and which therefore they knew little about.

The creative writers who saw themselves as inheritors of the *Bulletin* tradition remained convinced that the bush was the proper inspiration for a national literature. In Melbourne, Vance and Nettie Palmer tried to provide a radical continuity, seeking to encourage younger writers, but in spite of the apparent promotion of bush values going on around them, they tended to feel embattled. Partly this was because of the sheer difficulty of making a living as journalist-cum-writers in a society which still lacked so much of the cultural infrastructure of literary journals and patronage; but partly, too, it stemmed from their feeling that the war had ideologically blighted the earlier nationalist promise. The war-time transformation of the *Bulletin* from a broad radicalism to a conservative populism pointed to their dilemma; the *Bulletin* maintained its role as a guardian of literary nationalism, but there was now a disjunction between its political and literary pages.

Perhaps the crux of their problem was that, unlike populists such as Idriess, they were uncertain of their audience. Whereas the earlier *Bulletin* school, so much centred on the ballad and slice-of-life short story, had deliberately maintained a popular dialogue with its readership, the Palmers and their circle were attempting to intellectualise this tradition, yet somehow with expectations of retaining its mass appeal. Nettie Palmer discerned this:

> Confidence is surely one of the main things lacking in our
> writers up till now [she wrote in 1927] particularly our
> novelists. They never seemed quite sure of themselves or their
> public, never were fully convinced of their own point of view,
> or that there were people to communicate with whose minds
> were as adult as their own.[24]

She was too loyal to have been thinking of her husband Vance,
whose often laboured novels succeeded neither as high art nor
popular fiction. In fact her remarks were made in the context of
praising the novel *Working Bullocks* written by their friend, Katharine Susannah Prichard. Prichard was notable for her attempt to
imaginatively encompass Aboriginal experience, as in *Coonardoo*
and the play, *Brumby Innes*, but she, too, seemed unsure of the terms
on which she should engage the reader, the preachiness of her naïve
but missionary Communism at times sitting oddly with the clichés
of historical romance.

The self-conscious attempts in the 1920s to found a national
drama, with which these writers were associated, amply demonstrated the gulf between artist and audience. Louis Esson, whose
particular ambitions were as a playwright, had been persuaded by
the Irish writers, Synge and Yeats, and the example of Dublin's
Abbey Theatre, that what was needed were 'plays on really national
themes', plays that would 'help *to build a nation* in the spiritual
sense', rather than 'so-called intellectual drama, abstract and cosmopolitan', by which he meant Galsworthy, Bennett and Shaw.
Yeats advised them to get a theatre going 'no matter how small', and
this they did with the aptly named Pioneer Players.[25] Although some
productions had a modest success audiences were indeed small and
the theatre necessarily amateur. The Players petered out after a few
years, disappointed not so much by the size of their audiences as by
the lack of ferment in the stalls. There was no simple formula for
creating a national drama, and Dublin's Abbey Theatre, a product of
a unique Anglo-Irish culture, could not be transplanted in Melbourne.

There were writers, of course, who were not interested in these
nationalist assertions. Norman Lindsay, and the group which
gathered round him in Sydney, disowned, at least in theory, the
importance of place. Introducing a collection, *Poetry in Australia*,
Lindsay wrote in 1923:

> ... we must accept the accident of geographical isolation, and
> label our poetry 'Australian'.

Beyond that we have no concern for these variations in
degree of rock and mud which pass for national distinctions on
Earth.[26]

Yet Lindsay was, in his own way, a cultural isolationist who rejected
contemporary Europe, seeing modernism in art and literature as
symptomatic of a collapse in civilised values. In this sense he was
much less cosmopolitan than the nationalists, who kept open their
European lines of communication. Lindsay himself was an artist
and writer of many talents, a perpetual adolescent who saw pagan-
ism as a liberating force, but whose artistic creed was conservative
and imaginatively constricting. He was also an anti-nationalist who
made a profitable sideline out of charming cartoon characterisations
of Australian animals, and whose children's book, *The Magic Pud-
ding*, set in the bush, has been hailed as an Australian classic.

Lindsay shared with the nationalists a deep suspicion of American cultural influences which seemed to be reshaping the urban
environment. For Vance Palmer the suburb with its 'picture
theatres, gramophones, motor cars and villas' was 'without pride of
ancestry or hope of posterity', and he deplored jazz and cinema
(though he was later to do some film reviewing). Lindsay, who by
the 1920s was living in the Blue Mountains, disliked visiting Sydney
where he saw in people's faces apathy and defeat; he also personally
resisted the new technology of telephone, radio and motor car. It
became fashionable to regard suburbia as the Australian blight.
D. H. Lawrence's *Kangaroo*, published in 1923, contributed with its
depiction of 'this litter of bungalows and tin cans scattered for miles
and miles'. Lawrence's *alter ego*, Somers, and his wife Harriett,
travel to their first home in Sydney in a hansom cab, down 'the long
street, like a child's drawing, the little square bungalows dot-dot-
dot, close together and yet far apart, like modern democracy': their
house, they discover, is called 'Torestin', which Somers at first takes
to be an Aboriginal word.[27]

The new technology which was changing suburban life was
American-dominated, but the American influence was evident in
other spheres too. The search for an Australian style in house
architecture had in the 1890s resulted in a local adaptation of 'Queen
Anne' style, the 'federation villa', as it has come to be called. Whilst
sometimes incorporating elaborate embellishments, including art
nouveau, the federation villa drew on the country homestead tradition, and flowed on into a 'Colonial Revival' style. But in the 1920s
builders and architects turned increasingly to the American West

Coast for marketable styles appropriate to Australian conditions, and the new post-war suburbs were created in the image of the Californian bungalow and, to a lesser extent, the Spanish Mission house.

Yet whatever the American influences, this suburbia had already acquired its own character, as Lawrence's appraisal indicated. Californian bungalow and Spanish Mission house, as much as art-deco picture houses, electric trams and soda fountains, were incorporated into and became part of its culture. This was the environment in which most Australians lived, yet intellectuals, seeing only a mediocrity of sameness, preferred to ignore it. A few writers such as C. J. Dennis and the novelist, Louis Stone, had exploited the larrikin pushes of the inner suburbs of the pre-war period, but it was a children's writer, Ethel Turner, who had probably written more about urban life than anyone else. Vance Palmer's *The Swayne Family* confronted Melbourne suburbia, but from a position of hostility. 'Was there something about the town itself', young Ernest Swayne wonders, 'with its dull, middle-class dignity, its geometric streets, flat suburbs, featureless surroundings, that sucked all the passion out of people except the passion for conformity . . .?'[28] Palmer, if not his readers, knew the answer. Even fiction inspired by the Depression often focused on the bush, rather than the city where hardship was greater.

It is possible that this alienation from their urban environment helps explain the failure of 'serious' writers to communicate with a larger audience: they were not writing about the Australia with which most of their readers were familiar, runs the argument. Yet, as has been pointed out, the popular landscape writers succeeded for apparently the very same reason – that they were introducing readers to the unfamiliar, even the legendary. What is involved here is a question of genres and the expectations attaching to them, and, more generally, the level of cultural engagement. When one considers the popular successes in Australian writing – the *Bulletin* literature, the children's books of Ethel Turner, Mary Grant Bruce, May Gibbs, Dorothy Wall (and Norman Lindsay), *The Sentimental Bloke* and his successors, the travel adventures of Idriess, Frank Clune and company – one is reminded that their authors all *chose* to locate them in popular literary traditions, and to that extent avoided the expectations of high culture. A reader choosing a travel book or a children's book already had an appreciative context in which to place it, while the digger, for example, with a paperback copy of *The Sentimental Bloke* in his pocket, did not have to worry whether this exercise in comic verse was in any sense 'literature'. Even the images of the Heidelberg school – the gumtree, or the river meandering across a bleached landscape – could be incorporated in a popular vision of Australia which had little need for the aesthetics of high art.

The lack of confidence which Nettie Palmer discerned in Australian novelists stemmed from their increasing literary serious-ness, because this immediately raised questions of cultural expecta-tions. And here the Australian artist – whether writer, painter or performer – was faced with the old dilemma of a colonial culture, the continuing cultural ties with the metropolitan society. The myth-building engendered by the Great War did not weaken ties with Britain, it only made them more complex. It certainly did not dimin-ish the widespread belief that London was still the Empire's cultural capital, and therefore that cultural standards had their ultimate source and legitimation there. On the one hand this created difficul-ties for the Australian public in evaluating the work of local artists which made claims as 'art'; but it was also a potent cause for cultural schizophrenia among the artists themselves.

For the mass of Australians at this time travel abroad was out of the question (the diggers, of course, being a unique case). But for the artist and intellectual travel was a challenge – and temptation. Most writers and artists and many performers travelled at some stage of their careers, usually to London, though for painters it was some-times Paris and for musicians Germany. There was an understand-able urge simply to experience the world – to behold the sights and landscapes which English and European literature had told them of, to see the paintings which had only been glimpsed in reproduc-tions, to hear the music of the masters performed in its original European context. They travelled also to test their competence as artists by universal standards; and sometimes they travelled to make the living which was denied them at home. Some, like Lawson and Lindsay, stayed only a year or so and then scuttled back to familiar surroundings. Some, like Streeton, Roberts, the Palmers and Esson, went for longer periods but returned to resume their work in Australia. There were others who left virtually for good. The pianist and composer, Percy Grainger, left at the age of thirteen, eventually settling in the United States; Henry Handel Richardson left at seventeen to pursue a musical career before turning to novel writing; novelists Martin Boyd and Christina Stead spent most of their creative lives abroad, though Stead returned in her last years.

Expatriatism became an issue in Australian culture, and one

which could divide the artistic community. Where lay the artists' loyalty? To their country, their art, their careers? It was also divisive in the sense that expatriates were often dispersed and lost sight of by the artists at home. So it was possible that Richardson's epic Australian trilogy, *The Fortunes of Richard Mahony*, passed largely unnoticed until Nettie Palmer's advocacy drew attention to it. Christina Stead, settled in the USA and removed from her Australian background, gave her best known novel, *The Man Who Loved Children*, an American setting, though it drew essentially on her childhood experiences. Her 'Americanisation' seemed symbolically to confirm the neglect which her works suffered in Australia.

Yet the expatriates often added an important critical dimension to the Australian experience. Richardson's *Fortunes of Richard Mahony* is not the conventional salute to colonial pioneers but an exploration of Mahony's decline and fall: in doing so she established that Australian literature could encompass the tragic. Living out a comfortable upper-middle-class life in England, Richardson did not cease to see herself as Australian, no matter how 'out of touch' she might have grown. Martin Boyd's novels, particularly *The Cardboard Crown* sequence, depict the dilemma of those who saw themselves as Anglo-Australians, and add a distinctive view both of provincial cultural deprivation and metropolitan arrogance. Perhaps the oddest case was that of Grainger, who returned only to make concert tours and supervise the building of his own eccentric museum and archive at Melbourne University. Yet this last gesture indicated how important he considered his oft-reiterated Australianness, which incorporated his own curious Nordic variant of race consciousness.

When journeying to England, the Australian, whether artist or not, already had an image of 'Home', instilled by upbringing and education. Robert Menzies, visiting England for the first time in 1935 to attend the Imperial Conference, recorded his arrival: 'At last we are in England. Our journey to Mecca has ended, and our minds abandoned to those reflections which can so strangely (unless you remember our traditions and upbringing) move the soul of those who go "home" to a land they have never seen. . . .' Mecca, indeed: and the first beholding of England could have almost a religious awe to it. The study of English history and literature prepared the visitor, but the experience of the countryside, particularly in spring, was still often a revelation. The educator Frank Tate, making his first visit to Britain at the age of forty-two, marvelled at bluebells and primroses, and observed of the countryside that 'there was nothing ragged and unfinished and new', the farms seeming to have been 'fertilized for centuries by human contact'. Yet he pointed out that Buttermere was not new to him; he 'had been there often enough through the magic of Wordsworth'. Menzies, still under the spell of it all, professed to understand England anew: 'The green and tranquil country sends forth from its very soil the love of peace and of good humour and contentment'. He was also enchanted to have tea with the Duke and Duchess of York, and to watch the royal children having a dancing lesson: amazingly, this was 'a real family, with real and intelligent people in it'.[29]

Menzies was an Anglophile, but there were many others whose sentiments were more confused, but for whom England nevertheless was an important experience. Yet sometimes a reaction set in, the sense of Old World decay displacing the wonder at countryside and historic monuments. English poverty seemed more chilling, more permanent, than that which Australians were used to. Tate was appalled by 'the hell of the slums' in the north, and the fatalistic acceptance of such pervasive misery: 'I can't imagine how an Australian can rest content in such a place as this'.[30]

The image and the reality did not always match. Even the dream-like perfection of English scenery could pall, and be subtly invoked to point up a contrasting vision of Australia. In one of the best known salutes to Australia, a poem recited by whole generations of schoolchildren, Dorothea Mackellar set the precedent:

> The love of field and coppice,
> Of green and shaded lanes,
> Of ordered woods and gardens
> Is running in your veins;
> Strong love of grey-blue distance,
> Brown streams and soft, dim skies –
> I know but cannot share it,
> My love is otherwise.[31]

Although the paean of praise for Australia which follows is remembered for its evocation of a 'sunburnt country' and 'The wide brown land for me', the poem stresses not only the expansiveness of this 'opal-hearted country', but its variety of scenery and moods, ranging from 'sapphire-misted mountains' to 'her jewel-sea', as if implying, with a nice reversal of images, that it is England, with its 'ordered woods and gardens', which is guilty of sameness. Yet the poem, written around 1908, was first published in the London *Spectator*, and for all its Australianness, was addressed in the old colonial manner, to an English audience (hence 'Is running in *your* veins').

For the great majority of native-born Australians who did not visit England, their attitude to 'Home' depended not only on the images purveyed through the various media but on their experience of the English in Australia. Immigrants were one thing, but there was also a traffic of quite a different order. Royalty began to tour more frequently: the young Prince of Wales in 1920, the Yorks in 1927 (when they inaugurated Canberra) and the Gloucesters in 1934. Such tours were epic presentations of the imperial link. Governors-general of the Commonwealth and State governors were regarded as Imperial appointments: when, in 1931, a Labor prime minister would nominate only Sir Isaac Isaacs, a native-born High Court judge and former radical politician, George V acquiesced but let his displeasure be known. (The fact that Isaacs was also a Jew did not help.) England provided the Anglicans with their archbishops and many bishops as well (just as Ireland did for Catholics): the presidential voice at an Anglican synod was likely to be refined southern English. The universities, still small institutions, had many English – and Scotsmen – on their staff, particularly occupying prestigious chairs. Private schools of note often looked to England for their headmasters. Many such visitors integrated themselves into Australian society, even identified with it, yet their voices carried a message of which they themselves might have been unaware, namely, that in an important sense cultural authority still resided in England. When in 1935 P. R. Stephenson published his cultural manifesto, *The Foundations of Culture in Australia*, he was provoked by an article written by 'an Englishman resident in Australia', Professor O. H. Cowling, in which he dismissed the possibility of an Australian literature, claiming that 'literary culture is not indigenous like the gum tree, but is from a European source'.[32]

This deference to the European, and specifically English, source was later dubbed 'the cultural cringe'.[33] Yet if one took the imperial link seriously – as middle-class Australia professed to do – it was understandable to seek, through such English appointments, to maintain ties with 'Home'. Anti-labor was in office federally for most of the period between the wars, and its leaders still tended to assume, and perhaps rightly, that an empire had no meaning without a hierarchical structure; consequently they did not embrace the Statute of Westminster, which proclaimed the autonomy of 'dominions', with enthusiasm. Although Australia had an External Affairs minister it had no diplomatic service of its own until the eve of the

Second World War. Australia made its representations to Britain which was then assumed to implement an imperial foreign policy. In 1931, in the depths of the Depression, the Anti-labor leader, Joe Lyons (who had recently defected from Labor), urged Australians to 'tune in with Britain', a slogan which neatly deployed the new language of radio in the imperial cause.

There was also an implied accusation here that Labor was not on the imperial wavelength. In the wake of the war, isolationism tended to suit the mood of political Labor. With the setting up of the Irish Free State that issue faded into the background, many Catholics having been perplexed and alienated by the civil war which inaugurated it. But in any case the cultural horizons of working-class Australia were more constricted, and workers had little to do with the local representatives of English authority in the form of governors, archbishops and professors. It was convenient for Labor to proclaim an isolationist Australianism, yet tacitly accept the forms of imperialism: here was another of the silent accommodations of the period.

The 'cultural cringe' gained much of its force from the growing dichotomy between high and popular culture which was itself a creation of the period between the wars. As has been remarked, the new agencies of mass entertainment were often characterised as degenerate, but it is salutary to recall the venom which the cultural elite could direct, for example, at popular music. W. Arundel Orchard, the English Director of the NSW Conservatorium of Music, inveighed against the wireless giving air to 'that abomination known as crooning, with its nauseating chromatic slides and verbal twaddle', adding dismissively that it was 'no excuse to say that some people like it'.[34] Mass entertainment was seen as endangering true cultural values, and a potent cultural snobbery was born. But in Australia the snobbery had added edge, in that it encouraged a turning to England, the source, as the arbiter of high culture.

In areas where these cultural standards were not seen as relevant, sport for example, an Australian ideology could be promoted with compensating enthusiasm. For a small nation which prided itself on the healthiness of its population, sport was ripe for myth-making. There was a tendency, when heroes failed, to seek scapegoats abroad. In the case of Les Darcy, the boxer, and Phar Lap, the racehorse, the United States was cast as the villain, popularly accused of destroying both. But the preferred enemy remained England, and cricket provided the classic confrontations. The 'Bodyline' tour of 1932–33 aroused considerable ill-feeling, culmi-

5.5　One local hero was the aviator Kingsford-Smith seen here seated in front of the radio microphone, with his partner, C. T. Ulm, casually on the edge of the desk. They all study the shrinking globe. Air travel could be seen as tightening the bonds of empire. Kingsford-Smith and Ulm were both members of the New Guard, discussed in Chapter 6.

nating in the Australian Board of Control's accusation that the MCC team, in its use of 'leg theory' bowling, had been guilty of 'unsportsmanlike' play. There were political repercussions, involving prime minister Lyons and British Secretary of State for Dominions, J. H. Thomas. But the claim, sometimes made half-seriously, that the controversy endangered the whole imperial relationship, misses the point. It was necessary for Australia to play England at cricket: the Australian anger was in large measure the expression of frustration in realising this. Hence in the end the Board of Control capitulated and withdrew 'unsportsmanlike'. The usual enmity could now be resumed, even if, for a time, without the customary good humour.

　　Nowhere, perhaps, was the oddity of the Australian relationship with England more evident than in the question of accent. A distinctive pattern of colonial speech dated back to the Currency generation, though its precise character then is hard to establish; but by the twentieth century the 'Australian accent', as even Australians tended to call it, had stabilised, with very little in the way of regional variation. Yet local attitudes to the accent were truly contradictory. Most people spoke with such an accent (even if the heaviness of it varied), yet few could accept it in a cultural sense. On the stage, for example, and on the Australian Broadcasting Commission (ABC) radio, the standard accent was Southern English. Partly this stemmed from the respect accorded touring companies despatched from the West End, and partly from the ABC's infatuation with its parent model, the BBC. But Australian actors and announcers never questioned the need to acquire the proper accent; usually they could turn it on or off at will. The Australian accent was only acceptable on stage (and cinema screen) in vaudeville and in 'low' comedy, such as the 'Dad and Dave' neo-hillbilly genre. This was a provincialism born of distance and dependence.

The ambivalence of Australian attitudes to Britain seemed magnified and dramatised by the events and concerns of the inter-war years, from the myth making of Anzac to the passions of the cricket pitch. There seemed, too, an element of gathering but inarticulate tension in the relationship, particularly as in the late 1930s the crisis in Europe escalated, and the vulnerability of the Empire was more than ever apparent.

For creative artists the question of loyalties was particularly disturbing, for the provincial-metropolitan nexus seemed more problematic, yet more confining than ever. At this time the young A. D. Hope wrote a poem which was, like Mackellar's 'My Country', to become something of a classic, though of a different order. It managed to combine some of the oldest cultural myths about Australia with an intellectual discontent which seemed utterly contemporary. So, in its opening line, the poem, in identifying 'A Nation of trees, drab green and desolate grey', draws on the colonial image of a landscape of gumtree monotony. Not only the land is monotonous, but its people too:

> The river of her immense stupidity
> Floods her monotonous tribes from Cairns to Perth.

But the anti-urban tradition is also endorsed: her 'five cities' are 'like five teeming sores'. Hope offers for our contempt

> a vast parasite robber-state
> Where second-hand Europeans pullulate
> Timidly on the edge of alien shores.

It is, he alleges, a land 'Without songs, architecture, history'. Yet the poem concludes by deftly exploiting anti-European isolationism:

> Yet there are some like me turn gladly home
> From the lush jungle of modern thought, to find
> The Arabian desert of the human mind,
> Hoping, if still from the deserts the prophets come,
>
> Such savage and scarlet as no green hills dare
> Springs in that waste, some spirit which escapes
> The learned doubt, the chatter of cultured apes
> Which is called civilization over there.[35]

It is all there – the suspicion of 'modern thought', even a Mackellar-ish dissatisfaction with 'green hills'. It mattered not whether the poem was, in a literal sense, true. (Even then Australia had songs, architecture, history.) But in it Hope had distilled a mood, a frustration, a vision. He called it 'Australia': the year was 1939.

6

Political institutions

The unique and, to many, the perplexing achievement of Australian democracy has been to combine an egalitarian tradition with the politics of class. The contradiction is more apparent than real. Lacking a titled aristocracy and leisured class colonial society encouraged an egalitarianism of manners. Such manners reflected not the absence of social stratification, but a means of coming to terms with it in the new setting. The egalitarian society became a popular myth capable of various uses – it could be handily deployed in comparisons with 'class-ridden' Britain, and similarly invoked to condemn the perceived absurdity of class rhetoric in Australia; but perhaps most importantly it influenced the form and style of political solutions to social problems. Hence industrial arbitration, which has become such a significant and distinctive institution of Australian society, owes much of its character and rationale to the legacy of social egalitarianism. For whilst recognising class conflict in its industrial form, arbitration purported to replace the inequalities of social structure with a system which magically transformed bourgeoisie and working class into legal parties, equal before the law.

Arbitration was also a political solution in the sense that it emerged from a party system in a state of transition. When the colonies federated in 1901 their political structures varied. In New South Wales, Queensland and South Australia something like a party system existed, aided by the emergence of vigorous Labor parties, but the structures still seemed provisional. In Victoria the severity of the 1890s depression and the political emphasis on recovery had discouraged polarisation, and the Labor Party lacked organisation. In Tasmania and Western Australia parties hardly existed at all. Yet within a decade those States with parties had moved from three- to two-party systems, and Tasmania and Western Australia had speedily adopted similar models. Federation itself seemed to encourage this uniformity, though the survival of the tariff issue in the federal arena delayed the reduction to two parties there until 1909. It had taken Labor a mere eighteen years, from its first New South Wales electoral successes of 1891, to establish its position as one of the two parties. Appearances also suggested that Labor had dictated the terms of political conflict, for although 'Liberal' was at first the preferred name of the other party, as a political force it was also known as 'Anti-labor'.

In Britain the two-party system was regarded as the norm, and the intrusion, first, of the Irish party, and then Labor, was seen as corrupting it. Australians inherited a tendency to see constitutional virtue in a neat political bi-polarity; in a celebrated metaphor Deakin argued the impossibility of playing cricket with three elevens on the field. But the fact that political parties had been late in developing in the colonies meant that Labor could hardly be cast as an intruder complicating an existing order. Furthermore both in parliament and the electorate Labor was the organisational pacemaker, and its methods were often imitated, if reluctantly, by other parties. By 1911, when Labor was in office in the Commonwealth and three States, the professionalisation of politics was irreversibly under way.

Labor was a trade union-based party. (Only in Tasmania was there the short-lived oddity of a parliamentary party pre-dating a union involvement in the organisation.) Although the Labor Party of each colony was a separate entity, the mobility of workers encouraged the development of similar structures: the party which mushroomed after 1901 in Western Australia, for example, owed much to the trade unionism of the 't'othersiders' on the goldfields. Trade unions not only helped mobilise a working-class vote for the new party, but also provided the experience in organisation for its leaders. The ethos of trade unionism, with its emphasis on solidarity, also carried over. So emerged, though not without some argument, the distinctive Labor mechanisms: the caucus, the decisions of which were binding on the members constituting it, and the pledge, which enforced this discipline. These mechanisms were supported both in parliament and the organisation by the militant sentiment of working-class unity. Just as a worker disloyal to trade unionism was nastily labelled a 'scab', so too was a Labor renegade commonly called a 'rat'. To its opponents Labor seemed an efficient machine, manned by political zealots. But the discipline of the party could also create internal stresses which at times caused damaging 'splits'.

The growth of trade unionism in the years before the Great War – much assisted, as we shall see, by the introduction of wage regulation – fed the infant party, its vote increasing from 18.7 per cent in 1902 to 50 per cent in 1910. In Sydney and Melbourne Labor's hold on the inner suburbs (now often identified as slums) tightened. The Labor vote could also take on a regional character, as in northern Queensland, the coalmining districts of New South Wales, and union towns such as Broken Hill and Kalgoorlie. Manual workers formed the base of this vote, but many public servants were also coopted, particularly when Anti-labor groups sponsored campaigns for retrenchment and economy. As the political base for middle-class radicalism shrank, eventually disappearing altogether in the fusion of non-labor parties, some of its supporters cast a sympathetic eye towards Labor, but the party remained thin in professional men. Lawyers, for example, were at first hard to come by, and Watson, in forming the first federal Labor government in 1904, had to recruit H. B. Higgins, a Deakinite, as Attorney-General.

Just as Labor's trade union base helped determine the structures it adopted, so too it conditioned its ideological outlook. One should not be surprised, therefore, that the labour movement espoused a form of socialism which was populist rather than intellectual. If the source was often the United States that was largely because the American populist tradition produced a marketable political literature with a New World orientation. Henry George's *Progess and Poverty*, published in 1880, offered in the single tax a means of democratising land ownership which won a ready audience in the colonies, where land seemed so abundant and yet so locked up, and the visit of this political evangelist in 1890 confirmed the interest. But perhaps most revealing was the taste for utopianism, evident in the vogue for polemical novels, such as Bellamy's *Looking Backward* (1888) and Donnelly's *Caesar's Column* (1892). A taste for utopianism was understandable in a new society, but Bellamy in particular became almost a password in the circles of colonial labour. His utopia had been achieved through painless evolution; it also drew on the tradition of Christian socialism. It was, on both counts, a convenient and relatively uncontroversial vision for the movement. The early Labor Party included a significant nonconformist, particularly Methodist, element; while later on the Catholic association with the party reinforced suspicion of more materialist brands of socialism. If socialism was simply 'the desire to be mates'[1], as one union paper put it, who could possibly object? and if socialism was,

6.1   The library at the shearers' camp at Barcaldine, Queensland, during the 1891 strike. It is part of the myth that the bush unionists were eager readers, with reforming and utopian authors such as Henry George and Bellamy being popular. Certainly the weekly *Bulletin*, at this time sympathetic to the labour movement, would have been read by some shearers.

in any case, inevitable, what damage could be done by short-term compromises?

This was an important consideration because the unions, with their bitter memories of the defeats of the 1890s, expected the party to achieve quick results, and in its early years 'support in return for concessions' became a rewarding political tactic. Militance in the industrial sphere did not necessarily carry over into the parliamentary party; on the contrary, many union leaders, who could, like W. G. Spence, appear warlike on the industrial trail, nevertheless embraced pragmatism and compromise in the political arena. Nor was this necessarily a case of virile unionists suffering political castration; it could also stem from their perception of the mode of operation which would be most productive in a particular context. Labor's kind of socialism could also draw on the colonial tradition which tolerated much more state intervention than allowed for by dominant British *laissez-faire* economics. In a sense, of course, this was not socialism at all, even if its rhetoric sometimes gave it such a gloss; but on the other hand, eclectic and populist though it may have been, Labor's ideology was something more than what the fascinated French observer Métin called 'le socialisme sans doctrines'.[2]

There were socialists both in the movement and the party who looked much more to the Marxist school. But even quite early in the history of the Labor Party they were disillusioned by its lack of ideological rigour. Such socialists continued to operate in the party, and not always on the fringes; Tom Mann, for example, as organiser 1902–04 did much to mobilise the hitherto backward Victorian branch. Increasingly, however, they concentrated on developing their own 'purer' organisations. During and after the war the mood of the movement, influenced by industrial discontent and American syndicalism, was for a time more sympathetic to an explicit socialist commitment and programme, but for the most part the party adhered loosely to its populist tradition, whilst focusing its energies on campaigns for specific reforms. The importance of the alliance with the Catholic Church, particularly after the Hughes split of 1916, strengthened these priorities. Just as industrial militance coexisted with political pragmatism, so too did the radical impulses of the political left have to accommodate themselves to the institutional conservatism of trade union and party.

Although there was a significant American ideological influence on the Australian labour movement, from Bellamy to syndicalism, its cultural heritage remained firmly British. Many of the union and party leaders were British born; indeed there were fewer native born amongst the early Labor parliamentarians than amongst their non-labor opponents. Visiting British labour figures such as Ben Tillett, Keir Hardie and Ramsay MacDonald were received with an enthusiasm and respect which was increased by the knowledge that they came to learn from the colonial experience. Labor members readily accepted the British parliamentary system, and, indeed, were noted for their earnestness and industry in learning its ways. But they also introduced a new professionalism – they were usually 'full-time' members, totally dependent on their parliamentary salary – which was ultimately to transform political life.

It was often said that the labour ethos encouraged a suspicion of strong leadership. Hughes, for example, reputedly predicted that he would never get his party's leadership. 'The brains are the trouble. Our fellows distrust 'em. They'd sooner have "Andy" Fisher. He's moderately supplied so they think he's safe.'[3] Hughes was wrong in his prediction; he succeeded Fisher in 1915. But one year later his personal and provocative style of leadership led him out of the party, an experience which reinforced a suspicion of leaders who were seen as being waywardly ambitious. What Labor did require of its leaders were the tactical skills and patience to deal with its institutional structures, particularly the caucus, which also elected the cabinet, and the conference, which ultimately controlled platform and policy. T. J. Ryan, premier of Queensland 1915–19, had an untypical background, being a teacher turned barrister, but his Catholicism helped steer him into Labor politics. He owed much of his success as leader to his shrewdness and diplomacy in party dealings; he was able to avoid the conscription split which destroyed other Labor governments.

In New South Wales J. T. Lang, a figure who has acquired mythic proportions in Australian politics, dominated the party for much of the 1920s and 1930s. Like Ryan, he lacked a trade union background (he was a suburban real estate agent) but gained his hold over the party through a combination of an effective and ruthless machine and his flair as a charismatic demagogue. In his first term as premier Lang's programme included widows' pensions and the 44-hour week, measures which accorded well with Labor's reformist, trade-union tradition. But when, after a spell in opposition, he returned to office in 1930, Lang found himself on a collision course with his federal Labor colleagues, refusing to accept the policies dictated by economic orthodoxy. He gained particular notoriety when his government repudiated interest payments to British bondholders, throwing New South Wales into crisis. Lang, aided by his powerful machine, mobilised working-class support for a populist crusade against evil 'money power', but his campaign also, as we shall see, mobilised his opponents. In the end he was dismissed by the governor in a situation which teetered on the edge of violent confrontation. Yet although Lang was a populist and a demagogue, and although his enemies called him 'the Red Wrecker', he was also assailed by the Communists as 'a social fascist', and it is ironic that he eventually destroyed the socialisation units* within his own party because they threatened his power-base.

Few would have disputed that the Labor Party was a working-class party, even if all working-class people did not support it; indeed, it was the frequent complaint of its opponents that it *was* a class party. Anti-labor, on the other hand, claimed to be national or classless: in 1917, when receiving Hughes and his Labor renegades, it adopted the 'National' label; fourteen years later, in the depths of

* Radical groups dedicated to promoting socialist policies.

6.2   Premier J. T. Lang, known as the 'Big Fella', seen here, centre, at the opening of the Sydney Harbour Bridge in 1931, with the governor, Sir Philip Game, who is in full imperial rig. Lang, not Game, officially opened the Bridge. Shortly afterwards Game dismissed Lang.

the depression and another political crisis, it re-emerged as the United Australia Party. Both titles were intended to contrast with the sectionalism of 'Labor'. Yet although different interests and ideologies merged together in the 'fusion' (as it was called) the initial *raison d'être* of Anti-labor was the perceived necessity to match Labor's political organisation: even the denial of class had class implications.

In parliament the fusion brought together protectionists and freetraders, liberals and conservatives: protection was acknowledged as the national policy, but now lost much of the reformist impetus which Deakin had given it. Most parliamentarians conceded that in the electorate the new party would be heavily dependent on the employer organisations which had expanded greatly since federation. And so it proved to be. In the 1910 election, for example, seen at the time as a crucial test, the Victorian Employers' Federation held the party purse strings in that State; it had even gone to the trouble of raising money in London for the campaign.

After the war employers tightly controlled the raising of funds for the National Party.

Beyond the employers, however, was a range of organisations which helped mobilise middle-class voters to the Anti-labor cause. Women's leagues were formed, their leaders sometimes drawn, paradoxically, from the old anti-suffrage movement. Often these leagues achieved considerable influence, and in many ways women had more say in Anti-labor politics than in the Labor Party. (On both sides, however, candidature for parliament, let alone election, was extremely rare.) Farmers' organisations also became more political, and were swung behind the Anti-labor alliance. Even sectarianism was tapped, and militant Protestant organisations, designed to stem Romish influence, directed their support to the new party. The anti-Catholic tradition became part of the ambience of Anti-labor for more than half a century. Middle-class suburbia, permeated by Protestant respectability, was the social heartland of the party. According to one leader, addressing the first United Australia Party NSW convention in 1932, it was the middle party, based on the middle class, which had always saved Australia in time of distress.

The Great War created a new source for Anti-labor sentiment – the diggers. Hughes himself had through his identification with Australian soldiers (and gnome-like stature) earned himself the nickname, 'The Little Digger'. The Returned Servicemen's League always proclaimed itself to be non-political, but the labour movement's ambivalent attitude to the war was not easily forgotten. Diggers often professed a scepticism of party politics in general, believing that their service had not been adequately recognised, and just as roughly half the diggers had voted against conscription, no doubt many from working-class backgrounds remained sympathetic to Labor. Nevertheless Anti-labor was better placed ideologically to exploit both the material dissatisfaction of the diggers and the nationalist yearnings of Anzac.

Ideologically the party placed much emphasis on its hostility to socialism, a socialism which was depicted, not as a homegrown tradition ('the desire to be mates') but as an unAustralian intrusion, propagated by foreign agitators and revolutionaries. Yet Anti-labor had its own uses for state intervention. Protection, even though still resented by interests such as the rural sector, was maintained, even strengthened, while state enterprises were rarely dismantled. The Commonwealth Bank, for example, set up by Labor in 1911, was retained, but placed under a board which, it was argued, would be free of political control; in fact the composition of the board ensured that the bank would harmonise with private interests. In the Depression the board of the government's own bank was able to dictate policy to an embattled Labor administration.

But perhaps the unifying theme in the ideology of Anti-labor was its concern for property and its rights. Whereas Labor looked to the wage-earner, Anti-labor appealed to the property owner, whether the representative of capital, the farmer or the suburban house-owner. Labor tended to be suspicious of home ownership, which made it easier for its opponent to speak as if the interests of all property owners were the same. During the Depression the extent to which people's property was seen as under attack – both from economic misfortune and revolutionary challenge – helped motivate a revival of middle-class Anti-labor forces.

Leadership had a special significance for the Anti-labor cause. Without the leader, there was, in a sense, no party, for the initiative, both in making policies and cabinets, lay with him. Party structures, as such, offered few constraints, the parliamentary wing being virtually autonomous. Yet this apparent freedom of the leader, as compared with his Labor counterpart, was often illusory. The powerful interests which funded the party assumed that they had a right, at the very least, to exert an influence in policy areas that concerned them. Moreover the high expectations which attached to the leader could easily invite disappointment; and once the leadership was in dispute, ugly vendettas could break out.

Between the wars Anti-labor's two longest-serving leaders illustrate different aspects of its concept of leadership. Whilst the old liberals had in 1917 accepted Hughes's leadership of the new National Party as a war necessity, they did not warm to either his abrasive style or populist values, both of which could be seen as part of his Labor heritage. In 1923 Hughes was discarded, and Stanley Bruce was caterpulted into the prime ministership after a mere four years in parliament. Part of Bruce's appeal to Nationalists was that he was not seen as being a politician in the conventional sense at all. A Cambridge graduate, he had served in the British, not Australian, Army, and was a successful Melbourne businessman. According to legend, his leadership qualities having been recognised, he was drafted, almost against his will, into parliament. Bruce was, for many middle-class people, an impressive figure, acceptably English in manner, while businessmen were jubilant that at last one of their own breed, rather than a political wheeler-dealer, was at the helm. He presided over a government committed to a policy of develop-

6.3   Prime Minister Joe Lyons and his wife Enid proudly displaying the extent of their family. The visual suggestion of regimentation could be seen as reflecting an aspect of the culture.

ment, summed up in the slogan, 'Men, Money and Markets': all three were to be British.

Bruce was defeated in 1929, and two years later, in the depths of the Depression, the Nationalists looked to a different kind of leadership in Lyons. Here was another ex-Labor man, but from a different school to Hughes. A schoolteacher by training, he hailed from Tasmania, where Labor politics were set in a more conservative, small-town mould, which contrasted with the hurly-burly of New South Wales which had created Hughes. Whereas Bruce was the Anglo-Australian proponent of capitalist development, Lyons was the healing unifier in a time of social stress. Bruce was often characterised as the aloof gentleman who wore spats: to cartoonists Lyons was a kindly koala presiding from a gumtree. Lyons' leadership of the United Australia Party, formed to expel Labor from office and inaugurate the economic recovery, also reflected an important gesture from Protestant Anti-labor – for the new prime minister was a Catholic (and with a Catholic-sized family of eleven children). Yet although conservatives were thankful for the role that Lyons played, many still hankered for that other, more commanding leadership which Bruce represented; and during the years he served, appropriately enough, as high commissioner in London, there were intermittent attempts to recall him to the prime ministership. Bruce himself remarked privately that Lyons, although 'a marvellous election leader, . . . was not competent to run a Government between elections'.[4] Lyons died in office in 1939, tired and disillusioned; Bruce stayed on in London, becoming one of the few Australians to receive a peerage, taking the title Lord Bruce of Melbourne.

In spite of recurrent instability, with Labor splits in 1916 and 1931 and corresponding realignments of its opponents, the politics of Labor versus Anti-labor survived, but with one major modification. After the Great War a third party emerged, and soon established itself as a semi-independent wing of Anti-labor. This, the Country Party as it was then called,* was stimulated into being by primary producers' concern about the war-time marketing schemes for their produce. It was not that these schemes were necessarily disadvantageous to them, but rather that they alerted farmers and graziers to their need for a political voice. The Country Party, however, drew on a longstanding rural tradition which saw politics as urban dominated. So protection was widely seen as a policy which benefited manufacturers and urban workers, but penalised primary producers. In a time of renewed urbanisation, this anti-city feeling, which could encompass some hostility to 'big business', served as a powerful focus for a party which had to cater for the needs of diverse rural industries.

In this sense the Country Party was not new. In the days of more fluid politics, short-lived parliamentary 'country parties' had come together for particular purposes. But now that politics had been professionalised, and the party order formalised, the rural sector feared that its interests could be overlooked. It was necessary, therefore, for the Country Party to have autonomy, even if, in practice, it would submerge that autonomy in Anti-labor coalitions. Although the Nationalists resented the newcomer, they very quickly came to terms with it. When the Country Party's first electoral successes threatened to split the Anti-labor vote, preferential voting was hastily introduced: so another element in Australian political tradition was, in this quite casual but self-interested manner, set in place.† Then in 1923, the Country Party having assisted in

---

* In recent years re-christened the National Party.

† After some experimentation with different systems most States followed the Commonwealth with preferential voting. Queensland, however, retained first past the post voting till 1963, while Tasmania had in 1907 opted for proportional representation.

HIS ONLY HOPE.

6.4 This cartoon, in the *Pastoral Review*, 1913, already conjures up the dream of a Country Party, which will, presumably, remove the burden from the shoulders of the man on the land.

the political demise of Hughes, a coalition between the two Anti-labor parties was negotiated which set the precedent for subsequent deals. Although the new order was not to be without its strains, only in Victoria, where factional politics continued to thrive, was the unity of the Anti-labor forces seriously affected – and there Labor was too weak to take full advantage of the division. Basically what Prime Minister Bruce and his Country Party deputy, Earle Page, established in 1923 was a joint policy of 'protection all round': the tariff wall which sustained manufacturers would now be offset by a generous system of bounties giving the rural sector matching benefits. Here was another accommodation with which Australians would live for many years. The blatant sectionalism of the Country Party was often to offend political commentators, but their reaction misses the point. As a party it made no claims to be national: it was in fact a self-conscious faction with the Anti-labor movement which realised that party status and party organisation could give it the political clout which mere lobbying could not. As such the Country Party was a cultural product of the disjunction between the urban majority and the rural minority.

There were always those who professed to despise 'party politics' and, unable to accept the logic of history, looked for alternatives. Such critics drew on a colonial cynicism about 'politicians' (in their mouths the very word could sound like an insult). Partly this reflected the lack of a longstanding political tradition; the sudden advent of democracy in the 1850s was seen as having made parliament a prey to opportunists and demagogues. The early introduction of the Chartist reform of payment of members (Victoria led the way in 1871) also encouraged among some of the well-to-do an elitist contempt for politics, which should have been a calling for gentlemen but had become a business for hirelings. Thus was Australia characterised as being plagued by politicians, just as some other countries were by clergy or soldiers. In the twentieth century the raising of parliamentary salaries would always provide the occasion for anti-political feeling to assert itself. Federation itself offered an opportunity to strike a blow against politicians. Now that the States had less business to conduct they would, it was argued, need fewer politicians, and 'reform' movements, dedicated to economy both in parliament and public service, were launched. Constitutional referenda also seemed to be an irritant, and, although the Constitution has never enjoyed the public status of its American model, proposals to amend it have tended to be seen as serving the interests of politicians and rejected accordingly.

Politicians were only too well aware of this cynicism, and the apathy to which it could contribute. One response was the introduction of compulsory voting, first in Queensland in 1915, then in the Commonwealth in 1924; other States followed. The self-conscious uneasiness with which parliamentarians thus attempted to enforce democracy is reflected in the 'conspiracy of silence' surrounding the passing of the Commonwealth legislation: introduced in the Senate as a private member's bill, it went through the House of Representatives with almost no debate, and with no comment from government ministers. Yet there has never been a serious move to abolish compulsory voting, the denial of freedom perhaps seeming too trivial to merit resistance; for in practice it is not 'voting' which is compulsory, but attendance at the polling booth.

The extent of apathy should not be exaggerated. (It is possible, for example, that one of the attractions of compulsory voting for politicians was that it immensely simplified electoral campaigning.) And dissatisfaction with party politics could itself stimulate political activity. Some people proposed unrealistic panaceas, such as cabinets elected by parliament, or 'national' governments. Proportional representation was sometimes seen as an antidote for party politics, though in Tasmania, where it has been used since 1909, the party system has remained very stable, in spite of the opportunities afforded independents.

In its emergence after the war the Country Party benefited from rural suspicion of party politics, which tended to be seen as part of the urban culture: indeed, in its very sectionalism, the new party claimed to speak for all country people, townspeople as well as primary producers. New States movements likewise exploited the association of party politics with the capital cities which allegedly neglected outlying country areas. The return of Labor to office in New South Wales in 1930, under the defiant leadership of Lang, gave an immediate impetus to new States movements in the New England and the Riverina districts. Once the crisis which Lang symbolised had passed, the movements lost much of their drive.

While in any indictment of party politics Labor was the principal culprit, Anti-labor also received critical attention. Particularly was this so in the Depression, when the National Party had failed in what many saw as its essential purpose, namely, to keep Labor out of office. The organisations which now sprang up often identified themselves as 'peoples' movements, just as the reform movement had in the wake of federation: if they did not actually blame party politics for the Depression, they certainly characterised it as preventing recovery. The most notable was the All for Australia League, which was, the *Sydney Morning Herald* reported, 'a new non-party political organization ... conceived primarily to purge politics'. It claimed, as its name implied, to be formed 'to draw together citizens of every class in a spirit of patriotism'.[5] Yet the League's middle-class origins were evident in it being launched in one of Sydney's wealthiest suburbs, while its 'non-party' status was ceded a mere three months later when it merged with the Nationalists and other groups to form the United Australia Party under Lyons. So could anti-political sentiment serve party ends.

In the period between the wars the critique of party politics also merged into a critique of democracy. Sometimes this could take apparently innocuous forms, as with the new respect for 'experts'. So Mrs Herbert Brookes, daughter of Deakin and a leader of the Australian Women's National League, could assert the need for 'an advisory board of businessmen, economic experts and a few experienced women to undertake scientific investigations and to advise the Government'. The example of Fascist Italy, and later on Nazi Germany, also raised the question of leadership and commitment. After a visit to Germany in 1938, Menzies, while admitting that totalitarianism was 'not suited to the British genius', nevertheless expressed admiration for the 'really spiritual quality in the willingness of young Germans to devote themselves to the service and well-being of the State'; later he was to speak of Australia's need for 'inspiring leadership'. In the mid 1930s William MacMahon Ball, hardly a conservative, also conceded that 'Stalin, Hitler and Mussolini have discovered an altogether superior technique of leadership', and suggested that 'if we are to make democracy a living reality, we must discover the technique of arousing the same kind of emotion as is undoubtedly aroused in Europe'.[6] It seemed that even leadership was a matter of *technique*, for which there were appropriate *experts*.

Such comments reveal a concern not only about leaders but the led. It was often the electors' self-interest which was blamed for democracy's apparent failure to solve the problems of the Depression. J. A. McCallum identified a 'submerged stratum' of society which was 'readily responsive to the mass bribe and the sadistic pleasure that comes from making the comfortable classes uncomfortable': he blamed this 'stratum' for 'much that now masquerades as Labor policy'. Such a diagnosis could easily lead to a eugenicist prescription. So the 'Psychologist' and 'Physician' who authored a book on 'Australia's national decline' entitled *Whither Away?* could similarly lament that 'it is to this flotsam and jetsam of human society that we pander with our democratic laws', but conclude that 'degeneration in a race can only be remedied when the nation thinks and acts with one voice'.[7] The 'flotsam and jetsam' were not part of that 'nation': they would be taken care of with compulsory sterilization and certificates of fitness for marriage.

This middle-class dissatisfaction with democracy was not always spelt out in such extreme terms, but it was a pervasive

6.5 In this scene from the Brisbane general strike of 1912 special constables stand at the ready with bayoneted rifles. This kind of middle-class 'law and order' was to take a more concerted form after the First World War, when fears of civil disorder grew.

presence in the 1920s and 1930s, and political life was conducted in its shadow. The war had seen the federal government assume unprecedented authority under the defence power of the constitution, and when peace came there was a school of conservative thought which argued the continued need for 'strong' government. However Australia's commitment to the structures of federalism posed a problem in both a practical and ideological sense. On the other hand, the fear of civil disorder which was also, in large measure, a legacy of the war resulted in various shadowy organisations, dedicated to 'law-and-order'; these sometimes took on the character of private armies. The election of a Labor government in New South Wales in 1920 occasioned the formation of the King and Empire Alliance, dedicated to 'combat the forces of disloyalty in our community'. The Alliance appears to have had a military dimension which provided D. H. Lawrence with the basis of the neo-fascist digger organisation in *Kangaroo*. In Melbourne in 1923 when police went on strike a 'special constabulary force' of some 6,000 was recruited, many of whom were diggers; when the strike had collapsed, elements of this 'force' seemed to have become the White Guard under the leadership of General Sir Brudenell White.[8] The secrecy of these groups, which, for the most part, were never put to the test, accounts for the fact that for many years it was assumed that Lawrence had simply transposed his Italian experience to an Australian setting.

One such organisation, however, did for a short time achieve public prominence, and raises important doubts about the Australian commitment to democracy. When Lang came to office in New South Wales in 1930, with unemployment close to 20 per cent, there was immediate middle-class alarm. The All for Australia League was one response: but another and more sensational reaction was the sudden mobilisation of the New Guard. This organisation was 'New' to distinguish it from a pre-existing 'Old' Guard (sometimes called the Movement) which probably had a line of descent going back to the King and Empire Alliance. Its leaders were mostly ex-service officers whose shared war experience alienated them from the older generation of business and professional men who dominated the Old Guard, a generation which they tended to characterise as lacking leadership and vitality. The New Guard group did not see themselves as 'political'. As Eric Campbell, its founder, put it, 'for all I cared, the politicians of all brands could have gone and boiled their heads or suffered death from the boredom of listening to the dreary pronouncements of their political opponents'; he was more concerned with securing 'economic independence by building a mighty practice [as a solicitor] and an occasional developmental activity on the side'.[9] But in 1931 they felt the need to intervene in a crisis which they deemed the Old Guard incapable of resolving. Organised along military lines with 'localities', and with Campbell installed as Chief Commander, the New Guard expanded rapidly, perhaps enlisting as many as 50,000.

According to the attestation paper its members had to sign, the New Guard offered 'unswerving loyalty' to King and Empire, and while standing for 'sane and honourable representative Government', proposed the 'abolition of machine politics' and, most significantly, the 'suppression of any disloyal and immoral elements in Governmental, industrial and social circles'. How was this to be done? The attestation paper merely noted that the Guard would 'take all proper and necessary steps to effect any or all of its principles'. Campbell himself believed that while the New Guard would act in case of 'civil strife', it would also intervene to prevent any attempt at socialisation, 'constitutional or unconstitutional'.[10] Nor were the All for Australia League and the New Guard seen as alternatives: many respectable citizens belonged to both. Sir Sidney Snow, one of the businessmen founders of the AFA, told Campbell that the New Guard was the fighting wing and the AFA the political wing of the same brand of thought.

Overall the New Guard indulged more in bluster than action. Members drilled in secret, and sometimes broke up Communist meetings. One Captain de Groot, an antique dealer, scored a symbolic triumph for the Guard when at the opening of the Sydney Harbour Bridge he slashed the ribbon with his sword before Premier Lang could perform the ceremony. There is evidence that a section of the Guard may have planned to kidnap Lang, but for whatever reasons such a coup was not attempted. And, as with the new states movements, the governor's dismissal of the Lang government in May 1932, subsequently endorsed by the electorate, deprived the New Guard of the sense of crisis which had fostered it. Nevertheless the fascist potential of the organisation is all the more interesting for its relative isolation from European ideology. Looking back in 1934, Campbell confessed that he 'became a Fascist without knowing what Fascism was'. His own authoritarian style of leadership caused some disaffection in the ranks, and the ambiguity of the New Guard's aims disguised a tension between those who wanted to develop the fascist initiative, with appropriate salutes and uniforms, and those who preferred a more discreet and defensive posture. Yet the concern with the paraphernalia of European fascism (which sometimes could seem faintly ridiculous in the antipodean setting) should not obscure the fact that much of the New Guard's neo-fascist vitality had indigenous roots. Campbell and his cronies drew on the digger, petty-bourgeois sense of social grievance; they even claimed that the New Guard was internally democratic (egalitarian?), just as the AIF was said to be, though of course no army can be other than hierarchical. There was always a strong element of military nostalgia and boy scouts' high-jinks in the Depression escapades of what Campbell termed 'that rather unique and happy fellowship called the New Guard'.[11] Its very maleness – so often taken for granted – accorded with Australian social tradition. Just as war was 'men's work', so too, it was implied, was the new politics of fighting subversion. The new war was to be conducted in an urban setting, and the structure of the New Guard, with its 'localities', reflected the structure of Australian suburbia.

That the New Guard petered out in 1935, and that it was confined to New South Wales, has given it the appearance of an aberration, something not really part of the Australian political culture. Yet the evidence of other such organisations suggests that it was by no means exceptional, and that middle-class disillusion with democracy was a continuing factor. When, in the context of the Depression, Labor had been safely banished, the need for this disillusion to be translated into action lost its urgency. Apathy could work both ways: whilst at times it might endanger democratic processes, at other times it could, in a passive sense, protect them. But the end of the New Guard did not spell the end of middle-class ambivalence towards democracy: another crisis was always capable of reactivating it.

Perhaps part of the irritation with democracy stemmed from the realisation that the party system had stabilised into a kind of permanence: in spite of Labor splits and Anti-labor transformations the system remained basically the same. Arbitration was another institution which had become a fixture, and it too was, from time to time, a cause for frustration, particularly in Anti-labor circles. But arbitration was considerably modified over the years, and became something rather different from what its founders had intended.

In its origins the intervention of the state in industrial affairs was justified as a means of replacing 'brute force' (strikes and lockouts) with 'reason' (a tribunal or board imposing a wage award or determination), and was a response to the unrest and dislocation of the early 1890s. At another level it was a means of adjusting the industrial balance of power which had, in the depression of that decade, tipped dramatically in the employers' favour. This aspect appealed to the labour movement which had little difficulty in overcoming inherited British qualms about the state intervening in trade union affairs. Once labour leaders appreciated that arbitration in particular was predicated on the existence of organisations on both sides, they realised that it would stimulate the revival and expansion of trade unionism, and most became ardent supporters. In the triangular politics of the 1890s and early 1900s – Deakin's 'three elevens' – arbitration was one of the social reforms which middle-class radicals enacted with enthusiastic Labor support.

The Commonwealth Arbitration Court, founded in 1904, set the pace in this new state initiative, particularly under the dynamic presidency of H. B. Higgins, 1907–21. Higgins, an Irish-born lawyer, had gained a reputation as a stubborn and individual radical, who did not flinch from unpopular causes, such as opposing federation on the terms negotiated (he thought the constitution too 'provincial') and condemning the Boer War. Although a Protestant by upbringing, he was a strong supporter of Irish Home Rule, and was respected alike by the labour movement and the Catholic community. As a KC and leader of the equity bar, Higgins seemed well qualified to explore what he called 'the new province for law and order'.[12]

Higgins saw arbitration as much more than a procedure for settling industrial disputes. His very first case gave him a unique opportunity to map out his approach. The Commonwealth had recently enacted 'New Protection' legislation which required manufacturers, to escape excise duties, to pay their employees 'fair and reasonable' wages, to be certified accordingly by the Court. The case, then, involving H. V. McKay, the manufacturer of the Sunshine Harvester, was not an ordinary arbitration proceeding, but compelled Higgins to decide what constituted a 'fair and reasonable' wage for an unskilled labourer. His starting point was that the legislation was designed to benefit employees, intending 'to secure them something which they cannot get by the ordinary system of individual bargaining'. He concluded that the only appropriate standard was 'the normal needs of the average employee, regarded as a human being living in a civilized community'. These 'normal needs' included provision for a wife and children, and Higgins made a somewhat primitive calculation of a household budget for a family of 'about five persons'.[13] Thus was established the basic wage.

The Harvester Judgment, as it was called, became the cornerstone of the court, to be built on by subsequent decisions. The basic wage was sacrosanct. If a firm could not afford to pay it, then it was better that it close down, rather than exploit its employees. (Margins, however, could legitimately be adjusted according to the prosperity of an industry, because this did not imperil the basic needs of the worker.) Understandably this uncompromising doctrine alienated employers, but it made the court popular with trade unions, who sought to 'federalise' their disputes in order to bring them within its jurisdiction, for Higgins's minimum awards were notably higher than those set by most state tribunals. Less obvious at the time was the extent to which *Harvester*, in enshrining a family wage, led to an elaborate stratification of 'male' and 'female' occupations, which would prove a formidable barrier to equal pay.

In the years before the Great War a return to prosperity meant that industry, the hostility of employers notwithstanding, was able to cope with the pressure on wages. The apparent success of arbitration, and wage regulation more generally, attracted attention abroad, and contributed greatly to the gathering reputation of

Australia – and New Zealand, which had earlier led the way in state intervention in industrial disputes – as a 'social laboratory for the world'. Whilst the image of the 'working man's paradise' had not been entirely discarded, the depression of the 1890s had seriously weakened it. That the 'paradise' had now become a 'laboratory' reflected the shift from a romantic to a scientific perception. 'Experts' and politicians in the United States, Britain and Europe examined the 'experiments' being conducted in the 'laboratory', and argued as to whether the results could be applied in the Old World. In Britain some liberal imperialists saw such colonial experimentation as one of the benefits of Empire. Sir Charles Dilke, for example, presided over a British anti-sweating campaign, which drew largely on colonial experience, resulting in the introduction in 1909 of 'trade boards' (later, wage councils) based on the Victorian wages boards.

Arbitration, however, was not often copied abroad; it remained a distinctively Australasian institution. What often seemed, in the Australian context, the advantage of arbitration – parliament's shedding of a difficult responsibility onto a quasi-judicial tribunal – was, to British officials, a weakness, for they saw government as thus losing an industrial and economic power which it might at times have reason to exercise. But in Australia politicians found that the judicial solution satisfactorily distanced them from a potentially dangerous issue. In any case the Constitution had only given the Commonwealth industrial responsibility through its limited arbitration power. Although Higgins lamented parliament's 'shunting of legislative responsibility' in leaving it to him to define 'fair and reasonable', he seized the opportunity to develop the court as a powerful, autonomous institution.[14]

The legal apparatus of arbitration also seemed suited to the cultural climate. British trade unions remained immensely wary of state intrusion into the industrial arena, but in Australia the labour movement was much more historically conditioned to state initiatives, and, although retaining some suspicion of the class credentials of judges, was more easily persuaded that the law could be mobilised to its advantage. The technical parity which the system accorded employers and workers also satisfied the egalitarian temper which Australians credited themselves with. The whole master-servant relationship, with its echoes of the convict past, was subtly translated into a legal dispute between parties which had to argue their case before an impartial judge, who was characterised as somehow representing the public. This 'public' had a decidedly middle-class image (by inference it excluded employers and trade unionists), but it was a concept with a powerful political appeal. It was difficult to argue against a system which so ostentatiously invoked the public interest.

For Higgins the court, representing the public, became the arbiter of the standard of living. In 1911 the journal *Melbourne Punch* described him as 'the real ruler of Australia just now' who controlled 'the citizens' in terms of 'their pockets, their hours of working, their presents and their futures'. It saw Higgins as having 'without deliberate intention created a new public opinion'.[15] This was, of course, an exaggeration: the court had jurisdiction over only a minority of workers. But it was true in the broad sense that this new institution – which comprised not only federal but six state systems – had established a powerful presence, and that Higgins had helped create a climate of public acceptance.

The war marked an end to this mood of optimism. Social and industrial unrest undermined the authority of the Arbitration Court. Trade unions grew restless with the court's legalism, while socialists preached that arbitration was a bourgeois institution designed to ameliorate the class war. Employers, on the other hand, urged that the court discipline recalcitrant unions, de-registering them if necessary. Some employers argued that Australian economic recovery after the War demanded that the entire system be dismantled: if any form of wage regulation were needed they preferred the homelier Victorian wages boards. Meanwhile the Hughes government pursued an erratic policy, at times by-passing the court by setting up special tribunals to sort out particular disputes. Irritated and frustrated by all these attacks, Higgins resigned the presidency in 1921.

Yet the system survived, even if pressure from Anti-labor governments gave it a more conservative character. Much of Higgins's Promethean sense of mission was lost, and the court showed less interest in improving the workers' lot. Nevertheless trade unions, whatever criticisms they offered, found in it some degree of security, while employers gradually came to accept its permanence, and concentrated on developing its disciplinary role. There was now a mutual realisation that arbitration had not, and, indeed, could not, abolish strikes and lock-outs; it could at times resolve them, but generally its regulatory role was to impose some sort of coherence on industrial relations. In 1929 the Bruce-Page government, which had long been preoccupied with labour problems, attempted to simplify things by virtually closing down the Commonwealth Court and leaving wage regulation to the States. There was immediate uproar, and Hughes and a few rebels helped defeat the government in the House of Representatives; the ensuing landslide victory of Labor at the polls very much confirmed the institutional inviolability of arbitration.

Arbitration had thus become part of a complex economic and political accommodation. Although the New Protection, which affirmed that if manufacturers merited protection so did their employees, had, in its literal form, been invalidated by the High Court, it continued in a broader sense to provide an ideological underpinning for wage regulation. Manufacturers, farmers and workers all claimed entitlements to the 'benefits' of state intervention. And while both capital and labour had reasons for dissatisfaction with the way the arbitration system worked, both nevertheless hoped to use it to their own ends.

By 1929 the system had lost much of its international glamour, and few would have claimed that Australia was still a 'social laboratory'. The pre-war reformist energy had been either dissipated or deflected into less ambitious concerns. One reason for the Bruce-Page government's suicidal attack on arbitration was its sensitivity to the advice of economic 'experts' both at home and abroad who tended to make wage regulation a scapegoat for the difficulties being experienced by the Australian economy in the late 1920s. In the wake of the government's expulsion from office, the emphasis now had to be on making the court responsive to the wisdom of the economists. In 1931 the court took heed of the 'expert' advice and cut real wages by 10 per cent. Although introduced as a temporary sacrifice, it was a symbolic departure from the *Harvester* standard.

The Depression not only confirmed that the 'social laboratory' was a thing of the past, it also identified the concerns which the laboratory had neglected. Dating from what seemed the halcyon days of the 'working-man's paradise', Australians had tended to assume a right to work. In the face of unemployment workers looked to governments to provide jobs. Although the 1890s depression directed the attention of legislators to the problems of industrial strife, sweating and poverty, surprisingly little interest was shown in unemployment insurance, Queensland being the only State to introduce such a scheme. Workers themselves continued to emphasise the need for work rather than relief, and in their resentment of charity often made little distinction between relief offered by public and private authorities. Trade union leaders expressed hostility to 'money doles', because, as the secretary of the Melbourne Trades Hall put it, 'a man loses his manliness under such a system'.[16] This was part of the colonial inheritance which could prize independence even in the context of the employment relationship. Such an attitude assumed a state role in regulating conditions of work, but at the same time proved an obstacle to providing more positive forms of state social welfare. The persistence of unemployment throughout the 1930s forced a rethinking of this attitude, whilst consolidating the over-riding importance for the labour movement of the elusive goal of full employment.

Both parties tended to accept a balance between state and private enterprise. While Labor had created the Commonwealth Bank, which operated alongside trading banks, in 1932 an Anti-labor government established the Australian Broadcasting Commission which, unlike the BBC, coexisted with commercial broadcasting stations. The state had always been important in providing facilities such as railways and electric power, and the comfortable coexistence of private and public enterprise, theoretically in competition with each other, represented an accommodation which transcended party politics.

The Depression did little to disturb this accommodation (which was later to provide the model for aviation) but it did direct attention to the weaknesses of federalism. Just as industrial relations were characterised by the inefficiency of competing Commonwealth and State regulatory systems, so too was economic and financial responsibility shared. Prior to the collapse of 1929 this hardly mattered, for the need for a national economic policy was not recognised. The Depression crisis therefore required a convoluted series of negotiated policy settlements – not only between Commonwealth and State governments, but also involving the Commonwealth Bank, the Arbitration Court, and, of course, the imperial interest as represented by the Bank of England's Sir Otto Niemeyer, who visited Australia in 1931.

While the Great War had demanded a greater Commonwealth role, the coming of peace saw a return to old federalist assumptions. The Loan Council, established in 1924 and given teeth by the Financial Agreement of 1929, brought together Commonwealth and States in the approved federal manner, but led, in practice, to a shift of power to the Commonwealth Treasury which provided the Council's administration. It was now becoming clear that given the Australian people's reluctance to formally amend the Constitution any centralising of power in the Commonwealth depended on either the wielding of financial influence or on the judicial interpretation of the Constitution by the High Court. This body, envisaged by the federal fathers as a priestly guardian of the federal compact, gradually came to accept that the changing needs of society might call for a more dynamic view of the Constitution. Various High Court decisions effectively increased Commonwealth power, but what the court gave, it could also take away. A change in membership or in the political climate could affect the court's outlook, and there was no guarantee that its decisions would continue to favour the Commonwealth cause. Here, then, as with the Arbitration Court, was another powerful autonomous body which had become part of the institutional structure of Australian politics. In one sense the High Court was making federation workable; but it was also changing its very nature. The people having failed at referendums to modernise the Constitution, the court took over, and most Australians seemed unperturbed by its assuming that role.

The States were often annoyed by the shift of power to the Commonwealth, but there was not much that they could do about it; in any case they remained divided by old competing provincial interests. Western Australia, most isolated of the States, briefly flirted with secession during the Depression when farmers' resentment towards the tariff, which protected eastern manufacturing industry but penalised them, reasserted itself. There had always been an element in the West which saw the colony as having been hijacked into federation by the goldrush influx of t'other-siders, and this provided a base for secessionist feeling which Depression disillusion could then build upon. The issue was, however, a potentially dangerous one for the political parties, which preferred in 1933 to put the question to a referendum. The people voted two to one for secession, yet simultaneously elected to office Labor, the party with the least enthusiasm for implementing it.

The aftermath was revealing. How in any case could secession be realised? A handsome, official volume was prepared, presenting *The Case of the People of Western Australia* for secession; the Commonwealth dutifully replied with *The Case for Union*. A Western Australian delegation journeyed to London to deliver jarrah-bound copies of its *Case* to the Imperial Parliament, but a Joint Select Committee of the two Houses declined to act upon the petition. There being no question of Western Australians launching a civil war, the secession vote now provided the occasion for financial haggling between Commonwealth and State. A Commonwealth Grants Commission was set up to systematise the making of Commonwealth grants to the less populous, 'claimant' States, Western

Australia, South Australia and Tasmania. As the Depression lifted, the secession movement lapsed.

There was a sense in which Western Australia's argument was not so much with the Commonwealth as such, as with the eastern States which it saw as dominating federation. This helps explain the curious anomaly that while the West was the only State to launch a serious secession movement, it nevertheless maintained a record of voting 'Yes', usually against the national trend, to constitutional amendments extending Commonwealth power. Secessionism was an expression of the West's distinctive *mentalité*, which incorporated a nostalgia for an independent past: once it came face to face with the institutional realities of Australian federation its limitations were exposed. So, too, the periodic resurgence of new states movements in New South Wales and Queensland always foundered on the difficulty of negotiating the constitutional hurdles, which included the consent of the State to be dismembered.

Federation therefore contributed to the force of inertia in Australian politics. Insofar as Labor was more unificationist than its opponents, the Constitution worked to frustrate its policies, but the fate of Western Australian secession and the new states movements point to other ways in which the structures of federalism have been politically restrictive. If Australians generally accepted federation, it was in a passive sense. The Constitution was not venerated, and for most Australians probably remained a mystery, though hardly a tantalising one. For all its inefficiencies, federation seemed to provide a tolerable *modus vivendi*, with the popular bonus that its checks and balances provided an opportunity for anti-political sentiment to periodically assert itself.

Although the Constitution could at times also thwart the policy initiatives of Anti-labor governments, the institutional complexity of federation was generally congenial to political conservatism. Australian historians have sometimes seen Labor as the party of initiative in Australian politics, and its opponents as the parties of resistance, but such a model implies a value judgment about the policies pursued by the two political forces. In any case, Labor's capacity for initiative was always a limited one, whether in the days of 'support in return for concessions' when it was often dependent on the policy concepts of middle-class radicals, or when, having graduated as one of the main parties, it dissipated much of its energy in internal wrangling. The Labor split in the Great War ushered in a period of conservative domination of federal politics (although at a state level Labor often remained powerful). It was ironical that the only Labor government of the inter-war period, the Scullin government 1929–31, was in no position to 'initiate' policies, being thwarted both by the constraints of the Constitution and an Anti-labor majority in the Senate; in the end it implemented the programme dictated to it by the financial establishment. Only in the sense that the Labor Party's emergence was crucial in creating the Australian party system can it be credited with a role of 'initiative' denied to other parties.

In spite of the furore of the Lang crisis, the Depression in the end consolidated the party system, whilst in the short-term strengthening its Anti-labor bias. But the social tensions of the Depression also exposed potential deviations across the political spectrum. The New Guard gave strident voice to a usually dormant neo-fascist tendency, while the Communist Party, hitherto a marginal group, gathered impetus from the Depression and began to establish a significant base in the trade union movement. Douglas Credit, with its populist middle-class appeal, also made an impact, though never gaining the foothold that it did in Canada and New Zealand.

Both the Great War and the Depression were events which dramatically impinged on the Australian consciousness. Both were world catastrophes which seemed, from the local perspective, inexplicable. According to the narrator of George Johnston's *My Brother Jack* the Depression came 'like a great river flooding or changing its course' with 'the insidious creeping movement of dark, strong, unpredictable forces'.[17] The combination of War and Depression had a profound impact on the lives and outlook of a whole generation of Australians – yet this impact was largely contained within a range of political institutions already established. This reflected the underlying reality that the Australian social structure changed relatively little between 1914 and 1939. The drift to the cities continued (temporarily checked by the Depression tendency for men to travel the bush), and secondary industry gained in importance. But the class structure remained basically the same, and the Depression only served to heighten the contrast between middle- and working-class experience. For although middle-class people were not exempt from Depression hardship, they were better placed to withstand it: for workers the margin between what Higgins called 'frugal comfort' and poverty was always less. Unemployment was high, peaking at 28.1 per cent in 1932, a rate second only to Germany's. Whilst this is not the only criterion, and whilst environmental factors may have mitigated the effects of unemployment – the introduced rabbit fed many, becoming in consequence rather despised as a food – it remains true that as an exporter of primary products and an international borrower Australia was particularly vulnerable to the Depression. If the revolutionary moment of truth which Lang seemed to create proved illusory, then so too did the talk of unity and equality of sacrifice. The political instability of the Depression marked not the weakening but the strengthening of the politics of class.

The Depression had briefly thrown up the possibility that politics might be taken into the streets of suburbia and country town: once parliamentary institutions had reasserted their dominance, the accommodations of Australian political culture similarly came into play again. There were adjustments, of course (like the 10 per cent cut in real wages), but the party system, industrial arbitration and federation all channelled social conflict into certain forms, whilst simultaneously treating it with the historical legacy of the 'social laboratory', that nostalgic inheritance of the egalitarianism of manners which retained an emotional appeal for most Australians.

Perhaps the figure of Joe Lyons – together with his high-profile wife, Enid – best encapsulates the political atmosphere of the period. A man of some integrity and egalitarian instincts, Lyons lacked political imagination and could see no alternative to the conventional economic wisdom of the 'experts', and was vulnerable, in a time of crisis, to the appeal of consensus politics. In spite of the part he played in the Scullin Labor government's downfall, Lyons was protected by a kind of innocence which seemed to minimise the venom which Labor usually reserved for its 'rats'. In the end Lyons was betrayed by those who had helped lure him from the Labor fold; as the newspaper magnate, Sir Keith Murdoch, put it, 'He has lost his usefulness; he is a conciliator, a peace man and, of course, a born rail-sitter'. Consensus politics had gone out of fashion: there had, in reality, been precious little consensus, even within the United Australia Party which Lyons led.

His wife, Enid, had always been an important factor in Joe Lyons' career. Murdoch was not being sarcastic when he noted that 'Lyons and his wife are quite determined to remain in office'.[18] But as a mother of eleven children and a creature of family-oriented culture, she could have no political career of her own, save through her husband and his memory. When, four years later, she entered parliament as the member for her husband's former constituency, Enid Lyons made less impact than she had as her husband's consort. This was a comment not so much on her ability as on the expectations of a culture which, having conceded women political rights, did not seriously envisage that they would exercise them.

_7

Relationships and pursuits

Faced with the evidence of a declining birthrate, a New South Wales royal commission set up in 1903 extolled 'the benefits of large families', and claimed that it was recognised that ' "only" children and members of small families are less well-equipped for the struggle of life'. British emigration earlier in the nineteenth century had been conditioned by a Malthusian concern for over-population: now, in the context of imperial rivalry and racial fears, the Anglo-Saxon nightmare was 'race suicide'. The royal commission blamed all classes for the falling birthrate: at one end of the scale, the factory system was seen as subjecting women and girls to 'physical and nervous strains' which impaired 'their subsequent reproductiveness', while amongst the middle class a selfish addiction to pleasure was detected. Women were especially reprimanded: the commission expressed 'grave misgivings that so many women do not realise the wrong involved in the practices of prevention and abortion'.

While the commission recommended that 'articles designed to enable sexuality to be dissociated from its consequent responsibility' be outlawed, at a moral level it seemed stumped. The churches were invited to undertake a crusade directed at 'the conscience of married people', and the government was urged to implement land settlement policies which would check the evils of urbanisation. That both proposals were such clichés reflected the dilemma of those exercising moral authority – the clergy, doctors and other 'experts' – when faced with an historical phenomenon beyond their control.[1]

Contraceptives were not outlawed; the Protestant churches had little impact on 'the conscience of married people' on this matter; and schemes for closer settlement, which was a continuing colonial ideal, did not stem the drift to the cities. As in much of the western world, the family was undergoing a radical transformation. By 1914 there was a greater acceptance that the falling birthrate was irreversible, and concern about the future of the race was expressed more in terms of child welfare policies. The eugenist influence was evident in fears that the unfit (usually assumed to be found mostly among the poor) were outbreeding the fit. However in Australia the eugenics movement retained a degree of environmental optimism, and a preference, therefore, for reformative rather than prohibitive policies; given the nation's convict origins this emphasis was perhaps understandable. Only in the 1930s did the harsher aspect of eugenics come to the fore.

Significantly, Higgins's 1907 *Harvester Judgment* had nominated three children as, so to speak, a 'fair and reasonable' family. A burst of family-making after the war did not prevent a further decline of the birthrate from 1925, reaching a trough in 1935. In the comic 'Ginger Meggs', launched in 1921 and destined to become an institution, the Meggs family is limited to two children, a marked contrast to the *Seven Little Australians* of Ethel Turner's 1894 classic. From the 1920s a large family was likely to serve as an indicator of Catholicism, for, unlike Protestants, Catholics took their church's opposition to birth control seriously.

The emergence of the new, smaller family required an ideological reinterpretation of the home. The shrinking number of children to bring up was offset by a greater emphasis on the responsibilities of parents, particularly the mother; while the modernising of the house in which the family lived expressed a dedication to ideas of efficiency and management. Home and family were placed under the microscope, and a new range of experts made their recommendations. The authority of the medical profession was never greater, but the doctors were now reinforced by child psychologists, infant welfare sisters, dieticians and the like. Domestic science – its very name capturing the spirit of the new ideology – was introduced into the school curriculum for girls, so that they could acquire the skills needed to manage the modern home. Architects asserted the contribution they could make to the new order. A magazine launched in 1922 by a group of architects and artists called *For Every Man His Home* claimed that the owner wouldn't 'get anything approaching a simple, up-to-date building unless he employs and trusts an architect'.[2] Journalists passed on much of the wisdom of the experts through the pages of the magazines which burgeoned after the Great War, catering particularly for a new public of women readers.

Technology was providing the physical means of reshaping the suburban home. The war had seen building costs almost double,

7.1   Marriage, Australian style: a country wedding, *circa* 1940. Formality, frills and fuss, even in modest surroundings; in nineteenth-century style, the husband is seated.

and cheaper, mass-produced materials were therefore preferred to traditional methods requiring the skills of tradesmen. The members of the now fashionably small family could enjoy, and came to expect, more privacy: children might now have their own bedrooms, though the sleep-out (an adaptation of the verandah) was a common compromise, often thought to be 'healthy'. The introduction of gas and electricity into the home reduced housework, and architects and builders responded by opting for the simplicity which they saw as consolidating this trend. In particular the kitchen was transformed into a hygienic laboratory, designed for efficient operation by the housewife on her own: it was, therefore, smaller, abolishing the central table which had previously allowed for kitchen sociability. In this modern kitchen were beginning to appear the appropriate new manufactured foods, such as breakfast cereals, processed cheese, and even that great Australian institution, launched in 1923, Vegemite.

Elsewhere, however, the vogue for efficiency was relieved by what was called 'genuine bungalow feeling'[3], a brand of cosiness which the Californian bungalow, with its smaller windows and featured fireplace, especially marketed. The house also tended to be narrower, to allow for a driveway down the side to that new appendage, the garage. Whereas the traditional colonial house, flanked with verandahs, seemed to open out into the world, the new cosy bungalow conveyed a sense of self-containment.

The image of the cosy modern bungalow, complete with garage and car, represented the aspirations of post-war suburbia – or, at least, of the professionals who supervised its development. The reality, particularly in terms of the houses people actually lived in, was often different. However something of the new ideas and new appliances, often subtly interwoven, affected the lives of most people. As Donald Horne noted, the 'literature' on babies which his pregnant mother referred to was 'like the brochures handed out with the new electrical appliances'.[4]

What went on inside the home – how the family adapted to its smaller size and responded to the ideological pressures to which it was subjected – is problematical. Writing in 1913, Jessie Ackermann, an American journalist and Women's Christian Temperance Union reformer, thought 'the first striking feature of the husband in Australia' was 'his assured position as head of the home', but this was more a matter of the respect accorded to him than of a dominion vigorously asserted. In practice the home was the woman's domain, and Ackermann noted the widespread working-class practice of the husband handing over most of his pay packet to his wife for her administration. She also noted, with disapproval, a tendency for wives to use guile in 'managing' their husbands. She would not have cared for the advice offered by the journal of the Anglican Mothers' Union in 1918:

'How to Cook Husbands'

A good many husbands are entirely spoilt by mismanagement in cooking and are not tender and good. Some women keep them too constantly in hot water, others freeze them, others put them in a stew; others roast them and others keep them constantly in a pickle. . . .

Having outlined the correct techniques, the anonymous 'expert' concludes that 'thus treated you will find him very digestible and that he will agree nicely with you'.[5] So could the language of domestic science be used to suggest that while the housewife was like a

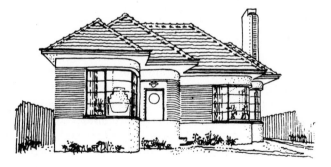

7.2   Three images of the suburban home: California Bungalow, Spanish
Mission, and Waterfall Front. This last version, with its curved corners and
'moderne' finish, was beginning to be fashionable at the onset of the
Second World War. These illustrations are taken from Robin Boyd's
Australia's Home; Boyd is discussed in Chapter 10.

servant in cooking for her husband she could also, as the presiding spirit of the home, consume him.

Regardless of the roles which society assigned to husband and wife there is evidence to suggest that within the family the wife/ mother was often emotionally dominant. At the end of his 'Joe Wilson' stories Henry Lawson confesses that he had intended his hero to be 'a strong character', but that 'the man's natural sentimental selfishness, good-nature, "softness", or weakness ... developed as I wrote on'. Joe's wife, Mary, is sentimentalised as a character, reflecting Lawson's ambivalence to women, but she is nevertheless portrayed as providing the strength and steadiness which the wayward hero lacks; indeed, in 'Joe Wilson's Courtship' Mary's interest in her suitor is expressed in terms of 'it was a pity that something couldn't be done for' him. However it is in one of Barbara Baynton's macabre *Bush Studies* that the official roles are most dramatically reversed: Squeaker is a waster and petty scoundrel, his wife, 'Squeaker's Mate', a figure of stoic nobility. While Steele Rudd's *On Our Selection* series presents, in Dad, a patriarchal pioneer, it is interesting that his sons are characterised as loutish or weak, while the daughters are depicted as being much more positive. In urban society the father lacked even the aura of pioneering. 'Ginger Meggs' presents the archetypal suburban family: while John Meggs's formal authority is acknowledged, he is, as one interpreter has put it, 'another diminished Australian father', while the 'ample proportions' of his wife, Sarah, 'symbolize the solidity of the unit of which she is the centre'.[6]

The Great War and depression often confirmed the sense of paternal decline. The father depicted by George Johnston in the autobiographical *My Brother Jack* is harsh and violent to his wife and two sons, but it is a violence born of impotence, for 'he was frustrated by his failure to have made anything of his life'. Their house is haunted by the war; the hero's mother has herself served as a nurse and a number of maimed survivors board with them, and, as the author surmises, 'those shattered former comrades-in-arms ... would have been a constant and sinister reminder [to his father] of the price of glory'. Donald Horne's father believed that 'the men who had volunteered to fight the Huns or the Turk were the only real men in Australia': eighteen years after demobilisation he suffered what was then called a 'nervous breakdown', attributed to his war service. He recovered his sanity but not his family position. Mother and son 'treated him with the honour due to a constitutional monarch'.[7]

If the war psychologically maimed many of its survivors, the Depressions threatened to undermine the father's role as bread-winner. Unemployed, he was, during the day, a foreigner in his own house, while the family's plight made greater demands on the mother's management skills. Some working-class women were able to get the work, paid less of course, which was denied their husbands. In Melbourne it was a symbolic irony that unemployed ex-diggers helped build the Shrine which commemorated their fallen mates.

Disappointed men clung to a tradition of mateship, a domain of male values from which women were largely excluded. Whether or not mateship was born as a response to the pioneering hardships of the bush, as is the conventional wisdom, it soon became a part of the colonial culture, as much at home, say, in the folklore of trade unionism as in rural mythology. Anzac took over the value of mateship, giving them a patriotic dimension and, incidentally, reinforcing the male exclusiveness of the tradition.

Mateship, at one level, was a form of male sociability, an escape from the domestic environment. Pubs were basically a male preserve, and according to one social historian, for many workers 'their time in the pub at the end of each day was all that made life bearable; life without beer was unimaginable'. This drinking routine could be 'as fundamental to survival as food and sleep; it was more cathartic than sex'.[8] The custom of 'shouting' – no drinker could leave a group before having 'shouted' a round of drinks – was an established ritual. Sport was in large measure an extension of this male world, because although women were permitted to watch and, in restricted forms, participate, the overriding ethos was masculine. The race track, cricket ground and boxing stadium were venues where men could feel entirely at home – even if accompanied by women.

At another level mateship was an intense, personal experience, a one-to-one relationship. In colonial society, with its relative absence of women, the homosexual overtones of mateship (even the very word 'mate' carrying its sexual innuendo) have been remarked upon. This ambiguity became part of the culture, particularly evident in the competition between 'mate' and woman for man's affections. One can see this satirised in 'Ginger Meggs' in an episode in which Ginger talks his mate Benny into wagging it, but then deserts him when presented with the opportunity of escorting his girlfriend Min to school. Benny is left lamenting: 'And he calls himself a FRIEND! Gee! Would you think a feller could sink so low as to leave his best mate for a bloomin' girl!' Even in the enchanted world of the

7.3   Almost an Australian Romeo and Juliet: Ginger Meggs, with attendant pets, tries to impress his girlfriend Min. A shilling was big money – more than the price of a seat at the local cinema.

gumnut fairies, *Snugglepot and Cuddlepie*, the motif recurs; Snugglepot cannot forsake his foster-brother Cuddlepie for Ragged Blossom, and the dilemma is finally resolved when 'Snugglepot built a new, big house, and took Cuddlepie and Ragged Blossom to live with him', in this case mate appearing to take precedence over wife.[9]

The ambiguity of mateship necessarily engendered a profound suspicion of overt homosexuality. In the cities a discreet homosexual subculture existed, though most people were unaware of it. Even someone like the artist-writer Norman Lindsay, with his bohemian reputation, was capable of being shocked by homosexuality. When his friend, the painter Gruner, confessed his 'weakness' to him – it was the time of the Great War, and Gruner, who was thinking of enlisting, feared the temptations of such a male environment – Lindsay was so stunned that he only managed to reply, 'Look, I think it's best to dismiss such a thing from your mind'.[10] Both were so embarrassed by this exchange that the subject was never referred to again.

Mateship also made men shy with women. The segregation of men from women in situations designed to bring them together became legendary. As one white-collar worker recalled of the 1920s:

When I went dancing, the men got up one end of the hall and the girls up the other and it was only when the music started that the men would all make a dash to get a girl who could dance well or who was good looking. It used to be just a rush like a team of draught horses. And when the dance was over you might be polite enough to lead the lady back to her seat, but you wouldn't sit with her, you'd walk back to the men again. It was 'sissy' to talk to women . . .

This emotional distance between the sexes seemed to be reflected in literature, and one critic has judged of this period that 'few local writers managed to depict relationships adequately, especially relationships between men and women'. The espousal of manliness by a writer such as Vance Palmer disguises an unease with women and a distaste for what he perceived as feminine values. His wife, Nettie, at times grew irritated with the lack of intimacy between them, complaining once that his letters to her were 'not the letters of any one who could imaginably be a lover of the person to whom they are written'.[11]

Yet perhaps this sexual reserve was part of a more general emotional reticence. Even mateship, no matter how much reliance men placed upon it, was characterised by things unsaid. Others have echoed Hans Heysen's complaint that 'too few of us Australians open our heart and mind to each other, although we very often desire to do so'.[12] More than traditional Anglo-Saxon reserve seemed to be involved. It has been said, for example, that Australian poets have to a large extent been 'externalisers', and the implication is that the materialist concerns of a provincial culture discouraged a pursuit of deeper realities.

The other side to this emotional reticence was the good humour and cheerfulness which often characterised casual social encounters. Australians gained the reputation of being friendly, informal. D. H. Lawrence found himself both attracted and repelled:

A perpetual, unchanging willingness, and an absolute equality. The same good-humoured, right-you-are approach from everybody to everybody. 'Right-you-are! Right-O!' Somers had been told so many hundreds of times, Right-he-was, Right-O! that he almost had dropped into the way of it. It was like sleeping between blankets – so cosy. So cosy.

Lawrence was recognising part of the social code of egalitarianism which enforced a camaraderie of manners, a 'mateyness' which could be either cheerful or sardonic. Yet this camaraderie could be seen as symptomatic of the retreat from intimacy, which Lawrence called 'the profound Australian indifference'.[13]

The characteristic setting for Australian life (as distinct from myth) was suburbia. (And many country towns were now approximating to the suburban standard, with the appropriate amenities.) But suburbia was not an undifferentiated mass, and the inner suburbs were a world apart from the newer middle-class suburbs which dominated the imagery of home and family. In Sydney and Melbourne particularly, life in these working-class suburbs was certainly rougher, and housing often dilapidated and squalid. 'Pushes' (gangs) conducted their battles on the streets, while rats invaded houses. Residents of these deprived suburbs nevertheless often resented their environment being dismissed as 'slums'.

In this bleak urban environment working-class family life was subject to disruptions which harked back to the nineteenth century. Many a child grew up without one parent, or sometimes without both, childbirth, illness or even accident being to blame. Such children took their luck with step-parents, or were foisted on, at times, unwilling relatives; sometimes they were committed to institutions, or farmed out to foster parents. One such survivor, Jean Brett, recalls that her mother died when she was five, and to this day she does not know the cause: with her father away at the Great War she and her sister and brother were put in an orphanage. When her father, now a stranger to them, returned, the three children joined their grandmother, who had a family of twelve; later, the grandmother 'dished us out to the rest of the family'. They rejoined their father sometime after his re-marriage, though in fact 'he didn't want to take us at all', and their new stepmother was more concerned with her own children. Years later her father, still bearing the scars of the war, was to commit suicide.[14] An upbringing characterised by such dislocation and deprivation could be debilitating, even if accepted with equanimity, and mocked the cosy magazine images of family life. Even so, family ties helped survival, while suffering, particularly in the circumstances of the Depression, could engender a communality of hardship.

Towards the end of the 1930s the slum clearance projects beloved of middle-class reformers began to be implemented, sometimes with the support of Labor party leaders, but were received uneasily by residents who felt they had little say in the fate of their own communities. Perhaps the distinguishing characteristic of working-class people, emphasised by the Depression, was a sometimes paralysing lack of social confidence. Trade unions and Labor Party gave working men (but hardly working women) nominal access to political power, but this was necessarily for the few, and the ghetto-like existence of inner suburbia psychologically imprisoned many working-class people, giving them the additional handicap of a sense of social inferiority. Egalitarianism across classes had little meaning beyond such social customs as the use of 'mate' by men as a form of casual address.

Rural society had its own distinctive poverty. In the wake of the Great War soldier settlers were encouraged to take up farming on land which was often too marginal and on blocks too small to support them. Undercapitalised, and faced in the 1920s with falling prices for farm commodities, these new settlers were especially vulnerable to debt and bankruptcy. A government inspector noted of one failed settler that 'he and his family had existed, not lived, poorly all through, more like animals than human beings'. The result of such plight was often 'domestic trouble', with wives 'breaking down' under the strain, or marriages disintegrating. One wife grimly labelled her husband 'a rank failure', who had left her to battle her own way in the world.[15]

For the children of the poor, in city or bush, education offered limited opportunities. After the energy expended in the controversy of the 1870s and 1880s which saw the creation of the state school system and, as a consequence, a separate Catholic system, political interest in educational reform withered. In working-class suburbia, where there was usually a higher than average proportion of Catholics, children divided into the two systems, both of which were impoverished. Catholic parish schools were 'ricketty, unpainted, crowded buildings which never saw enough money . . . staffed by over-worked and under-prepared men and women'. The state schools in the inner suburbs were probably worse; in Richmond, Melbourne, even before the Great War they were 'grossly overcrowded, unsanitary and already falling to pieces'.[16] Neither system made much provision for secondary education before the 1920s (though a few Catholic colleges enjoyed 'public school' status) and the church schools were often an influential lobby in resisting state entry into the field. Few working-class people would even have entertained the idea that their children might find their way to a university. The widespread indifference to education frustrated reformers and permeated even the labour movement: Queensland, where Labor was in office for much of the period, was probably the most lethargic of the States in educational reform. Yet education was also a rich area of political patronage: in Victoria, for example, the influence of the rural lobby was reflected in a huge imbalance in 1921 between country and city secondary school facilities.

Education also served to divide children – boys from girls, rich from poor, Protestant from Catholic. All these divisions had important implications for Australian culture. Sexual separation (even within schools which were co-educational) not only assumed different kinds of education for boys and girls but also reinforced the old social barrier between men and women. The children of the well-to-do were effectively segregated in the church-run private schools, in praise of which the editor of the 'egalitarian' *War History*, C. E. W. Bean, later wrote *Here, My Son*. These schools usually clustered together in middle-class suburbs, and the advent of state high schools paradoxically reinforced their social appeal. And in separating, for the most part, Catholic and Protestant, schools effectively socialised children in the traditions of sectarianism. Going to a state school in a country town, Donald Horne believed that the convent children 'were different physically from us; their faces were coarser than ours – more like apes'.[17]

In working-class suburbs Protestant congregations felt embattled, both by the Catholic integration into the community (often evident in local government) and the predominant social atmosphere of beer and betting. But in middle-class suburbia Protestant morality was able to assert itself. Pubs were fewer, and in some districts forbidden altogether. And if Protestants were slack in church attendance, they nevertheless sent their children to Sunday School. Masonic temples, still being built in the 1920s, were important agents in expressing Protestant solidarity at a local level. In the Meggs household religion might not, at first glance, appear to play much part, but the Protestant ambience is subtly suggested. Ginger may regard Sunday School as an imposition, but he is eager to be included in the annual picnic; John Meggs, it turns out, is a mason. That Ginger's main oppressor, the larrikin bully Tiger Kelly, is so clearly identified as of Irish background adds a sectarian dimension.

Although the Protestant-dominated temperance movement failed to secure prohibition, the atmosphere of national sacrifice engendered by the Great War made possible the introduction of six o'clock closing of hotels in most States. Here was a classic Australian compromise. With the increasing separation of home from workplace which characterised the growth of suburbia, drinking now became primarily an after-work social activity for men who, after frantically drinking against the clock in pubs which resembled large urinals, then surrendered themselves to home, family and evening tea. The home was not, by and large, a place for drinking. Only, perhaps, the rich and, at the other extreme, the down-and-out, integrated alcohol into their dwelling places.

The accommodation reached between the hedonism of the 'workingman's paradise' and the morality of Protestant wowserism* was symptomatic of Australian social practice. Thus most approved, or at least accepted, strict laws relating to drinking and gambling, while at the same time sardonically acknowledging sly grog, off course SP betting and two-up as an authentically Australian sub-culture. On both sides the making of gestures was often more important than argument or conversion: so, for example, many Protestant churches in Melbourne held their Sunday School picnics on Melbourne Cup Day as a kind of protest against this pagan festival.

The home was the centre for entertaining. Few Australians dined out at restaurants, though 'a day in town' might encompass the excitement of lunch, either genteel or basic. Saturday cooking prepared the way for Sunday visits from relatives. If food was simple – the Sunday leg of lamb perhaps being the symbolic aspiration of most Australians – celebrations or special occasions saw an extravagant multiplication of rich cakes, biscuits and meringues. The pavlova meringue (for the invention of which there are rival Western Australian and New Zealand claims) reflected both the sweetness of the popular tooth and the pride of the modern kitchen. Cards and musical evenings were popular; the arrival of the pianola, gramophone and wireless all reinforced the home focus for entertainment.

The wireless in particular became a popular medium, seen as having a symbolic significance in a country of such great distances as Australia. In city and country families listened intently to the evening's fanfare of radio serials, which as well as 'Dad and Dave' (adapted from Steele Rudd's *On Our Selection*) included titles such as 'Fred and Maggie Everybody', 'People Like Us' and 'Houses in Our Street'; perhaps one of the most memorable was 'Martin's Corner' which was about a family who ran a corner shop. The great interest in test cricket was cleverly exploited by the ABC: in 1934, with the aid of coded messages and studio sound effects, it first simulated direct broadcasts of matches being played in England. The nation sat up through the early hours of the morning, enthralled by the sound of the commentator's pencil 'batting' to a background of recorded crowd noises.

* A 'wowser' is a prudish teetotaller or killjoy. According to one disputed theory it is an acronym of 'W(e) O(nly) W(ant) S(ocial) E(vils) R(emedied)'.

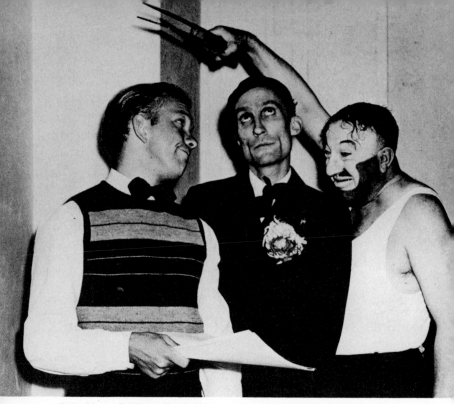

7.4   Harry Griffiths, Eddie Finn and Roy Rene ('Mo') mugging it for a
publicity photograph for a production of the Colgate Palmolive Radio Unit,
probably in the 1940s. Mo was a popular vaudeville performer who later
turned to radio.

'Going out' usually meant either to the cinema or dancing. The
1920s saw the building of grand picture palaces in the capital cities,
temples of architectural pastiche which were called 'theatres', and,
indeed, often retained a theatrical component with a live orchestra,
wurlitzer organ and stage acts. The 'legitimate' theatre was now an
increasingly middle-class preserve, specialising in musical comedy;
vaudeville, however, survived and was still capable of producing a
comedian with the popular appeal of Roy Rene 'Mo', whose
humour represented an extraordinary fusion of Australian, English
and Jewish elements.

    But it was the suburban or country town cinema which enter-
tained most Australians most often. This institution was democratic
in its relative cheapness; it entertained children at noisy Saturday
'arvo' matinees as well as adults at night; and, paradoxically, in spite
of the pagan glamour of Hollywood life it attracted fewer moral
objections than live theatre – one of the first feature length films had
been a religious epic made by the Salvation Army in Melbourne. For

a time a lively film industry existed in Australia, but as film budgets increased the industry was effectively squeezed out by cinema chains which accepted American control of distribution. By the 1930s only a remnant survived which produced mostly 'B' class supporting films. What most Australians saw on their cinema screens was standard Hollywood fare with a leavening of British and a locally-made newsreel as an overture.

During the inter-war period dancing became particularly popular with the young. In the cities huge art-deco palaces of dance like Cloudland in Brisbane and the 'Troc' (Trocadero) in Sydney injected American glitter and American music into the mainstream of Australian popular culture. Not only the young participated, and in the suburbs and especially in the country, dances were communal affairs, usually 'dry', although the men might intermittently retire to the pub, or elsewhere, for alcoholic stimulus. While dancing had sexual overtones, and was taboo for some Protestants, it could also be promoted as a healthful activity.

The wide diffusion, if not quality, of education had helped give Australians the reputation of being great readers. Although public and university libraries were often meagrely endowed, circulating libraries, both municipal and commercial, catered for the needs of many, with shelves marked 'Wild West', 'Romance', 'Detective', and so on. After the Great War the appeal of the popular press was enhanced by the much greater use of photographs, but magazines, aimed at particular markets, now supplemented many people's reading. In 1933 the *Australian Women's Weekly* was launched, ironically enough printed on presses originally intended to produce a labour newspaper. Planned to have 'an unswerving Australian outlook', with an appeal for 'every Australian home from the outback to the industrial suburbs',[18] the *Weekly* had, within a decade, become an Australian institution, boasting a massive circulation. Of a different order was *Man*, which, with its girlie cartoons and 'tasteful' nudes, was based on the American *Esquire* and catered for a racier male-cum-barbershop clientele. Yet interestingly both the *Women's Weekly* and *Man* in their early years fused their popular appeal with more serious political concerns – the *Weekly* with a moderate but committed feminism, and *Man* with an informed discussion of national and international issues. Both were destined to shed these concerns as their markets burgeoned.

Although in the 1930s the motor car was a rarity in working-class suburbs, it was beginning to affect middle-class leisure patterns. A Sunday afternoon drive into nearby country was becoming

7.5   The front page of the first issue of the *Australian Women's Weekly*, 10 June 1933. Society and fashion dominate, but feminism establishes a presence.

part of the suburban weekend. By 1938 the car had already created a vogue for caravanning, which coupled the freedom of the road with a family-centred privacy. Caravan holidays also meant an escape from the tyranny of spartan hotels and regimented boarding houses, though for many the holiday resort boarding house or private hotel (the distinction was a nice one), in the mountains or by the sea, still beckoned once a year. Some of these summoned up a contemporary ritziness; most, however, were rambling bungalows, with long wide verandahs, creaking corridors and distant bathrooms. At such guesthouses the pleasures of holidaying were severely regulated – promptness at meals, for example, being a requirement – but most 'guests' seemed to accept, and, indeed, perhaps even to depend upon, such regimentation.

The sense in which Australians assumed a need for cultural conformity is reflected in attitudes to minorities. At the best of times there were always those, like trade unionists, who resisted immigration programmes, but if there *were* to be immigrants then the general preference was for Britishers. While this was historically understandable it encouraged a narrowness of vision. The oft-made boast that Australians were 98 per cent of British stock not only ignored the fact that the Irish-born might not wish to be so counted, but also defined all Australian-born citizens, even if of non-British descent, as 'British'. Homogeneity was to this extent manufactured, and its proclamation was calculated to intimidate racial minorities. The White Australia policy ensured that Asians were kept out, but the entry of small numbers of southern Europeans – Italians, Yugoslavs and Greeks – aroused hostility. As early as the 1890s some Italians had entered the sugar industry in Queensland, but in the 1920s the European trickle became noticeable, though quotas ensured that it was still numerically dwarfed by the arrival of 261,000 British migrants. In the late 1930s refugees from Nazism, mostly Jews, added a new strand.

Even when such European immigrants attempted to meet the demand to assimilate promptly, their 'foreignness' guaranteed that they were treated with suspicion. It was always tempting to seize on them as scapegoats, projecting social discontent onto pushy 'foreigners'. So in 1934 on the Kalgoorlie goldfields grievances over wage levels were directed not at mine owners but European immigrants, and for two days angry mobs, unimpeded by police, smashed shops and set fire to miners' huts, leaving parts of Kalgoorlie and neighbouring Boulder a devastated wasteland. The attitude to European immigrants at this time seemed less tolerant than in the

7.6   Another aspect of the continuing imperial relationship – immigration.
These Barnardo Homes boys are arriving from England in 1924.

nineteenth century, as if the memory of the Great War itself induced
an aversion to the idea of Europe. Jewish refugees were even
advised by a local Jewish agency of their responsibility to the older
community:

> Above all, do not speak German in the streets and in the trams.
> Modulate your voice. Do not make yourself conspicuous
> anywhere by walking with a group of persons, all of whom are
> loudly speaking a foreign language. Remember that the

welfare of the old-established Jewish communities in
Australia, as well as of every migrant, depends on your
personal behaviour.[19]

Although for Australian Jews anti-semitism had been an irritant – as,
for example, in their exclusion from some establishment clubs – it
had not been a serious bar to their social advancement. It was all the
more ironic, therefore, that they should share the apprehension of
other Australians about the newcomers.

Few Australians saw immigration as socially beneficial. To be an
immigrant entailed a certain stigma. On the High Court, Isaacs – a
Jew, incidentally, who was proudly Anglo-Australian – advocated
as legal doctrine 'once an immigrant always an immigrant', meaning
that the Commonwealth could always invoke the power to deport.
His concern was that 'persons who are criminals, anarchists, public
enemies or loathsome hotbeds of disease' might defy and injure the
'entire people of a continent'.[20] Not all his colleagues went as far as
this, but Isaacs' characterisation of foreigners as a source of corruption reflected a widespread view.

Aborigines could hardly be treated as immigrants; but, more
tellingly, they could be ignored, their very existence almost ex-
punged from the national consciousness. So the Constitution laid
down that they should not be counted at the census as members of
the Australian population. As late as 1928 it was possible for an
inquiry to exonerate police in Central Australia who had shot thirty-
one Aborigines as a reprisal for the alleged murder of a white man. It
was still widely assumed that as a race the Aborigines were dying
out, but by the 1930s there was the beginning of an agitation, led
principally by anthropologists and church missionaries, to recognise a positive responsibility for the welfare of Aborigines. This
alliance of European religion and science was epitomised in the role
of anthropologist A. P. Elkin, who had started his career as an
Anglican priest, and whose work pioneered an understanding of
Aboriginal religion. For the first time a pro-Aboriginal lobby, operating through the Association for the Protection of Native Races,
began to be heard. In 1939 the Commonwealth Government, which
controlled the Northern Territory but had no direct responsibility
for Aborigines in the States, adopted a more enlightened and informed policy, recognising Aboriginal rights, though still seeing
them in an assimilationist context.

Yet stereotypes changed slowly. When Charles Chauvel, one of
the few Australian film directors in the 1930s, made a film in north-

ern Queensland, it was a melodrama in the Hollywood African mode called 'Uncivilized'. (In 1954 Chauvel made the much more sympathetic – though still melodramatic – 'Jedda', for which he consulted Elkin.) In 1938 when Australia celebrated its sesqui-centenary some Aborigines were rounded up for the re-enactment of Governor Phillip's landing at Farm Cove. The official programme, with no irony intended, described how 'the first boat to land will carry a party of men who will put the Aborigines to flight', adding that 'Governor Phillip will arrive in the second boat'. Other Aborigines, however, had declared a Day of Mourning, and meeting elsewhere solemnly protested 'the Whiteman's seizure of our country'.[21] It was a symbolic occasion which signalled Aborigines' intention to speak for themselves. Meanwhile anthropologists, who in the past had undertaken field work on the assumption that they were collecting data about a dying culture, now had a more positive vision. 'The extinction of the aborigines is only inevitable if we allow it to be so', wrote W. E. Stanner in 1938.[22] But no matter how important these changes, the great majority of Australians, living in the cities, had no experience of Aborigines and therefore, while capable of expressing humanitarian concern about 'natives', had little alternative but subscribe to the old 'Stone Age' stereotype. The crude attempts of the Jindyworobak school of writers to draw on Aboriginal culture only underlined the distance between white and black, and the extent to which 'our' culture could not embrace 'theirs'.

Writers, artists, bohemians, were themselves marginal members of society. While in Sydney and Melbourne they had their haunts, only perhaps Sydney's King's Cross, where 'foreigners' tended to congregate, had a more cosmopolitan flavour. If artists and eccentrics were tolerated it was in the sense that their existence was not noticed. The freedom which they enjoyed, and which had made Australia attractive to some European refugees, was neutralised by a general indifference. The amateur ethos was dominant. Australians were great participants in and followers of eisteddfods, but they looked askance at professionalism in the arts.

The marginality of artists, together with the nostalgic adherence to old images of bush and bushman, made for conditions uncongenial to modernism. European artists among the trickle of immigrants therefore often had a profound effect on local painters who had been starved of such stimulus; Danila Vassilief, Josl Bergner and Sali Herman helped introduce the possibility of artists interpreting the urban experience. Bergner also painted Aborigines who had been largely ignored by artists since the early days when they had been part of the exotic detail of an unfamiliar landscape. Even the 1938 visit of the Russian Ballet had modernist implications: Bernard Smith, later to emerge as a leading cultural critic and art historian, 'sat on the edge of his seat transported into another world, enchanted by the colour of Benois and the music of Stravinsky'.[23] In 1939 an exhibition organised by the Melbourne *Herald* brought to Australia a significant collection of European modernist masterpieces: it not only was a revelation to many young artists but also suggested, in the widespread public interest it aroused, that the artist might have a future in Australian society. The Contemporary Art Society, founded in 1938, challenged the conservative, Royal Academy-oriented establishment which, in its adherence to traditional values, had helped stifle the creativity of the young.

Women were also victims of the pressure to conform – in their case to the limited range of roles permitted them. Technically granted their political rights, they were expected to concentrate their talents and energies on home and family. Those who sought other outlets were often patronised or even ignored. Yet women were notable contributors in both literature and painting in the period between the wars, and it is possible that their marginality may have in itself been a creative stimulus. Certainly they had less reason to perpetuate the old male-dominated myths of the bush. Women writers like Katharine Susannah Prichard and Eleanor Dark began to explore the dynamics of Australian relationships between the sexes, while women painters such as Margaret Preston and Grace Crowley were often more receptive to modernist influences.

There was nevertheless a tension between the isolationism of a conformist culture and the intrusive pressures of the modern world and its technology. The concern about 'Americanisation' demonstrated this. Upholders of the British connexion and those seeking to elevate an Australian identity could agree in seeing American films, music and magazines as a corrupting influence, which threatened to undermine cultural values. Yet the attraction of the American offerings could not be denied. So in 1938 the *Women's Weekly* could complain that 'we are in danger of becoming a cultural suburb of Hollywood'[24] while still devoting more than four pages to Hollywood gossip and reviews. It was ironic that 'Americanisation' should be feared as a pervasive and levelling mediocrity, when the culture it invaded possessed a conformism of its own. In fact the American values of mass entertainment were absorbed in a way that did not so much 'Americanise' society as create a disjunction between the images of popular fantasy and the reality of Australian life – but then, such a disjunction was a characteristic of American society itself.

That Australian culture before the Second World War was characterised by powerful pressures to conform – whether to the values of Anzac, home and family or social egalitarianism – did not mean that cultural differences were not important. Just as the Great War had exposed the interwoven antagonisms of class, race and religion, so too did the Depression accentuate the disparity between middle-class and working-class environments. Yet in spite of sporadic outbursts of open hostility – as in strike violence and the contrived games played by the private armies – the characteristic feature of Australian society between the wars was the extent to which it institutionalised the cultural accommodations which had been reached. So Catholic and Protestant were joined together by a regulated code of mutual hostility; men and women married and raised families yet lived much of their lives in separate cultural spheres; employers and trade unions ritualised their no longer new conflict in the workplace and courtroom; middle class and working class shared the same cities while respecting each other's territorial limits; and the city's domination of the bush was matched by its capacity to sustain an increasingly improbable rural dream. A culture should be identified not so much by any sense of shared values, which may often be artificially induced, as by the means it develops to reconcile, or at least accommodate the dissonant forces within it. Because the period between 1890 and 1939 saw economic growth of such modest proportions, with the two depressions providing long pauses of contraction, it was a time for coming to terms with the Australian condition, and therefore a time for the articulation of rites, codes and customs, while at the same time adapting to the now more insistent intrusions of the modern world. It was this process which saw the construction of an Australian culture, rather than the conscious strivings of the polemicists to define and project a national identity.

An important example of this process was the emergence of the beach culture. Although in the nineteenth century the beach had been a place for recreation, its pleasures were no more than tasted. The sun was something to be protected against with hats or parasols, while the crashing surf was there to be admired, not experienced. The twentieth century saw the beach transformed. From about 1904 surf bathing began to be permitted on Sydney's beaches,

7.7 Charles Meere's 'Australian Beach Pattern', painted in 1940, splendidly captures the robust physicality of the beach scene, yet also suggests the self-absorption in the pursuit of pleasure. Men are topless in woollen, belted trunks; the man wearing a hat on the deck, top left, may possibly be the beach inspector, responsible for enforcing the regulations concerning dress.

but was soon a cause for moral controversy. In 1911 Catholic Archbishop Kelly, while acknowledging that surf bathing was 'an invigorating and healthy pastime', nevertheless condemned 'the promiscuous commingling of the sexes'. The mayor of a seaside municipality replied to the archbishop, arguing that 'women who surf mix with the men more from a sense of safety than a desire to besport their figures in full view of admirers'; in any case he believed that 'the beauty of the human form had at all times appealed to the world's greatest painters and sculptors, and surely we, living in an enlightened age, can be permitted to add our quota of admiration without shocking our modesty'.[25] The enthusiasm for the surf seemed unstoppable, and in 1906 led to the forming of the Bondi Surf-Bathers' Lifesaving Club, the first such organisation in the world.

After the Great War the beach became the symbol of Australia at pleasure. It is an image which can be interpreted at several levels.

The crowds which congregated on the sand turned their backs on the continent, city and bush alike. The beach could be likened to a grandstand from which the occupants viewed in the foreground the narrow margin of human pleasure, and beyond, the oblivion of endless sea and sky. The hedonism which was latent in the colonial tempermanent now had its most dramatic flowering, for while the sun was embraced with a passionate passivity, the beach also created a sociability of a new, sensually self-conscious kind.

Yet the beach did not lack those determined to impose order upon it. It was a natural focus for wowsers, for whom dress and behaviour were a constant concern, and Archbishop Kelly's comments suggest that while Catholic authorities could traditionally look with a tolerant eye on grog and gambling, the beach confronted them with more alarming temptations. Perhaps even more revealing than the continuing guerilla war between the forces of pleasure and morality was the dramatising of the beach as a military parade ground. The lifesaving movement mushroomed, clubs multiplied and a whole ethos was born, which was amateur, manly, martial. The essential task of saving the lives of the pleasure-seekers gave

SNAPPED (1929)
This beach always makes me sad. I lost my best boy
here two seasons ago.
What! Shark?
No—sheila.

7.8   This 1929 *Bulletin* cartoon is 'smart' both in its depiction of fast life on the beach and its contemporary style. 'Sheila', however, is a term used more by men than women.

rise to beach drill and competitive sports. The beach was the new frontier of urban Australia, and the uniformed lifesavers who (literally) patrolled it were promoted in an Anzac tradition.

The beach also provided a kind of Australian promenade where the young and healthy cheerfully displayed themselves. The male swagger of the lifesaver was matched by the cult of the beachgirl. Beach beauty contests punctuated summer newspapers, presenting local adaptations of glamorous Hollywood images to an audience of suburban voyeurs. In the world of the beach pleasure and duty were subtly juxtaposed. The hedonism of sun and surf was moderated by the discipline of the frontier: the common ground lay, perhaps, in the elevation of extrovert health and fitness. The beach suited the Australian temperament; it was a place for physical expression, not emotional intimacy.

When in 1941 Japan bombed the American fleet at Pearl Harbor, and the Second World War suddenly began to impinge on the Australian consciousness, the beach took on a new significance as a foyer for a possible invasion. Pits were dug to swallow up the expected tanks, and the breakers were met by huge strands of barbed wire. The view from the grandstand was suddenly disturbing, for out of the bleached nothingness of summer threatened an Asian invader. The endless miles of glittering beaches had become a symbol of Australia's vulnerability.

Part 4

The culture questioned: 1939–1988

8

Dependence

> Fellow Australians. It is my melancholy duty to inform you
> that, in consequence of the persistence by Germany in her
> invasion of Poland, Great Britain has declared war upon her,
> and that, as a result, Australia is also at war.

It was Sunday evening, 3 September 1939, and gathered around
their wireless sets Australians were hearing the solemn voice, laden
with a sense of historical occasion, of their young Prime Minister,
Robert Gordon Menzies. On Lyons' death in April Menzies had
attained the prime ministership, but not without an ugly personal
attack from Country Party leader, Earle Page, which drew attention
to his failure to serve in the Great War. Now, in announcing the new
war, Menzies called for 'calmness, resolution, confidence, and hard
work', implying a very different mood from that of 1914. Yet he still
identified Australia as a 'Dominion' of the 'Mother Country', and
the formula of words chosen deliberately suggested that Britain's
declaration automatically committed Australia.[1]

The terms of Menzies' address to the nation disguised the fact
that a reassessment of Australia's role in its region and the world at
large had already begun. In a speech following his appointment as
Prime Minister Menzies had emphasised that while in its approach
to European affairs Australia had to depend on British guidance, in
the Pacific we had 'primary responsibilities and primary risks'. The
Australian perspective was necessarily different, for 'what Britain
calls the Far East is to us the near north'. It followed that in its
immediate region Australia needed its own diplomatic representation, and in 1940, ambassadors to Japan, the United States and
China were appointed. And although, for Menzies, the unity of the
British Empire remained a prime consideration, implicit in this
diagnosis was the realisation that British concern with European
events might be at the expense of Australian – and imperial –

interests in the Pacific region. Furthermore, the External Affairs Minister had made it clear that although in the situation of 1939 Australia supported British policy in Europe and therefore felt bound by it, this did *not* mean that 'in any and every set of circumstances' a British declaration of war 'should or would automatically commit Australia to participation in that war'.[2] In 1914 Australian loyalty had been unquestioning as the eager AIF sought admission to the European world at war: in 1939 the commitment to Britain, although similar in form, was made in the context of an emerging assessment of Australian priorities.

The despatch of troops to the European theatre was conditioned by concern about Australia's own defence. While appointing an ambassador to Japan reflected a need for good relations with this Pacific power, it could not disguise fears of Japan as a potential aggressor, fears which grew with the fall of France in 1940, for this was seen as likely to tempt Japan to enter the fray. Yet for many Australians the war continued to seem somewhat remote, and some concern was expressed by those in authority that commitment and morale were weak. They found some evidence in a report by anthropologist Elkin, based on a survey, which concluded that 'apathy and antagonism' to the war effort were not limited to a particular social class, and that often they had their roots in 'the depression years'.[3]

Perhaps one reason for the guarded response to the conventional appeals for patriotic unity was the perceived intensification of conflict among the politicians themselves. The 1940 federal elections resulted in a dead-heat between the main parties, with two independents choosing to keep the Menzies-led Anti-labor coalition in office. Although Anti-labor leaders, influenced by the advent of a national government in Britain under Churchill, called for a similar regime here, they did so in full knowledge of Labor's traditional fear of losing its identity in alliances or coalitions. They could calculate that the war was capable of dividing the Labor Party, just as it had in 1916. Labor joined the War Advisory Council, set up to provide an official channel of communication between government and opposition, but that was as far as it was prepared to go.

In this delicately poised situation, it was the Anti-labor parties which began to show signs of disintegration, so that pious calls for a national government on their part began to seem less plausible. Menzies' leadership, which had never been unquestioned, now came under fire: his acknowledged ability and eloquence were not sufficient to overcome the suspicion provoked by his ambition and arrogance. But uncertainty about leadership was symptomatic of a

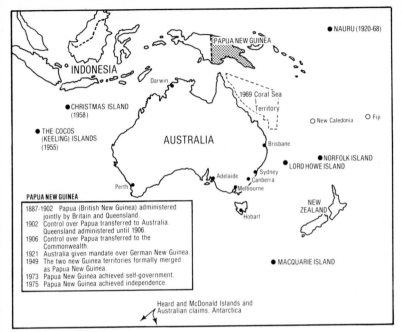

Map 6   Australia's overseas territories (source: J. C. R. Camm and
J. McQuitton (eds.), *Australians: A Historical Atlas* (Sydney 1987)

deeper malaise in the UAP, which had been hastily fashioned in the
depression crisis, and which lacked coherence in organisation and
ideology. When Menzies abandoned office in August 1941 the UAP
was so debilitated that it conceded leadership of the coalition to its
junior ally, the Country Party, but within a month the two independents withdrew their support and this government also collapsed.
Thus Labor assumed office little more than two months before Japan
bombed the American fleet at Pearl Harbor.

The new Prime Minister, John Curtin, had been largely responsible for rebuilding and re-uniting the Labor Party, and since
the dead-heat of 1940 had carefully prepared the party for the
responsibilities of government. Curtin was to die in office in July
1945, before the war was over, and this element of self-sacrifice has
helped make him, as one historian puts it, 'a secular saint, virtually a
martyr, in the Australian tradition'. A pacifist by temperament,
Curtin might have appeared an unlikely war leader. But while he
could not relish war in the Churchillian manner, he had the capacity, through example and commitment, to inspire others. Many
remarked on his outward coldness and loneliness, yet one of his

political opponents remembered him as 'a kindly warm-hearted man'. In earlier years he had had an intermittent problem with drink. His drinking had expressed a longing for what he once called 'the humanity of fellowship', and becoming a teetotaller was a bitter acknowledgement that that fellowship was illusory.[4] He was a man who subsumed disappointment in dedication; but he was also a skilful politician and a masterly parliamentarian.

Although the entry of Japan into the war was not unexpected, Pearl Harbor was an immense shock. Within a couple of days the British HMS *Prince of Wales* and *Repulse* had been sunk; Hong Kong fell on Christmas Day; and Singapore, which had always been regarded as the lynchpin of imperial defence in the Pacific, was suddenly seen as vulnerable. The Australian nightmare of an Asiatic invasion had taken alarming shape. The one advantage of Pearl Harbor, from an Australian point of view, was that it ensured the USA's participation in the war. However the lack of a formal alliance, and Roosevelt's commitment to a 'beat Hitler first' strategy, made for uneasiness and anxiety, whilst Australia's own preoccupation with the Pacific was also a cause for strain in its relationship with Britain.

It was in this context that Curtin wrote a New Year's message for the Melbourne *Herald*, published on 27 December. Curtin, who had been a journalist in his youth, began by quoting the Australian poet Bernard O'Dowd:

That reddish veil which o'er the face
  of night-hag East is drawn . . .
Flames new disaster for the race?
  Or can it be the dawn?

It was an appropriate image of apocalyptic crisis, but it was Curtin's belief that it was within our power to 'provide the answer'. Part of Curtin's message therefore concerned community morale:

In the first place the Commonwealth Government found it exceedingly difficult to bring the Australian people to a realisation of what, after two years of war, our position had become. Even the entry of Japan, bringing a direct threat in our own waters, was met with a subconscious view that the Americans would deal with the shortsighted, underfed, and fanatical Japanese.

But the part which was to attract attention was that in which he asserted Australia's need to have 'the fullest say', together with the United States, in the Pacific struggle:

Without any inhibitions of any kind, I make it quite clear that
Australia looks to America, free of any pangs as to our
traditional links with the United Kingdom.

We know the problems that the United Kingdom faces. We
know the constant threat of invasion. We know the dangers of
dispersal of strength, but we know, too, that Australia can go
and Britain still hold on.[5]

Given Labor's historical lack of enthusiasm for the imperial connexion, expressed more in gestures than any argued alternative,
this public turning to 'America' aroused Anti-labor concern, but the
wider community seems to have accepted the realism of Curtin's
diagnosis. Churchill, understandably, was cross, and Roosevelt
also, it seems, privately expressed 'the greatest distaste' for Curtin's
statement, which suggested 'panic and disloyalty'.[6]

The context of Curtin's remarks makes it clear that he was not
advocating any abject dependence on the United States: on the
contrary, the article was an urgent call for sacrifice directed to
Australians. 'I demand [emphasis added] that Australians everywhere realise that Australia is now inside the fighting lines.' Only
those who knew the peculiar strength of the Australian attachment
to Empire and 'Home' could fully appreciate why Curtin might feel
it necessary to stress, even 'distastefully', the new political realities.

This New Year's message in a Melbourne evening newspaper,
which Curtin himself can hardly have expected to gain such exposure, has subsequently come to be regarded as one of the critical
documents of Australian history, cited as a 'turning point' in Australia's relationship with Britain. In fact ties with Britain were, as we
shall see, to remain strong, but Curtin's message, in its recognition
of British inadequacy, might have tempted 'the somewhat lackadaisical Australian mind' (Curtin's own phrase) to surrender itself
to a more fundamental psychology of dependence. This was not
Curtin's intention, yet some of his words were capable of encouraging it. The self-conscious dismissal of 'any inhibitions of any kind'
suggests a kind of abasement, while 'Australia looks to America'
ambiguously conveys a hint of presumptuous expectation. Perhaps
Roosevelt was right in detecting a hint of panic: after all, Curtin
himself was concerned with identifying the problem of morale.
There is evidence, too, that Curtin was later to concede privately
that the appeal had been a mistake.

Since 1941 Australia has 'looked to America', and in doing so
has comfortably avoided taking much responsibility for its own

8.1 General MacArthur, with Prime Minister Curtin on the left and Governor-General Lord Gowrie on the right, on the occasion of his being given the Knight Grand Cross of the Military Division of the Order of the Bath.

survival. Unwittingly, Curtin might have administered 'the somewhat lackadaisical Australian mind' a drug rather than a tonic.

In February 1942 Singapore fell. A few days later the bombing of Darwin caused such local panic that a royal commission was appointed to investigate. The arrival of General MacArthur in March – he had just been appointed supreme commander of the allied forces in the south-west Pacific – provided a measure of reassurance. Australia was to be the base for the eventual counter-offensive against Japan. MacArthur conveyed an image of glamour and strength, and he and Curtin, dissimilar as they were, struck up a rapport. As American troops arrived the alliance took tangible shape. On to the slouching, well-mannered visitors were projected Australian hopes – and resentment.

Nevertheless the Labor government, which had a massive election win in 1943 and was confirmed in office in 1946, sought, within the alliance framework, to establish an independent foreign policy. Instrumental in this was Herbert Vere Evatt, the pugnacious and controversial external affairs minister. A lawyer by training,

Evatt had had a brief career in New South Wales politics before being appointed to the High Court bench at the age of 36. A learned and innovative judge, Evatt found time to write several books on subjects ranging from the Rum Rebellion to the dismissal of premier Lang in 1932; however his energies demanded wider outlets, and in 1940 he seized on the war situation to justify his stepping down from the bench to enter federal politics in the Labor interest. When Japan entered the war, Evatt saw to it that unlike 1939, Australia made its own formal declaration. He was always eager to assert Australia's interest in the allies' conduct of the war, often irritating both the United States and Britain. As planning for the peace began, Evatt emerged as a busy and determined spokesman for the small nations, seeking to ensure that their interests were not overlooked in the deals negotiated between the Big Five (the United States, Soviet Union, Britain, France and China), and at the San Francisco conference in 1945 had some success in modifying the Great Powers' dominance in the creation of the United Nations. After the war Australia was sympathetic to the emergent post-colonial countries, particularly Indonesia, and in 1948 Evatt's international role was recognised in his election as President of the General Assembly of the United Nations.

It was remarkable, however, that while Labor was criticised in 1941 for turning too abjectly to the United States, in the post-war era it was the government's failure to cement the American alliance which attracted political censure. Evatt's independent policy was overtaken by the Cold War and the politics of anti-Communism. With the fall of China to the Communists in 1949, the United States was increasingly preoccupied with the threat of international communism, while Australia still feared the resurgence of Japanese militarism. On the home front Anti-labor had risen phoenix-like from the ashes in the form of the Liberal Party, founded by Menzies in 1944, and seized on communism as an issue, pointing to the communist influence in the trade union movement, and linking it to the government's perceived socialist tendencies. In 1949 Menzies led the Anti-labor coalition to a decisive electoral victory, promising, amongst other things, to ban the Communist Party.

In this political transition there were some paradoxes. Labor, traditionally ambivalent towards the imperial connexion, found reason at times to reassert Commonwealth ties. Sometimes the motive was a pragmatic desire to maintain a counterweight to American dominance of the region; but sentiment was also a factor, particularly with Labour in office in Britain (1945–51), engaged in

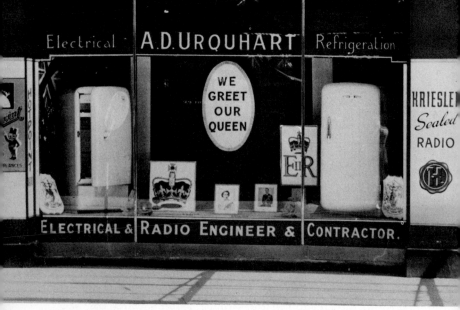

8.2   The coronation of Queen Elizabeth II is saluted by a loyal Western Australian retailer. 'My husband and I' (the phrase for which the Queen became well known during the 1954 royal tour) are dwarfed by two curved-top refrigerators, symbols of the new consumerism.

transforming the mother country into a welfare state. Chifley, who had succeeded Curtin as prime minister in 1945, was sympathetic to Britain's post-war economic problems. In 1947 Australia made a $A25 million gift to Britain to help in the balance of payments crisis, and one factor in Labor's defeat in 1949 was Chifley's reintroduction of petrol rationing, a measure designed to support sterling vis-à-vis the American dollar.

On the other hand the high priority the Menzies government gave to forging a formal alliance with the United States caused some tension in its relations with Britain. In 1950 Australia was anxious to be among the first to come to America's aid in the Korean War, a gesture made easier and more politically acceptable by the war being theoretically fought under the aegis of the United Nations. At one stage there was great alarm in the Australian cabinet when it seemed that Britain might beat them to the gun with an offer of land troops. It was a war which seemed to express the moral commitment of anti-communism, and American gratefulness for Australia's speedy response contributed to its readiness to sign the ANZUS Pact with Australia and New Zealand in 1951. This pact, partly designed to assuage Australian fears about the 'soft' peace treaty with Japan, seemed to be the guarantee of security which a nervous Australia

8.3   The Queen with the Lord Mayor, Frank Roberts, at the Brisbane State Ball. An eager phalanx of Brisbane matrons inspect their young sovereign and appear satisfied.

sought, but it deliberately excluded Britain. The British were miffed, but had little alternative but to accept the treaty.

In this context it seemed necessary to reaffirm the *sentiment* of the British connexion. Even during the war, when Britain's irrelevance to Australia's survival was so starkly demonstrated, concern for the fate of the mother country was considerable. Menzies, in spite of his private criticisms of Churchill, helped propagate the myth of the British leader, and Australians, both during and after the war, eagerly despatched parcels of 'Food for Britain'. Sentiment and nostalgia reached a peak, however, with the Royal Tour of 1954, the first tour of Australia by a reigning monarch. The young Queen Elizabeth, 'radiant' throughout a taxing schedule, was received with extraordinary rapture. While politicians and functionaries (and their curtseying wives) jostled at huge receptions, balls and garden parties to bask in the magic of royalty, a huge popular chorus of devoted subjects thronged the streets. Menzies hailed 'a second Elizabethan era in British history' in which Australians would share. In Sydney the *Catholic Weekly*, expressing joy, thanksgiving and gratitude for the Queen's visit, proudly noted that she was greeted by a Catholic premier and a Catholic lord mayor.[7] If, in practical terms, the British connexion now meant less, it could, for that very reason, be celebrated more universally, particularly when expressed in the person of 'a fairy tale princess', fresh from her coronation. It seemed a deliberate irony that the Queen should unveil in Canberra the Australian National Memorial commemorating the American contribution to the war in the Pacific.

Sentimental links with Britain were reinforced by emerging patterns of travel. The gathering impetus of post-war prosperity made overseas travel possible for more and more people. By the 1950s a working trip to Europe had become the ambition of many young Australians, and London usually provided the base for these expeditions. Thus while going 'Home' necessarily renewed old ties (and antagonisms), it also meant that the experience of Australians abroad tended to be filtered through English spectacles. In Australia the farewelling of travellers at the wharf, with cascades of streamers stretching across the water to the parting liner, became one of the great popular rituals. The democratising of travel might integrate Australia into the world, but it also acknowledged our persisting isolation. Given this condition it was not surprising that Australians should seek reassurance in the familiar cultural landmarks of the mother country.

The presence of many British migrants in Australia also helped rejuvenate the old connexion. When the Beatles toured Australia in 1964 the astonishing reception accorded them reflected more than the mere urge to witness the world's new pop phenomenon. The biggest crowds were in Adelaide, where there was a particularly large concentration of British migrants: for many, seeing the Beatles was to savour a glamourised image of their own culture.

Menzies' dominance as Prime Minister from 1949 to 1966, an achievement partly made possible by the split in the Labor Party*, meant he necessarily stamped his imprint on the post-war era. 'British to the bootheels' as he proclaimed himself, Menzies compensated for the American alliance by allowing Britain to test its atomic weapons in the early 1950s on the Monte Bello Islands off the coast of Western Australia and at Woomera and Maralinga in South Australia. And in 1956 Menzies briefly played a role in the Suez Crisis when he went to Cairo representing the London conference of users of the Canal which Egypt had nationalised. Menzies told President Nasser 'in the friendliest way' that it would be a mistake for him to assume that Britain and France would not use force.[8] Following the not unexpected collapse of this mission, Menzies over-ruled his external affairs minister, R. G. Casey, in giving Australia's sup-

* See Chapter 9.

8.4 Menzies, the imperial statesman, sharing the limelight with British Prime Minister, Anthony Eden, and former Prime Minister, Earl Attlee, in 1956 at the time of the Suez crisis. Suez destroyed Eden's career; Menzies was to enjoy a further ten years in office. Menzies made the most of his visits 'home', whereas he showed little enthusiasm for visiting Asian neighbours.

port to the ill-fated Anglo-French military intervention (made in collusion with Israel), even though this isolated Australia from the United States and, indeed, most of the world. Suez was an affirmation of the Britishness of Menzies – and of much of his middle-class constituency – and it was fitting that he should be rewarded with the Order of the Thistle in 1963, and succeed Churchill in the prestigious sinecure of Lord Warden of the Cinque Ports.

The popular celebration of the monarchy disguised the economic shift that was already underway, with the United States, and later Japan, looming larger in trade and investment. But from the Australian perspective, the real break with the past was signalled by Britain when it began negotiations in 1961 to enter the European Economic Community. Though it was not until 1973 that Britain joined the EEC, the move suggested that the mother country had lost interest in its 'dominion', just as the increasing pace of decolonisation had seen it shrug off most of the old empire. Australian imperialists felt betrayed: it was a grave blow to sentiment when travellers to Britain discovered that visitors from EEC countries received preference in passing through Immigration. Yet they could hardly complain, given Australia's own changing economic concerns.

At the same time Australia's relationship with the United States was evolving at different levels. The production of the first Holden car in 1948 by General Motors is generally regarded as a symbolic moment in this relationship. This development was greeted as demonstrating Australia's extending manufacturing base. And in spite of the enterprise being American it was also Australian in that the Holden was proudly claimed to be specially designed for local conditions. Interestingly, the impetus for the Holden did not come from Detroit, and General Motors had to be coaxed into the project: the capital was raised in Australia, though the profits were to flow back to America. The Holden, particularly in its FJ model, became one of the cultural artefacts of the post-war era. Although many still bought the smaller model English cars, the family-size Holden dominated the roads.

The expanding popularity of tennis – no longer a game confined

8.5   Prime Minister Chifley, a rather homely figure, looks pleased with the first Holden. Other dignatories inspect the interior.

8.6   Bringing the Davis Cup back from America. Lew Hoad, Neale Frazer, coach Harry Hopman, Rex Hartwig and Ken Rosewall pose proudly. Hoad and Rosewall in particular were the tennis heroes of the 1950s.

to the private courts of the well-to-do – provided a new forum for the American relationship. For a time the Davis Cup competition was dominated by the rivalry between the US Goliath and the Australian David, making an interesting comparison with the cricketing dialogue with England. The arrival of the 'Yanks' during the Second World War had given Australians their first encounter with the reality of American culture (as opposed to its Hollywood images), but the Davis Cup and its ceremonies gave a dramatised opportunity for comparisons. So the American tennis players were observed as personable and articulate, even if their utterances verged on the banal, while the Australians were often immature and incoherent, yet gutsy in performance.

Perhaps the emerging complexity of the American relationship is best seen in the tragedy of Vietnam. It was part of the Australian psychology – or at least the psychology of most policy-makers – that there was a prime need to keep America involved in the Pacific region. There had always been uncertainties as to how binding the ANZUS commitment was, and it seemed that Australia sought every opportunity to make the word flesh. In 1955 external affairs minister Casey suggested to Menzies that it should be tactfully drawn to Washington's attention that 'Australia would be sympathetic to the idea of an American base being established on Australian soil'[9]: the logic was that bases would, in a practical sense, commit the US to Australia's defence. So, too, the SEATO treaty, negotiated in 1954, and to which the US, Britain, France, Australia, New Zealand, Pakistan, the Philippines and Thailand were signatories, was welcomed as complementing ANZUS in engaging America in the region of Australia's concern.

When, in the wake of the French departure, the United States became gradually more involved in Vietnam, Australian diplomacy concentrated on encouraging the Americans in their commitment. Australia dropped hints that it would offer combat troops, before the US had even asked for them, largely to bolster American resolve to escalate its own military presence. Conscription was introduced in 1964, paving the way for the formal commitment of a battalion in April 1965. Ironically, South Vietnam itself was reluctant to welcome the Australian troops. Although Menzies spoke of 'the necessary request' from South Vietnam,[10] in the end that government was careful to accept the Australian offer rather than be seen as taking the initiative.

In the early 1960s Labor, under the leadership of Arthur Calwell, enthusiastically supported the American alliance, and insofar as it considered Vietnam at all, endorsed the sending of military advisers. Labor, however, baulked at conscription, and from 1965 the party became critical of the war, though uncertain as to how it should respond politically. Such doubts were heightened by the calamitous failure of Calwell's campaign to mobilise the anti-conscription vote. Harold Holt, Menzies' successor as Prime Minister, won a massive victory at the 1966 election, which was unusual for being dominated by issues of foreign policy. Holt, a cultivated if bland figure, had gone out of his way to support the United States President, L. B. Johnson, and in one celebrated effusion beamingly assured Johnson that in Australia he had 'an admiring friend, a staunch friend that will be all the way with LBJ'.[11] An appreciative Johnson visited Australia a month before the poll, attracting cheering crowds which rivalled the Queen's visit of 1954. The dissent of anti-war demonstrators seemed only to exaggerate the fervour of the majority who acclaimed the first visit of a serving American president. The American alliance had been personalised in a way unknown since the days of General MacArthur.

This enthusiasm for the alliance disguised the fact that Australia's commitment to Vietnam was relatively small. Whereas the American presence rose to over half a million troops, the Australian contribution peaked at about 8,000. Conscription was selective with a lottery of birthday dates deciding who would be called up. The government's policy, it has been sarcastically observed, was based on the assumption 'that Australians would fight to the last American'.[12] In the 1950s Casey's attempts to boost defence expenditure had met with indifference from most of his cabinet colleagues, and even during Vietnam the size of Australia's investment in defence was determined by an estimate of what was necessary to sustain the alliance. For if Australia did enough to support and encourage the US in policing the region, then it had little need to go beyond this in providing for its own defence. This reflected a cynicism all the more profound for it hardly being noticed. The effect, too, was to build the American alliance into domestic policy, for the cheap protection it gave Australia helped make possible the complacent affluence of the great majority who did not have to do the fighting.

When, in the late 1960s, disillusion with Vietnam began to seep through the community, there was a consciousness that this was an experience which we were sharing with the US. Those who condemned Yankee imperialism drew on the culture of the American protest movement, its music, its clothes, its drugs; they also learnt from its political example. The moratorium of May 1970, which saw the largest street demonstrations in Australia's history, was inspired by the American moratorium of October 1969. It was perhaps remarkable that the Vietnam issue was capable of mobilising such crowds in Australia, given the smallness of our commitment to the

war, yet that tokenism seemed to epitomise the hypocrisy of Australia's position, and provided a focus for the censure of a generation finding its voice. Protest, although part of an international phenomenon, had local roots.

It is perhaps not coincidental that the years of the Vietnam war also saw a fitful expression of nationalist values. Sometimes this meant a slackening of traditional bonds with Britain, though often this was as much effect as cause. Casey, elevated to a life peerage, was in 1965 the first Australian-born governor-general appointed by an Anti-labor government; with his impeccable imperial credentials – he had served during the war as British Minister of State in Cairo and Governor of Bengal – he was the perfect transitional figure.

Casey's appointment effectively established a new convention, so that what had once been controversial (as with Labor's appointment of Isaacs in 1931) gradually became the norm at both federal and state levels. Similar shifts of emphasis occurred in other institutions: The Church of England, for example, began to look for its archbishops at home rather than in England, and in 1981 transformed itself into the Anglican Church of Australia. A parallel transition was occurring in the Catholic Church, as the old generation of Irish-born prelates gave way to Australian-born successors. Such changes did not reflect an assertive nationalism, but rather the gradual, even reluctant, acceptance of autonomy in particular cultural spheres. Nor did they preclude the continuation of an underlying psychology of dependence, particularly in economic and defence matters, though they did render it more susceptible to questioning.

In the political arena nationalist rhetoric was coming into fashion. The development of Canberra – since its inauguration in 1927 little more than a country town of public servants – was given priority by Menzies, and in the 1960s it began to acquire the scale and monuments which could help identify it as a national capital. John Gorton, who enjoyed a brief but controversial term as prime minister (1968–71), projected an Australian larrikinish image, and his nationalism extended to the economic sphere with talk of government support for 'buying back the farm' from multi-national companies. When Gorton made his salute to the American alliance,

8.7 President Johnson at Canberra Airport in the dusk, 1966. The camera catches Prime Minister Holt appearing to bow deferentially to the President. This photograph by David Moore, available from the Australian National Gallery as a postcard, has clearly been seen as symbolising the American relationship.

he even tried to give it an Australian flavour, assuring a bemused President Nixon that 'we will go a-waltzing Matilda with you';[13] he also toyed with a 'fortress Australia' defence policy. But it was the advent of Labor to office in 1972, under Gough Whitlam, which saw the most dramatic flowering of what came to be known as 'the new nationalism'. Some of Whitlam's changes were symbolic, for example, the restyling of the Commonwealth as the 'Australian' Government, but overall he was seeking to convey both to Australians and the world a sense of our political independence. Whereas Anti-labor governments had assumed that good manners required that disagreements with Britain and the United States should not be publicly aired, Whitlam sought to establish a much more open stance, recognising too that those longstanding relationships were only part of Australia's foreign policy concerns. Labor took up Gorton's concern with ownership of Australia's economic resources, and the attempt to raise loans for development through unorthodox channels was to prove its undoing.

Some of the trivia of the new nationalism, such as the concern to find a national anthem to replace 'God Save the Queen', irritated some sections of the community, and there were fears expressed that Labor's ultimate aim was a republic. But in other areas the preoccupation with national identity was less controversial. The late 1960s saw a rapid expansion of subsidy to the arts, and this was largely justified in terms of the need to express an Australian culture. In the wake of the Queen's 1954 visit the first tentative foray into subsidy for the performing arts had resulted in the creation of the Australian Elizabethan Theatre Trust, the name firmly locating the endeavour in a British context. Ray Lawler's 'Summer of the Seventeenth Doll' was one of the first fruits of this Australian drama, yet it seemed that the aura which this play acquired derived in part from its being taken up by Sir Laurence Olivier and successfully staged in the West End. While such imprimatur would always have some appeal, by the time of the Whitlam government there was a greater acceptance of the arts as an expression of an indigenous culture. When, after decades of controversy and escalating expense, the Sydney Opera House was opened in 1973, it immediately became, for all its practical faults as a building, a symbol of the new cultural optimism. Its billowing, white sculptured form rising out of the waters soon eclipsed the Harbour Bridge as a motif for Sydney, even coming to serve on the travel posters as an image of Australia itself. The Opera House also conveyed a sense of the affluence which underpinned this investment in the arts.

8.8   The opening of the Sydney Opera House, 1973, with that other landmark, the Harbour Bridge, in the background. The imaginative design by the Danish architect Utzon emerged from a competition, but Utzon was ousted before the project was completed.

The dismissal of the Whitlam government by the Governor-General, Sir John Kerr, on 11 November 1975 was a dramatic culmination of three turbulent years, and an event which has already entered Australian folk-lore. The origins of this crisis were local, and lay in the refusal of interests opposed to Labor to accept its right, after twenty-three years in the wilderness, to govern, but it was not long before conspiracy theories had suggested a CIA involvement.* One immediate effect of the dismissal, however, was to stimulate a reassessment of the role of governor-general in the Australian political context. Kerr intervened to resolve a deadlock between House of Representatives and Senate over the passage of supply legislation, but it was one of the criticisms directed at him by Whitlam and others that in dismissing a government which still enjoyed the

* Whitlam's own account of *The Whitlam Government 1972–1975* does not rule out a CIA role, and relates how in 1977 President Carter passed on a message 'that the US Administration would never again interfere in the domestic political processes of Australia'.[14]

confidence of the lower house he was exercising a royal prerogative which the Queen herself would have felt, by convention, unable to use. According to this view, the monarchy, a British derived institution, was being misused by a determined and cynical Australian establishment. The result was to encourage a mood of republicanism in the labour movement, though it was never to be spelled out in a formal sense. It was, in any case, a paradoxical reaction, because according to Whitlam's argument it was the *weakening* of bonds with Britain which had made possible this abuse of the monarchy. And with conventions losing their force, only an amendment of the Constitution could ensure that 1975 could not happen again.

In some respects Australia was shedding its colonial past with little fuss: the Queen had become the Queen of Australia, appeals from Australian courts to the Privy Council were gradually abolished, and so on. Australia was also shedding its own small colonial empire, in particular Papua New Guinea. For many years it had been assumed that independence for New Guinea was a generation, even a century away, but as colonial empires around the globe vanished, this tropical outpost became an anomaly. Whitlam determined on the speediest of transitions, and independence was achieved in September 1975, less than three years after his accession to office and only two months before the demise of his government. 'If history were to obliterate the whole of my public career, save my contribution to the independence of a democratic PNG,' he was later to write, 'I should rest content.'[15]

Whitlam's attempt to reconcile an independent foreign policy with the historical logic of the American alliance created tensions which explain the plausibility of a CIA interest in facilitating a return to more reliable coalition rule. Yet although 1975 encouraged some on the left of the Labor Party to think in terms of dismantling the alliance, the practical difficulties of doing so were immense. The economic decline of the late 1970s and early 1980s was conducive to pragmatism in foreign as well as domestic policy, and when R. J. Hawke brought Labor back to office in 1983 the commitment to the alliance was carefully reaffirmed. The new Foreign Minister Bill Hayden (who had been the party's leader until displaced by Hawke on the eve of the election) sought, in the tradition of Evatt and Whitlam, to develop a more independent regional role for Australia, but where this impinged on the alliance the result was often not so much compromise as inconsistency. So, for example, the Government's professed interest in a nuclear-free south-west Pacific did not preclude it from welcoming visits by American ships which might be nuclear-armed.

It was this very issue which saw the ANZUS Pact threatened from an unlikely source. In 1984 New Zealand, so often taken for granted by Australia, also elected a Labor government, but one committed to implementing its anti-nuclear policy. Although the new government claimed to support the continuation of ANZUS it would not permit nuclear-armed ships in New Zealand ports, and the United States, refusing to divulge if any particular ship were so armed, decided that ANZUS could not function on those terms. In this confrontation between superpower and midget, Australia ostentatiously clung to the coat tails of Uncle Sam: as late as 1987 Prime Minister Hawke was still making a point of not visiting New Zealand.

The disintegration of ANZUS, at least in its original form, revealed the different world perspectives of Australia and New Zealand. Protected by its greater distance, New Zealand did not always share Australia's preoccupation with south-east Asia, and the American alliance, although important, had not been enshrined in its national consciousness to the same extent. New Zealand's residual sense of its own Britishness, which had not been disturbed by the kind of European immigration which Australia had experienced since the war, also contributed to a greater resistance to the American connexion. New Zealand's investment in the alliance never matched Australia's: it had, for example, no American bases comparable to those established on Australian soil. Given New Zealand's sense of isolation, an anti-nuclear policy had a much broader appeal, which was by no means confined to the left of the political spectrum.

This divergence in world views occurred at a time when in another sense the two nations were converging. Increasingly from the 1960s Australia, with its more obvious prosperity and greater cultural amenities, became a magnet for young New Zealanders, thousands of whom in effect migrated, particularly to Sydney. Traditionally Australia and New Zealand had waived passport requirements for each other's citizens: the end of this arrangement in 1981 was influenced by concern about possible drug trafficking, but also seemed to reflect a new complexity in the relationship. The New Zealand presence in Australia, although a subject for jokes, was generally accepted, because the cultural common ground was evident enough. But the coming of passports, and the estrangement of New Zealand from ANZUS, combined to transform it in Australian eyes into something more like a foreign nation. If this meant an erosion of the old familiarity, it also made New Zealand more interesting, even puzzling. It was no longer possible to dismiss the trans-Tasman neighbour as a British backwater, notable mainly for scenery and rugby. Its large and articulate prime minister, David Lange, seemed to capture the world's attention in a way that the supposedly charismatic Hawke might have envied. Whether or not one approved of its anti-nuclear policy, New Zealand had, over-night, asserted the independence which Australia had so long toyed with.

Yet insofar as the spell of ANZUS has been broken, Australia's own assessment of the alliance may be subtly affected. Recent defence planning has been placing greater emphasis on an assess-ment of Australia's local needs, on the assumption that the alliance cannot simply be taken for granted. At the same time Australia's support for US foreign policy has been juxtaposed against other aspects of the relationship. When in 1986 Australian overseas mar-kets were threatened by America's subsidising of its unsold wheat, the response was angry. Was this the way to treat a loyal ally? One farmers' organisation suggested that the government should not be afraid to use ANZUS in bargaining with the United States. Such rural pragmatism was very different from the critique of the alliance offered by radical ideologues. The government made a virtue of declining to regard ANZUS as negotiable, but nevertheless drew American attention to the pressure being placed upon it. The US made concessions; the immediate crisis passed. ANZUS survives because dispensing with it would still be too traumatic an ordeal. But its sacred aura has been tarnished.

In spite of the growth of a greater sense of cultural self-sufficiency, it seems to be part of the Australian temperament to be uneasy with nationalist gestures. The complexity of the relationship with Britain has meant that any assertion of Australian identity runs the risk of being interpreted as a rejection of the British heritage. The result has often been not so much a cultural division within the community (though that does, in shadowy form, exist) as a deep-seated sceptic-ism about the value of exercises in the ritual and rhetoric of national-ism. For a time it seemed that the power of Anzac had overcome this scepticism, or at least integrated it into an extraordinary day of mourning and carnival. But by the 1960s Anzac itself was under attack, and Alan Seymour's play 'The One Day of The Year' demon-strated the generational gap in attitudes. The attempts to develop another focus for national observance, as with Australia Day on 26 January, which commemorates the first white settlement of 1788, have met with yawns of indifference from a populace which prefers, appropriately perhaps, to dedicate the occasion to the pursuit of pleasure on a summer long-weekend. So, too, many Australians could not take the quest for a National Anthem seriously, and although grudgingly accepting the need for 'Advance Australia Fair' (how else could Australia be distinguished from Britain at the Olympic Games?) remain determined not to learn the words. The planning for the Bicentenary of 1988 has been marked by petty discord which has probably confirmed the innate scepticism about such occasions.

At the same time, however, the increasing exploitation of nationalism as a marketing device suggests a possible change in perceptions. While it is not surprising, perhaps, that the television extravaganza of 'world series' cricket should be promoted by the monotonous rorty refrain of 'Come on Aussie, come on', many other products and services now draw on quasi-nationalist images in their advertising. In much of this, the United States is the model: American marketing strategies, it would seem, have simply been adapted. At what level these messages are received is another matter. T-shirts bearing flags or emblems can be regarded as fun, without much absorption of the earnestness which usually underpins comparable American sentiment. On the other hand it may be that advertising is training Australians to be more at home with the ethos as well as the paraphernalia of nationalism.

The gradually accumulating economic crisis, brought on by the deterioration in world markets for minerals and primary products, and which culminated in the collapse of the Australian dollar in 1985–86, may also be having an effect on attitudes. In the Great Depression Britain filled the role of imperial schoolmaster, disciplining the wayward dominion, so that the question of recovery was inextricably bound up with the traditional relationship of dependence. In the 1980s it is a more mysterious entity, the international money market, which judges Australia; in particular a few Wall Street finance dealers who decided Australia's credit rating. Dependence now is less specific, and lacks the historic associations of the British connexion. In attempting to alert the public to the seriousness of the economic situation, Prime Minister Hawke compared the crisis to that which Australia faced in 1942. The task, as then, was to bring Australians together in a united effort until victory was won. But if, in 1942, Australia had looked to America, to whom could it look now? If prosperity had helped make possible the 'new nationalism', its evaporation could make independence seem a luxury. In a sense Australia was more alone than ever before, for even if it acknowledged an economic dependence on the United States, the United States had no obligation to accept the corresponding responsibility. It has become something of a truism that since 1942 Australia simply exchanged dependence on one global power for another, but the dependence had a different character and was based on a different cultural relationship. Imperialist Australians were hurt when they sensed that Britain had lost interest in its dominions, but with the United States such 'interest' was not there in the first place. And nor could the American success of, say, Paul Hogan's film 'Crocodile Dundee', noted with such satisfaction, create it, except in the most ephemeral sense. Australian dependence on the United States was not sustained by the kind of continuing dialogue which had been a natural part of the colonial-imperial relationship.

Even more problematic has been the relationship with Japan. The transformation of Japan from wartime foe (a target for both racial fear and contempt) into a major trading partner has been accomplished quietly and carefully, but for many years the cultural implications of the relationship were tactfully avoided. Australian interest in Japan was little more than polite, while Japanese investment in Australia was accepted for the benefits it offered; that Japan's graduation as a western economic power, rivalling the United States, might place Australia in another relationship of dependence has been for the most part ignored.

It might be the best of all possible worlds if Australia could gain the self-respect of independence without the accompanying trappings of nationalism. As it is, there is the danger that we might be conditioned to accept the trappings without the substance. Much has changed since the Second World War. The cultural cringe, which had so crippled creative endeavour, has certainly receded, and a more sophisticated society has more confidence in its own judgements. But old habits die hard. It is not easy to let go of the British connexion, whether in the form of traditional attachment to the monarchy or in equally traditional anti-English prejudice. So royal visits are amiably received, even if now peripheral in an institutional sense; while the habit of 'Pommy bashing' is still not unknown, as in the easy – and historically inaccurate – pillorying of the English officer caste in Peter Weir's film of 'Gallipoli'.

There is, no doubt, a measure of reassurance in both activities, for Anglo-Celtic Australians have a rich, inherited cultural context in which to locate them, a context relatively lacking for the dependence on America. The need for such reassurance is all the more understandable when one recognises the profound changes that have occurred since the Second World War, changes that have seen Australian society burgeon with a new diversity. No longer can it be assumed that the old Anglo-Celtic cultural hegemony will continue unquestioned.

9

Diversity

Welcoming American troops in 1943 Prime Minister Curtin stressed their similarity to Australians. He spoke of the 'kinship with men and women who, largely, spring from the same stock as ourselves'; 'our visitors speak like us, think like us, and fight like us'.[1] If the sentiment was understandable, Curtin was nevertheless wrong on all counts. Part of the fascination of the encounter lay precisely in discovering just how different the Yanks were. They not only spoke differently, but ate differently; and their elaborate manners, particularly in dating and courting, clearly distinguished them from Australian men. Furthermore, Curtin's reference to the shared 'stock' (modified only by the word 'largely') ignored the significant minority of black Americans, who were a subject for particular scrutiny, and took no account of the ethnic diversity of American society.

Australians had never experienced a foreign culture in quite this way before. There was no need to feel threatened by the Yanks, except, as was the case with some Australian servicemen competing for women, in a temporary sense. The visitors had glamour, self-assurance, money and a touch of mystery. Some 12,000 took Australian brides with them back to the US; but for most Australians meeting the Yanks was an opportunity to make cultural comparisons, and, if not to see what kind of a society Australia could become, at least to have the national imagination stimulated. It may have helped prepare the way for a more adventurous postwar immigration policy, even while giving many Australians a greater sense of their own culture.

The experience of the war, and the feeling that Australia had escaped invasion by the skin of its teeth, encouraged some soul-searching about the nation's future. The low birthrate demanded attention: as Calwell put it, 'our first task is to ennoble motherhood'.[2] Yet no one imagined that family patterns could be easily changed, and the demographic forecasts were depressing. A Labor government was forced, reluctantly, to consider the possible role of immigration in expanding Australia's meagre population of seven million. Calwell became immigration minister, and a programme was launched in 1947, with the grudging acquiescence of the trade unions; by this time there was reasonable confidence that full employment was sustainable, and therefore that immigrants would not threaten jobs. While the challenge of defending Australia was often cited as a justification for immigration, it was more the commitment to economic growth which ultimately provided its rationale. And although it was often imagined that migrants would assist in 'a return to the country', helping build a rural-based prosperity, increasingly it was appreciated by employers and trade unions that the newcomers would satisfy the labour demands of expanding secondary and tertiary industries, dutifully occupying the lower rungs of the ladder, and permitting the native-born workers to move up.

Between 1947 and 1969 more than two million migrants came. It hardly needed saying that British migrants were preferred, and some 880,000 were attracted, 84 per cent on assisted passages. But it was soon appreciated that the scheme could not be sustained from this traditional source, and alternatives had to be considered. Refugees from eastern Europe, 'displaced persons' as they were clinically dubbed, were accepted, with a nod towards humanitarian sentiment. 'Nordic' migrants from northern Europe were welcomed as being the next best thing to British, but soon substantial numbers of southern Europeans – Italians, Greeks, Yugoslavs and Maltese – were taken: more than half a million arrived over the 1947–69 period, three-quarters of them paying their own way. If southern Europeans were only grudgingly accepted, Asians were virtually taboo. It was Calwell who made the celebrated jest that 'two Wongs do not make a White', and it is revealing that he could still defend this racist pun, years later, on the grounds that it was really at the expense of another member of parliament, T. W. White.[3]

It might be thought that the increasingly confident growth of the post-war years assumed a need for change, but in a social sense the mood was conservative. Migrants were expected to assimilate, which meant coming to terms with 'the Australian way of life' with minimum fuss. Dubbed 'New Australians', they were expected to disperse into the community, to become invisible; any tendency to settle in clusters was deemed a failure of the policy, regardless of whether it helped migrants in adjusting to their new environment.

9.1   This was the frontispiece for *The Australian Way of Life*, published in 1953. A street scene is almost deserted of people except for a policeman and policewoman who appear to be keeping 'the Australian way of life' under observation. The image certainly does not accord with the idea of Australian society being hostile to authority. (See Chapter 10).

Australia had decided that it wanted immigration, but it did not particularly want immigrants. According to F. W. Eggleston, writing in a 1953 volume actually called *The Australian Way of Life*, Australians were 'fanatically determined' to protect their way of life, and therefore immigration could not be permitted to break down 'the common *mores* of a homogeneous community'.[4] What constituted this way of life was by no means clear, though the 'common mores' of which Eggleston spoke seemed to have a middle-class complexion.

There was little thought as to what immigrants might contribute, apart from their labour. Benign commentators sometimes conceded that migrants had added a welcome variety to Australian cooking, but were hard pressed to go beyond this. The great popular success of John O'Grady's 1957 novel, *They're a Weird Mob*, purportedly written by one 'Nino Culotta', demonstrated the assimilationist expectations. For all its sending up of Australian ways and its superficial sympathy with the immigrant experience, *They're a Weird Mob* ultimately told migrants they were on to a good thing. The message to New Australians, 'Well, don't be bludgers.* Hop in and learn', was all the more telling for ostensibly coming from an Italian mouth. 'Old' Australians could read the novel and feel they were being tolerant and understanding, while having their prejudices about Australian superiority confirmed. As late as 1969 the then minister for immigration, Billy Snedden, was still insistent that 'we should have a monoculture, with everyone living in the same way, understanding each other, and choosing the same aspirations'.[5] It had an authoritarian ring to it: woe betide the person who dissented and 'chose' (was there a choice?) other aspirations.

Growth, not diversity, was the preoccupation. The prosperity of the 1950s took shape in the multiplying vistas of suburbia. The home was more than ever the citadel of the family. The appliances of the consumer society now became much more widely available, the refrigerator and washing machine leading the way. The late arrival of television in 1956 reinforced the authority of the home; while the motor car, increasingly an adjunct of the home, was also designed for the family. Soon prosperity stimulated expectations for the next generation, and education became an issue; by the end of the decade the need felt for greater access to university education, presaged by the postwar scheme for ex-servicemen, had led to plans for new and larger tertiary institutions.

---

* In Australian slang, loafers.

9.2   John Brack's 'The Car' dates from the 1950s and portrays the small nuclear family, neatly cocooned in its shell of civilisation, on a drive in the bush. The car is not a Holden; the traffic indicator suggests the make is English.

This dedication of Australian society to the values of home and family, launched under the aegis of Labor's postwar reconstruction policies, was fully expressed in the Menzies years. The conformity which it required ('everyone living in the same way') was particularly at the expense of women, who had been called upon to enter the workforce in large numbers during the war, only to find themselves steered towards marriage and reproduction when peace came. Sometimes women seemed worse off than before the war. In medicine, for example, the preference given to ex-servicemen for university places meant that women doctors were scarcer than ever. It also seems no accident that there were fewer women painters of note than in the period between the wars.

After the dislocations of war, the churches sought to reintegrate themselves into the suburban order of home and family. New churches went up, buildings which, although often contriving to appear 'modern' in the now fashionable yellow brick, were usually traditional in inspiration. The Protestant churches sought to evangelise the new suburbia. In 1953 the Methodists launched their Mission to the Nation under the leadership of Alan Walker, and in 1959 Anglican and Protestant churches joined in sponsoring a much publicised crusade by the American evangelist, Billy Graham: more than three million people were claimed to have attended his open air meetings in Australia and New Zealand. A system of fund-raising was also imported from the US, via the Wells Organisation, according to which families were encouraged to pledge a regular weekly sum in support of their local church, the campaign usually being launched by a 'loyalty dinner'. The Graham crusade also reflected a degree of ecumenism amongst non-Catholics, and in 1957 Methodists, Presbyterians and Congregationalists had resumed discussions about union – the idea had first been mooted before the Great War – which would, twenty years later, create the Uniting Church. The Australian Council for the World Council of Churches, set up in 1946, also brought Anglican and Protestant churches together. In all this Protestant-oriented ecumenism, there was a sense of old ethnic religious loyalties giving way to a more homogeneous Australian Protestantism.

The Catholic Church, with its much more devout laity, was also able to exploit the prosperity of the 1950s to enhance its position in the community. The increasing affluence of working-class Catholics was to have political – and social – repercussions, but institutionally the church remained conservative. While technically standing to benefit from immigration from southern and eastern Europe, the

9.3　Billy Graham, an evangelist for his times, poses for a press photograph. Perhaps these young admirers had made decisions for Christ which was the climax of a crusade meeting.

Irish-derived church made few concessions to the different Catholic cultures of Italy, Malta and Poland. Looking back in 1967 Patrick O'Farrell, a notable Catholic historian and layman, observed that 'in Australian Catholicism, conformity is the eighth cardinal virtue'. It was 'small comfort', he added, 'to reflect that this is probably a generally Australian rather than specifically Catholic fault.'[6]

Censorship, although provoking some criticism from writers and academics, remained firmly intact, supported broadly by secular and religious authority. In 1958 the list of books banned on the recommendation of the Literature Censorship Board included not only traditional targets such as Boccaccio, de Sade, the *Kama-Sutra* and *Lady Chatterley's Lover*, but John O'Hara's *Butterfield 8*, Gore Vidal's *City and the Pillar*, J. P. Donleavy's *Ginger Man* and the original edition of Grace Metalious' *Peyton Place*.

The mood and values of this 'monocultural' society are neatly encapsulated in the Melbourne Olympic Games of 1956. This was an appropriate occasion for presenting Australia to the world. The residents of Heidelberg worked hard to present a spruce and friendly image of Australian suburbia to the athletes of the Olympic village, while an official barbecue, a demonstration match of Australian Rules football and a 'Meet the Australians Campaign' were all part of a self-conscious presentation of the 'Australian way of life'.

Although part of the rationale of this 'way of life' was that it was something to be protected from such foreign cancers as communism, as an international and 'non-political' gathering the Games technically had to rise above such considerations. However, the success of the 1956 Games was threatened by the atmosphere of international crisis engendered by the almost simultaneous invasion of the Suez Canal by Britain and France and of Hungary by the Soviet Union. Australia had shared in the strident anti-communism of the Cold War, which gained a local edge with the defection of a minor Soviet diplomat and KGB operative, Vladamir Petrov, in 1954. Two years later Games officials, including Wilfrid Kent Hughes who had a political reputation as an anti-communist, were urging peace and tolerance. Whereas eastern European migrants who had demonstrated against the Soviet Union in 1954 had been patted on the back in the media, Hungarian migrants who threatened action in 1956 were told that Australia was prepared to assimilate them 'AS HUMAN BEINGS', but was 'NOT prepared to assimilate their old-world hatreds and vendettas'. The *Official Report* was later to claim that it was 'Australia's very remoteness' which was 'perhaps the saving grace of the Games'. The notorious water polo final between the Soviet Union and Hungary, when the pool ran with blood, was not part of the Games which Melbourne, at least, wished to remember. The *Melbourne Herald* book of the Games simply referred to the match as 'hectic' and chose its pictures carefully.

The preferred image of the Games was the closing ceremony. The euphoria experienced by Melbourne as it seemed, for this short time, the centre of the world, culminated in the then unique idea of a final 'Ceremony of comradeship', during which national groupings would be dissolved in 'a hotchpotch of sheer humanity'. That the idea should have appealed to Australian officials – Olympic president Avery Brundage was less enthusiastic – might suggest that however much the Games were exploited as a national event, the Australian temperament retained a scepticism toward flag-waving. The emotion generated by this 'Olympic Armistice' was to be engraved on the memory of the huge crowd which shared it. But the idea itself came from a letter to Olympic officials written by 'an Australian-born Chinese boy', John Ian Wing.[7]

*   *   *

Even as it seemed that the values of 'the Australian way of life' were being consolidated, the prosperity of postwar society was unleashing processes which would ultimately transform it.

Thus the political ructions of the 1950s which seemed in the short term to strengthen the established order in fact signalled the end of one of Australia's long-standing cultural accommodations. Anti-communism as a political issue not only helped Anti-labor return to office in 1949 after eight years in opposition, but also helped destroy the old accord between Labor and the Catholic Church which had existed since the turn of the century. Menzies' attempt to ban the Communist Party came to grief in 1951 when a referendum narrowly but surprisingly refused to give the Commonwealth the necessary constitutional power. Although this was a victory for Labor leader Evatt, his party was increasingly divided about how the labour movement should deal with the Communists in its own ranks. Through a semi-secret Church-sponsored organisation called 'The Movement', Catholic unionists in the 1940s had been instrumental in launching an offensive to break communist influence in trade unions. The success of this campaign created a new problem, as the anti-communist zealots, not always sympathetic to traditional Labor mores, became a powerful faction seeking to control the party. In 1954 Evatt, whose leadership was under threat, shored up his position by publicly condemning the influence of The Movement, forcing a split in the party in 1955 when the right-wing faction defected to form the rebel Democratic Labor Party.

At the time the split was not seen as irreparable, but it became so. The DLP gave its preferences regularly to Anti-labor, on the grounds that this would eventually force Labor to come to terms with it, but in fact it served primarily to keep Menzies in office. Labor's traditional relish in faction fighting disguised the underlying social changes which conditioned The Split (as it came to be known, the capitals distinguishing it from other, less significant 'splits'). The historic attachment of Catholics to the party was being eroded by the gathering impetus of postwar prosperity. The Movement brought to the fore a younger generation of Catholics, more

9.4   Mrs Petrov, wife of the Soviet diplomat who had just defected, being hustled by Soviet officials to the waiting aircraft at Mascot Airport, Sydney, on 19 April 1954. In Darwin, approached by Australian officials, Mrs Petrov decided to stay with her husband in Australia. This potent image of the Cold War being acted out on Australian soil seemed to give anti-communism a boost: shortly afterwards Labor lost an election which it had earlier been given a good chance of winning.

ideological in their outlook and consequently impatient with the tacit compromise involved in the Church's relationship with Labor. The Movement's spokesman, B. A. Santamaria, was self-consciously an intellectual, interested in European Catholic thought and committed to rejuvenating Australian Catholic life. The Movement and its offshoots were influenced by the distributivism of Belloc and Chesterton, and advocated a Catholic variant of the Australian rural ideology, which emphasised the moral health of a peasant-type society. While the mass of laity did not necessarily share these enthusiasms, the DLP provided a convenient half-way house for middle-class Catholics who no longer found the cultural atmosphere of the labour movement congenial, but who could not bring themselves to vote for the Protestant-aligned Anti-labor parties.

At the time the political recriminations of The Split seemed evidence of a resurgence of sectarianism. Labor leaders attacked the DLP as a clerical party on the European model, while the exposure of The Movement and its Catholic Action associations reactivated some Protestant suspicions of Romish conspiracies. In reality The Split did not so much mobilise a Catholic vote as fragment it. Many Catholics maintained the traditional loyalty to Labor, so that Catholics were now divided in their allegiance. The result was often much bitterness at the level of parish and even family: Calwell, a Catholic who chose to stay with Labor, was denounced from the pulpit of his parish church.

From a Protestant perspective the Catholic Church was ceasing to be the monolith of old. At the same time the support given by the DLP to the Liberal-Country Party government meant that for the first time the Anti-labor coalition was dependent to a degree on Catholic patronage. In 1964 Menzies introduced a small but significant element of state aid to independent schools, thus signalling the end of the nineteenth-century educational settlement which had maintained the separation of Church and State. That Menzies, 'a simple Presbyterian' as he once called himself, could do this without incurring a politically damaging sectarian backlash, says much for the change in attitudes. The division between Catholic and Protestant remained significant, but the pursed lip silence of the old social accommodation had been broken. The Catholic minority was encouraged to examine its own cultural identity more openly and critically, and with less pressure to maintain traditional solidarity.

The accumulating migrant presence began to change society without many Australians noticing it. Assimilationist policies initially disguised the effects of immigration. Political parties, for example, assumed that dispersal was desirable, and resisted moves to create ethnic branches; so, too, the Scout movement saw few ethnic troops on the American model. And although migrant communities formed urban clusters, there did not develop the clearly defined ghettoes which characterised American cities. Partly this was because the prosperity of the period was infectious, and many migrants, seeking to acquire the trappings of success, were drawn into the expanding web of suburbia. To this extent the 'Australian way of life' was winning converts.

Nevertheless migrants were not so easily absorbed, nor, in sharing the fruits of prosperity, did they necessarily discard their culture. Whilst in the early years they understandably failed to penetrate the institutions of the host society, they were creating, or re-creating, their own institutions. For Greeks, for example, the Orthodox Church was of vital importance, while the family, such a pivotal institution in the immigrant experience, carried the essential Greek culture with it. The children of Greek migrants, in attempting to adapt to the ways of school and playground, became aware of their own 'Greekness'. The casual hostility experienced by migrants in the course of their daily lives was in some measure compensated for by the imprint they were beginning to make on their surroundings. They stimulated a transformation of the inner suburbs, which now became 'cosmopolitan' and 'colourful', a prelude to later gentrification at the hands of trendy Anglo-Celtic Australians.

Because they tended to be preoccupied with immediate survival, and because they were fragmented by language and culture, migrants could not easily make themselves heard. While their presence was changing the shape and appearance of Australian society, the cultural and political effects of immigration were necessarily delayed.

As migrants arrived the policy of immigration itself underwent subtle changes. The modest programme of aid to the undeveloped countries of south and south-east Asia which external affairs minister Spender helped launch as the Colombo Plan of 1950 brought large numbers of Asian students to study in Australia. They were only visitors, but the gesture of racial goodwill involved, even if patronising, seemed to make a symbolic dent in the White Australia policy. The administration of this policy was increasingly a cause for concern and embarrassment in Australia's foreign relations, and in 1958 the arbitrary dictation test was abolished. In 1966 the racial bar was relaxed to the extent that application for entry by

9.5   This is the Finke River Mission float in the Alice Springs Jubilee Day Parade in 1951, celebrating fifty years of federation. The *Centralian Advocate* thought it 'probably the best float in the whole function'. 'In a splendidly executed scene one saw the native in his aboriginal state [on the right] and his emancipation to further endeavour.' One might wonder how 'emancipated' these Aborigines look.

'well qualified people' would be considered 'on the basis of their suitability as settlers'.[8] Thus technically the White Australia policy had been discarded, but the numbers of Asians involved were small. At the same time the difficulty in keeping up the supply of immigrants in the 1960s forced the Immigration Department to recruit in countries not considered before, such as Turkey. So the first significant numbers of non-Christians since the Chinese of the goldrushes began to arrive.

Perceptions of Aborigines were also beginning to change. Although the war delayed the implementation of more enlightened government policies, it did extend awareness of discrimination. Gough Whitlam recalls how 'a young and keen Aboriginal member' of his RAAF squadron was constantly rejected in his attempts to join aircrew: it was Whitlam's first observation of such prejudice.[9] The work of anthropologists was also beginning to filter through to the popular consciousness. The ballet, 'Corroboree', to the music of John Antill, and Charles Chauvel's film, 'Jedda', seized on the picturesque and melodramatic, and were patronising by later standards (the Aboriginal heroine, Jedda, for example, is affectionately told by a white stockman that she is 'a nice piece of chocolate'); nevertheless they both reflected a greater recognition of the richness of Aboriginal culture.

The sentencing to gaol in 1958 of Aboriginal painter Albert Namatjira for supplying liquor to another full-blood Aborigine dramatically exposed the tragic potential of the cultural relationships which European settlement had imposed on Aborigines. Although Namatjira was brought up a Christian on a Lutheran mission, he still lived in a tribal community. However, it was the visit of a Melbourne artist, Rex Batterbee, which introduced him to the art of watercolour, and Batterbee organised his first exhibition in 1938. Namatjira's paintings of central Australia enjoyed a wide popularity, but were, at the time, coolly received by the art establishment, which saw his work as being derivative and not authentically Aboriginal. His success nevertheless made him a national figure, important enough to be brought to Canberra in 1954 to meet the Queen, and finally led to his attaining the citizenship usually denied to full-blood Aborigines. While his own family remained wards, Namatjira was allowed the illusion of autonomy. In European eyes the extended family which gathered around him and shared his prosperity were spongers, but to Namatjira such communality was part of his Aboriginal culture. That grog should be the issue for the intervention of the white man's law pointed to its insidious power to disrupt Aboriginal society, and to the overt moralism embedded in Aboriginal policy. Namatjira's sentence of six months' hard labour caused widespread controvery, and was later reduced. In the end he served two months in 'open' custody; shortly after his release in 1959 he died of a heart attack. At the very least it was difficult not to feel that Namatjira had been a victim of injustice, even if there was no simple remedy for his plight. But if Namatjira's death was on the national conscience, it would be some time before the art world would turn a more interested and sympathetic eye on the source of his fame, his paintings.

The exploitation of Aborigines by the pastoral industry, which paid them only token wages, began to attract attention. A gradual improvement in conditions culminated in a Commonwealth Arbitration Commission award in 1966 which at last gave Aboriginal workers the same wages and conditions as those enjoyed by white unionists. 1967 witnessed a momentary consensus about the need to right historic wrongs. A constitutional referendum decided, by an overwhelming majority, to abolish section 127 of the Constitution which laid down that 'in reckoning the numbers of the people of the Commonwealth . . . aboriginal natives shall not be counted'.[10] Thus Aborigines were belatedly recognised as members of the Australian community. Of more practical significance, the same referendum gave the Commonwealth a general power to legislate for Aborigines, a power it had previously only exercised over federal territories.

At the time of this symbolic referendum, Australia had enjoyed two decades of almost uninterrupted prosperity. Affluence, and the experience of English and European habits gained by travel, encouraged a questioning of wowserish regulation. The alliance of Protestantism, trade unionism and a home-based women's vote, which had sustained a range of practices from six o'clock closing of hotels to the maintenance of a 'traditional' Sunday, began to break down. The 1960s saw a new preoccupation with cultural amenities. The long process of liberalising liquor laws was launched; cinemas began to open on Sundays; the middle-class vogue for 'eating out' encouraged the mushrooming of restaurants; cities were planning or building new facilities for the arts; conservation emerged as an issue. Even the moves to relax censorship seemed as much motivated by the obstacle it offered to cultural consumption as by any commitment to libertarian principle.

Affluence also provided the conditions for a questioning of the dominant culture. The opening of Monash University in 1961 heralded a spate of new universities designed to cater for the expanded expectations of a post-war baby boom generation. Students were suddenly more numerous, and provided fertile ground for political dissent in the wake of Vietnam. In 1967 the Monash Labor Club impudently began to collect money for the Vietnamese National Liberation Front, provoking the university's censure and government legislation to prevent it. The next few years saw an escalation in student protest around the continent, fuelled in part by anger at the war in Vietnam and conscription, but also by the wider world experience of student revolt which catapulted into the headlines in 1968. Demonstrations became the expression of a new political culture. Their targets were not merely governments or their leaders, but a range of authorities perceived as oppressive, including the university administrations.

Protest helped create the climate for liberation movements. In relating how in 1969 a handful of women met in Adelaide at the University Refectory to launch the Women's Liberation Movement in South Australia, Anne Summers places the event in the context of student radicalism and acknowledges the American influence both at the level of feminist literature and the broader culture of protest. However, one of the influential books in publicising the women's movement, published in 1970, was written by the Australian born and educated Germaine Greer. In *The Female Eunuch* she drew little on her Australian experience, yet the book was permeated by a triumphant shedding of a provincial Catholic upbringing. Greer's ultimate message – 'Revolution is the festival of the oppressed'[11] – was one of hope, and the wave of feminist organisation in the early 1970s coincided with the enthusiastic build-up for Labor's advent to office in 1972. The Women's Electoral Lobby (WEL) was specifically formed to survey election candidates on women's issues: the immediate inspiration was an article in the American magazine *Ms* about such a survey of US presidential candidates. The academic fringe inhabited by many young feminists was reflected in the launching of the journal *Refractory Girl* in 1972. Summers herself, who, like Greer, was the product of a convent education, made one of the first attempts in *Damned Whores and God's Police* (1975) to provide Australian women with the history which male historians had denied them. In the wider community feminists agitated for justice in work and welfare, and took up issues such as abortion and child care.

Homosexuals also felt encouraged to assert their identity. In the late 1960s 'camp' venues became more common, and 'drag', which had once been confined to party games, took the form of theatre, appropriating a much older tradition of female impersonation. 'Camp' was still the Australian homosexual's self-identification, and the first attempt in 1970 at organising a political voice was called CAMP (Campaign Against Moral Persecution). The American example, however, proved difficult to resist. Mart Crowley's Broadway success, 'Boys In The Band', played successfully in 1969, and gained much publicity when presented in Melbourne – not for its theme of gay New York life, but for its language. ('Who do you have to fuck to get a drink around here?'[12] was one of the disputed lines: screw' was an acceptable substitute for the offending verb.) 'Gay' was already on the way to replacing 'camp', just as 'straight' would supersede 'square'; the first gay liberation group emerged at Sydney University in 1972. The adoption of much of the American-cum-international language and style of gay life did not prevent the Australian experience having its own input. Just as Germaine Greer was one of the missionaries of feminism, so was Dennis Altman's

9.6   The 'Aboriginal Embassy' in Canberra, 1972. In the background can be seen the Australian War Memorial.

Homosexual: Oppression and Liberation, published first in the US in 1971, a major contribution to gay liberation. Altman, a political scientist who had spent some time in America, acknowledged the influence of feminist writers, particularly Kate Millett; he also saw the 'peculiar . . . nature of sexual repression' in Australia as possibly motivating both himself and Greer to take up the pen.[13]

In the course of the 1960s Aboriginal protest had developed its own impetus, but the American civil rights movement was also an inspiration. Increasingly land rights became an issue, with the early focus being on the sparsely settled Northern Territory. In 1971 the cause received a setback when a Territory court declared that Aboriginal traditional ownership of the land 'did not form, and never has formed, part of the common law of Australia':[14] it was the old logic of conquest at work. When, on Australia Day 1972, Prime Minister McMahon made it clear that his government was not interested in remedying the situation, a tent appeared on the lawn facing Parliament House in Canberra. This 'Aboriginal Embassy', which lasted for six months, became the symbolic focus for the confrontation between the force of the conqueror and the spirit of the dispossessed.

There was a necessary separateness about Aboriginal protest, particularly insofar as the land rights movement was concentrated on regions far from the urban communities where student radicalism had burgeoned. Nevertheless the Aboriginal cause was in some measure integrated into the ideological mainstream of protest, even if there was an uneasy relationship between Aboriginal communities and the middle-class milieu of the counter-culture. For it was the counter-culture which provided the unifying theme for protest and liberation, deliberately setting out to subvert the conformist values of 'the Australian way of life'. Much of the cultural creativity of the late 1960s and early 1970s had its source in the intoxication of generational revolt. It could take the imported form of the musical 'Hair', which, according to its Australian entrepreneur, Harry Miller, was a mixture of 'flower power, brotherly love, several different kinds of mysticism, and the joys of sexual freedom and smoking pot'; its enthusiastic young director, Jim Sharman, also saw 'Hair' as revolutionary in theatrical terms, 'a work whose very existence vouchsafed the future'.[15] In less commercial guise, the energy of the counter-culture was apparent in the work of the Pram Factory theatre in Melbourne which, run as a collective, helped launch the playwrights Jack Hibberd, Alex Buzo, John Romeril, David Williamson and Barry Oakley.

One of the distinctive literary voices of the counter-culture was Frank Moorhouse, whose first collection of short stories, *Futility and Other Animals*, was published in 1969. Even the form of 'discontinuous narrative' used by Moorhouse reflected the ambience of the counter-culture. Although 'there is no single plot, the environment and characters are continuous'; the characters form 'a modern, urban tribe' which faces 'the central dilemma . . . of giving birth, of creating new life'.[16] One of Moorhouse's later stories, 'The American Paul Jonson', neatly suggests the interaction of politics, sexuality and cultural identity. The narrator, Carl, is a student, involved in the protest scene (later to be a draft dodger) and 'on' with Sylvia, another member of their group. One night in a hotel bar they get talking to the American Jonson; they bait him about civil rights and Vietnam, and there is even some later speculation about his being a CIA agent. However Carl's fascination with the American leads to a casual sexual encounter with him, and, almost against his will, he finds himself drawn into an intense relationship. That Carl's homosexual lover should be an American seems to encapsulate the dilemma: America is the enemy, the oppressor of Vietnam and the economic imperialist, yet America is also the disarming seducer, and the energising source of the protest culture.

The 'urban tribe' which Moorhouse describes was always a minority, even of its generation. Yet the questioning of conventional values, which the counter-culture helped stimulate, had much broader effects. The churches, for example, found some difficulty in maintaining traditional structures and allegiances. Orthodox religious observance seemed to be under challenge, particularly in face of the new taste for the eastern and exotic. There were significant defections from priesthood and ministry; nor were those who remained in the churches immune from the radicalising influence. In the 1950s there had been a resolute minority of Protestant clergy, the 'peace parsons' as they were sometimes called, who opposed the dominant anti-communism of the day, but the new generation of Christian activists was also seeking changes in the churches, their theology and liturgy. And, in the wake of Pope John XXIII's reforming Vatican Council of 1962–65 the Catholic Church was sharing many of these concerns.

Patterns of recreation were also affected. Nowhere was this better exemplified than on the beach. The rise of the new surfing cult – again, with a strong American infusion via Hawaii – threatened the hegemony of lifesaving clubs. Surfing was now an individualistic, even introspective pursuit, hostile to the regimentation and club atmosphere of the old order. Ardent surfies travelled the coast in search of waves, and the cult found convenient stimulus in the tribal hedonism of the counter-culture. Midget Farrelly, a surfboard champion at eighteen, saw something mystical at the centre of the surf experience, relating how 'this feeling of involvement in the waves' left him 'floating . . . I'm like a drug addict then'.[17] It was not the language of the uniformed lifesaver, bearer of the Anzac tradition.

The counter-culture incorporated a strong concern with the environment, reflected in the setting up of rural communes and the extension of 'liberation' to animals. However the conservation movement also tapped a wider community involvement. A growing National Trust and the emergence of resident action groups helped create an awareness of the built environment, while the Australian Conservation Foundation, established in 1965, focused on the natural environment. Conservation was no longer a bland publicity campaign for native flora and fauna but a highly political and contentious movement, which challenged the old bipartisan ethos of developmentalism. One of its most striking expressions was the

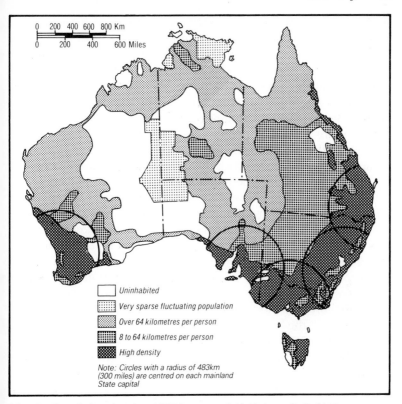

Map 7   Population density, 1971 (source: J. H. Holmes in D. N. Jeans (ed.), *Australia: A Geography* (Sydney 1987))

'green bans' movement, pioneered by the communist secretary of the New South Wales branch of the Builders' Labourers' Federation, Jack Mundey. In the early 1970s Mundey engineered an alliance between unions, National Trust and resident action groups, seeking to prevent developments which threatened the quality of the environment by imposing 'green' (i.e. 'black') union bans. This unlikely marriage between old-fashioned trade union militancy and 'trendy' middle-class interests reflected the changing agenda of political debate which affluence had encouraged.

There was, therefore, as the 1970s began, a strong sense of the old certainties of family and community being questioned. The accommodations which had characterised Australian society seemed to be disintegrating, but new accommodations remained to be reached. Technology was making its own contribution to this transformation. The advent of oral contraception – in an age of pills this was The Pill above all others – underpinned the 'new permissiveness'. As the young sought 'alternatives' the institution of the family came under critical examination. Age at marriage and of childbearing began to rise. The Family Law Act of 1975 simplified divorce, abolishing the notion of guilt; both divorce and *de facto* relationships became more common. Prosperity enabled the young to leave home and set up their own unconventional households; and as more and more people acquired their own cars, mobility increased other choices. The extent to which the media and entertainment industries catered for the new generation, identifying in it a profitable market, seemed a measure of its latent power.

The young were a minority, and at a time when many such minorities were asserting themselves, high expectations attached to the long awaited election of a federal Labor government. 'It's Time' was the simple slogan of the Labor campaign in 1972: you were left to complete the message to your own taste. Gough Whitlam convincingly played the part of a man of destiny. 'Men and women of Australia', he began his policy speech, symbolically echoing the words of Curtin thirty years before him: but he went on to target his programme at the huge swathes of new outer suburbs, which were relatively deprived of public amenities and services. He also carefully recognised the demands of the vocal minorities, such as the young, women,* migrants and Aborigines. Labor won, but its margin was relatively small – a majority of nine in a House of 125. Given the delay that is usual in the finalising of results under the Australian system of preferential voting, Whitlam could not resist the opportunity for the dramatic gesture. He and his deputy, Lance Barnard, formed an interim government, the 'duumvirate', which moved with lightning speed to implement some immediate decisions, the range of which suggested the new government's priorities: conscription was cancelled, draft resisters freed, the equal pay case in the Arbitration Commission reopened, the sales tax on 'the pill' removed, moves to recognise China announced, and plans to grant Aboriginal land rights initiated.

As a political and constitutional device, the thirteen-day duumvirate was not without its critics. However the dramatic urgency of its decisions seemed a necessary response to the long-held hopes of supporters, and an exciting promise of reform to come. It was as though Whitlam was determined to confound the sceptics who said that basically a Labor government would make no

* Technically not a minority of course, but projected as such in terms of power by feminists.

difference. Much of the character of the Whitlam government, particularly its magisterial and dramatic style, was established by the duumvirate. Less obvious at the time was its impact on Labor's traditional opponents in the establishment and business. While many had been prepared to tolerate an experiment in Labor rule – how, after all, in a parliamentary democracy with a two-party system could it be avoided? – the apparently reckless haste of the new government was profoundly disturbing. Almost from the beginning strategies were being devised for its removal.

There was, then, always a dichotomy between the expectations of Labor's supporters and the fears of its enemies. Many writers and artists found the new climate invigorating: some expatriates, including Germaine Greer, spoke of returning to Australia to live. The arts generally were to benefit from substantial increases in subsidy. So, too, many who taught in schools and the rapidly expanded tertiary institutions belonged to that section of the educated middle-class which had made a psychological investment in Labor's return to office. Labor's constituency in 1972 was significantly different from what it had been a generation earlier.

The focus of Anti-labor as it regrouped in opposition also reflected a change in social composition. The rural vote, although now a smaller proportion of the total electorate, was more Anti-labor than ever before, a factor emphasised by Whitlam's concentration on urban issues. Some Catholics began to penetrate the power structures of the Liberal Party; the DLP, it seemed, had served its historical purpose as a transitional home for Catholic conservatives, and entered a fatal decline. It is possible, too, that just as Labor was winning more middle-class votes, so too Anti-labor was becoming more attractive to some socially conservative blue-collar workers, who might not have shared Labor's new enthusiasms such as conservation, Aborigines and the arts. And as the climate of crisis increased between 1972 and 1975 the nervous and impressionable were drawn into the Anti-labor fold, persuaded that the Whitlam government was more trouble than it was worth. When the Senate withheld supply, and Whitlam decided to tough it out, gallup polls showed a majority disapproval of the Opposition's tactics, but when the Governor-General dismissed Whitlam and installed Malcolm Fraser as Prime Minister voters disregarded the constitutional issue and massively rejected Labor at the ensuing election.

The gathering recession of the 1970s undermined the prosperity which Whitlam had assumed in preparing his policies. As the optimism of two generations ebbed away, Fraser proclaimed his

9.7 The day after the dismissal of the Whitlam government: a Canberra demonstration with a galaxy of Labor personalities, including Whitlam, upper left, with head bowed; Jim Cairns, who had earlier been leader of the Vietnam moratorium movement, left foreground; and, at right, Bob Hawke, then president of the Australian Council of Trade Unions.

intention of taking politics off the front page. Fraser was a leader who commanded respect rather than admiration, but the divisive circumstances of his gaining office distracted attention from the continuities. Although some of Labor's policies, such as the Medibank health scheme, were dismantled, many of the cultural assumptions of Whitlam's programme were maintained. Diversity was recognised: Australia had become a 'multicultural' society, though what 'multiculturalism' meant remained vague. In 1976 Fraser legislated for Aboriginal land rights in the Northern Territory, but had less success in persuading the States to cooperate in making their Crown land available. Subsidy to the arts was maintained; when the Industries Assistance Commission recommended the scaling down of grants to the performing arts, Fraser rejected its advice. The new cultural agencies which had been created to administer and distribute subsidy, such as the Australia Council and the Australian Film Commission, continued unscathed. Yet in his rhetoric Fraser projected an image of conservatism and moral austerity summed up in his call for 'a rugged society' and his dictum that 'life isn't meant to be easy'.

Thus although 1975 spelled the end of the optimism associated with the experimentation of the counter-culture and the reformist programme of the Whitlam government, it was not until the 1980s that the new cultural issues crystallised. Labor's success in 1983 in ousting Fraser repaired some of the psychological damage caused by the events of 1975, but did not signal a resumption of the Whitlam programme. Indeed the ostentatious moderation of Hawke's approach, with its appeal to consensus, was a political response to the new ideological and economic climate. While Labor's policies on employment and welfare acknowledged the party's traditional constituency, in the economic field the government accepted the priorities of its opponents, even taking up financial deregulation with the enthusiasm of the convert.

While the new social perceptions of the late 1960s and early 1970s could not be undone, the preoccupation with economic recovery encouraged a tendency to interpret them as luxuries. The women's movement had achieved some notable successes, not least in simply establishing gender as an issue. Yet while equal pay had been technically achieved, and while 'equal opportunity' had become a respectable password in the professions, in the new economic climate women were particularly vulnerable to unemployment and psychological discrimination. The bitter Victorian nurses' strike of 1986 amply demonstrated the lengths to which women workers would have to go to overcome the institutional resistance to recognition of their claims, even with a Labor government in power.

For homosexuals the achievement of some measure of liberation was undermined by the fortuitous arrival of the AIDS virus, which first attracted scare headlines in 1983. AIDS, mysterious and horrific, was the ultimate stigma, associating homosexuality with disease and death, and was exploited in these terms by the moralists of the Christian Right. The institutions of the gay community which liberation had created were important in devising strategies to fight the AIDS virus, but such solidarity could not disguise the psychological blow which AIDS had dealt the gay affirmation of sexuality; in a broader sense, it also served to discredit the permissive society. In 1987 Frank Moorhouse looked back on his own homosexual experiences as 'romantically pre-AIDS': for him, it seemed, homosexuality was a thing of the past, 'a fascinating, strange, romantic cult'.[18]

Perhaps Aborigines had the most cause for disillusion. Dependent politically on white conscience and goodwill, they saw the promise of land rights being eroded. As mining companies stepped up their campaign for unfettered development, Labor, mindful of an anti-Aboriginal backlash at the polls, seemed to lose its enthusiasm for land rights: the Western Australian government virtually washed its hands of the matter, while the Hawke government watered down its commitment. Anti-labor, which ten years earlier had passed the Commonwealth legislation, was now seeking to exploit hostility to land rights.

Migrants, too, were to discover that the short-lived recognition which had been accorded them was not undisputed. Immigration policy since the war had been regarded as bipartisan, and White Australia had been abandoned with minimal intrusion of party politics. Now multiculturalism became a subject for controversy, and the political accord which had sustained the immigration policy was threatened. In 1984 the well-known historian and writer, Professor Geoffrey Blainey, launched a campaign to reduce the immigration intake, and in particular its Asian component. Blainey was not proposing a return to White Australia, but his argument that the intake of non-Europeans was testing community tolerance became confused with alarmist claims that the government had replaced White Australia with a 'surrender Australia' policy. Blainey and his supporters claimed that immigration had been treated as a taboo topic: his critics warned of the racism which his campaign was unintentionally stimulating. For a time some Liberals flirted with taking up Blainey's crusade, but in the end caution prevailed: the government made some minor adjustments to the intake, and the controversy died down almost as suddenly as it had flared up.

However, the questioning of multiculturalism continued. In his curiously titled apologia *All for Australia** Blainey described, with some nostalgia, what Australia was like before the war. Growing up in a country town, he could not recall hearing a foreign language before he was ten, or seeing a Jew until he was thirteen (how, one wonders, could he be sure?); he first met an Aborigine when hitch-hiking around Australia at eighteen. 'I prefer our present world, but I do not deride that vanished world,' he wrote.[19] The implication was that, although one could not go back, pursuit of the multicultural path would sever us from this Anglo-Celtic heritage. Blainey has also emphasised his own colonial roots, his eight English and Celtic great-grandparents all living in Victoria at the time of the goldrushes.

---

* Was Blainey making a reference to the All for Australia League, the conservative middle-class movement of the 1930s Depression? The cover, depicting multicoloured rows and rows of faces also suggests that the title might be a play on words: are these hordes all bound for Australia?

Blainey's hostility to multiculturalism could also be seen in the context of the emergence of a loosely-knit group of conservative ideologues, some of whom in 1986 formed a 'thinktank' called the H. R. Nicholls Society. Dedicated in particular to the abolition of the industrial arbitration system, this society took its name from a little known Hobart newspaper editor who, having in 1911 said some unpleasant and possibly libellous things about the Arbitration Court's president, Higgins, was unsuccessfully prosecuted for contempt of court. In attacking the arbitration system, the New Right was seeking to undo a cultural accommodation which had been unchallenged since 1929.

Diverse and sometimes inconsistent elements were lumped together as belonging to the New Right. Business-oriented free marketeers, whose concerns were principally economic, campaigned for low taxes and deregulation. The longstanding forces of social conservatism, drawing both on old Catholic values and new Protestant fundamentalism, found rejuvenation in the changed climate of debate. At the same time the debilitated rural sector, sensing political neglect by all parties, but particularly alienated by the urbanism of Labor, provided fertile ground for populist conservatism.

It was as though the prolonged recession of the 1970s and 1980s had seen the gradual accumulation of stresses which only now were revealing themselves. The tolerant pluralism of the multicultural society, so recently asserted, was exposed as fragile and even illusory. The consensus reflected in the 1967 referendum on Aborigines, and in the shedding of assimilationist ideology, had evaporated. But while there was this harking back to the social mores of the Anglo-Celtic cultural order, the opportunity was also recognised to reshape old political institutions, such as industrial arbitration and even the party system itself. The 'New Right' programme was, therefore, a compound of cultural nostalgia and capitalistic aggression.

While the impact of the new conservatism was, as the Bicentenary approached, uncertain, it was clear that Labor's chosen theme for 1988, 'Living together', had already taken on an ironic ring. Old social divisions seemed sharper than before. The bush was more alienated from urban Australia than ever, while outlying states such as Queensland and Tasmania, with Anti-labor governments and populist premiers, were following a quite different political path from the south-eastern crescent. With more than a decade of unemployment, and with social welfare under attack, the gap between middle and working class Australia was widening. While political energy was expended in devising tax cuts which would primarily benefit the middle class, the poor were left to carry the burden of the recession. Colouring these divisions was the new dichotomy between those who accepted and embraced ethnic diversity, and those who sought to maintain the hegemony of the old Anglo-Celtic order.

In the postwar period prosperity had become a habit, a habit which now has to be unlearned. For some, of course, the prosperity continues. In contemporary Australia the headlines are captured by half a dozen or so entrepreneurs who thrive on a chess game of takeovers and mergers, to the applause of stock exchange and financial press. The phoney excitement and glamour of this board-room drama, with its attendant entertainments such as the America's Cup, form a striking contrast to the problems of national insolvency, poverty and dispossession. It is possible, though, that just as the effects of postwar prosperity were delayed, emerging ultimately in protest, liberation and counter-culture, so too might economic decline take time to bear its bitter fruit.

10

Vision

In dramatising Australia's isolation the Second World War fuelled what one historian has called the 'national obsession' with defining an Australian identity. In 1943 Vance Palmer declared that 'the next few months may decide not only whether we are to survive as a nation, but whether we deserve to survive'. While he lamented that 'there is very little to show the presence of a people with a common purpose or a rich sense of life', he nevertheless affirmed that 'there is an Australia of the spirit, submerged and not very articulate', which was 'sardonic, idealist, tongue-tied perhaps' but was 'the Australia of all who truly belong here'.[1]

Palmer was writing in *Meanjin*, which, launched in Brisbane in 1940 as a humble eight-page journal, was to survive to become part of the postwar literary scene. In the same year Adelaide saw the emergence of *Angry Penguins* which, although not similarly destined for longevity, also reflected the encouragement which the war gave to cultural creativity. Isolation had its benefits, and the publishing industry was stimulated by the difficulty in importing books. The war itself was to affect many writers and artists profoundly. For the painter Sidney Nolan, stationed at Dimboola in Victoria, it meant confronting a challenging landscape: he recalls that he went into the army 'as a kind of abstract painter with my thoughts on Paris but I gradually changed right over to being completely identified with what I was looking at and I forgot all about Picasso, Klee and Paris and Lifar and everything else and became attached to light'.[2]

The intelligentsia was still a small community, dispersed across the continent, but it seemed as if the dislocations of war created an atmosphere conducive to disputation. In 1944 there were two controversies, both perceived as relating to modernism, which have become the stuff of legend. In January the New South Wales Gallery broke with conservative tradition and awarded its annual Archibald Prize to William Dobell for a strikingly gaunt portrait of fellow artist Joshua Smith. Some outraged members of the Sydney Royal Art Society organised a legal challenge, on the grounds that Dobell's painting was not a portrait as required under the terms of the Prize but a caricature. The courtroom entertainment that followed seemed a crucial public test for modernism and the decision in favour of the Gallery and Dobell was hailed as evidence of a new maturity. In fact Dobell, a painter in the classical tradition, was hardly a modernist, and the conservatism of the Gallery's trustees had been only momentarily dented. The case was more notable for the destructive ordeal it posed for its central characters, particularly Dobell and Smith, whose friendship was a casualty.

The other imbroglio arose from the poems by one Ern Malley published with some fanfare by *Angry Penguins*. They had been submitted to the journal by Malley's sister, Ethel, who reported that she had found them among her brother's things after his death, and, knowing nothing of poetry herself, was told by a friend that the poems were 'very good' and 'should be published'. She added that 'he was very ill in the months before his death last July and it may have affected his outlook', and enclosed 'a 2½d stamp for reply, and oblige'. It emerged that the Malley poems were a hoax, concocted by two poets of traditional persuasion, Douglas Stewart and James McAuley, who, observing 'with distaste the gradual decay of meaning and craftsmanship in poetry', had determined on 'a serious literary experiment'. The *Angry Penguins* of Melbourne (to where the journal had migrated) found themselves ridiculed in the press at home and abroad, but mobilised a counter-attack, enlisting support from Herbert Read amongst others, arguing that the poems, regardless of their underlying intent, had literary merit. As Max Harris put it, 'the myth is sometimes greater than its creators'. No one now disputes that the poems contained memorable images ('I am still/ The black swan of trespass on alien waters'), nor that they were self-evidently written by talented poets. At the very least they were, as one critic unsympathetic to *Angry Penguins* has judged, 'brilliant concoctions'.[3] Whether or not the hoaxers had been too clever by half, the controversy, like that surrounding Dobell's portrait, illustrates the predeliction of conservatives within the provincial intelligentsia for defending their interests by recourse to the institutions of law or 'public opinion'. In the Dobell case the ruse failed, but with Ern Malley it succeeded, at least in the short term. An appropriate coda was provided by the Adelaide police prosecution of the editors for publishing poems which were 'indecent, immoral or obscene'. It was a nice reminder that the semantic subtlety of the literary argument was lost on the upholders of conventional morality.

The energies of this small artistic-literary world were to produce more positive results, particularly in painting. In 1945–47 Sidney Nolan painted his Ned Kelly series which imaginatively exploited the mythic potential of the bushranger folk-hero. While Nolan was juxtaposing the iron helmet motif of Ned against an image of the

10.1   Nolan's 'Ned Kelly', but this time without the armour. This well-dressed version is distinguished by the piercing eyes.

10.2   Arthur Boyd's 'Melbourne Burning', painted in the wake of the War and Hiroshima, yet suggesting, too, something of the artist's alienation from contemporary Australian society.

bush landscape (which, after all, was the Australian artist's traditional concern) his colleague Arthur Boyd was expressing a Bruegel-like apocalyptic vision in an urban setting, as in the tumultuous 'Melbourne Burning' (1946–47). Although the work of such artists did not pass unnoticed at the time, the full measure of their achievement was not appreciated till much later.

In poetry 1946 was notable for the publication of first volumes by James McAuley, one half of 'Ern Malley', and Judith Wright. McCauley converted to Catholicism in 1952 – it was a time when such a 'conversion' was still a remarked-upon phenomenon – and became a conservative intellectual as well as major poet. In 1976 he was to look back 'with some affection on that shy humorist Ern Malley, who offered promises of portentous meanings that never arrived', yet admit that he still felt within him 'the tension between the modern and the traditional'. Wright, on the other hand, in her depiction of the landscape, with its strong sense of history, has been said to have had 'the same kind of impact that the paintings of Nolan, Boyd and others had in the art world'.[4]

As peace and prosperity settled on the land, many artists and writers, recovering from the enforced isolation of war, were tempted to travel, and expatriatism received a new impetus. There took place what one art historian has called 'the radical diaspora', its effect heightened by the advent of the disillusion of the Cold War. John Reed, a patron and organiser of the *Angry Penguins* group, later observed that 'some organic change seemed to take place in the community, a lessening of sensitive awareness, or perhaps a mere dissipation of energies into numerous channels, irrelevant to creative talent'.[5]

Yet even if in the short term there were grounds for pessimism, prosperity also enabled the gradual building up of the infrastructure which could support future cultural endeavour. The beginning of sustained subsidy to the performing arts has already been noted, but the 1950s also saw the emergence of new journalistic forums, with the launching of *Quadrant* (the Australian equivalent of *Encounter*, later to be edited by McAuley), and two reviews, *Observer* and *Nation*. In the art world the number of commercial galleries multiplied. No longer were exhibitions held in 'cheerless halls': in 1965 it was noted that the *cognoscenti* now patronised stylish galleries which were 'white-washed cottages, renovated terraces or smart facades in once frowsy and out-of-the-way corners'.[6] The growth and improving standards of the ABC's symphony orchestras, and the establishment of the Musica Viva Society to promote chamber music, helped provide a context of musical life more encouraging to composers. But perhaps of most significance was the growth of the universities, which increasingly were able to provide the intellectual apparatus for the study of Australian society and culture.

Nowhere was this better exemplified than in the emergence of Australian history and literature as respectable academic concerns. Before the Second World War both had been largely ignored by the universities: now they were 'discovered' by a wave of young teachers who passed their new-found knowledge on to their students. There was an understandable tendency to look for and define a tradition, located usually in the cultural coalition between the *Bulletin* school of writers and the labour movement, to which were coopted the Heidelberg painters. This radical nationalist tradition, as it came to be called, was convenient ideologically, as many of those pioneering the study of Australian society and culture saw this project as part of a contemporary radical programme.

In 1954 Vance Palmer published *The Legend of the Nineties*, the very title proclaiming its historical agenda. Four years later A. A. Phillips' *The Australian Tradition* examined the *Bulletin* school in the colonial context, and focused attention on the longstanding 'cultural cringe' which had inhibited the development of the 'tradition' he, like Palmer, was promulgating. While not academics themselves, Palmer and Phillips were associated with the new academic environment, particularly through *Meanjin*, now based at Melbourne University, which gave it modest financial support. Then in 1958 Russel Ward's *The Australian Legend* identified the typical (as distinct from average) Australian, and sought his origins in an ethos which, deriving from the convicts, was forged in the encounter with the environment of bush and outback. Ward's book, widely read by students and general public, reinforced the historic association of the bush with a collectivist, proletarian ideology. Meanwhile other historians were sketching in the history of the labour movement in terms of its institutions, projecting the Labor Party, even as it languished in opposition in the long Menzies years, as historically the party of initiative which set the political agenda.

While not all accepted the claims being staked by the legend-makers, they seemed in the 1960s to hold the cultural initiative, particularly as many conservatives still shunned what they saw as the parochialism of Australian studies and fixed their academic sights on Europe and Britain. There were signs, however, that some Australians found it difficult to identify with the historical image of Australia being presented. It was often writers, paradoxically, who felt most deprived, and a number ventured into autobiography, deliberately seeking to create the history which they lacked. Hal Porter subtitled his *The Watcher on the Cast-Iron Balcony* (1963) *An Australian Autobiography*, thus clearly identifying the nature of the exercise. In writing *The Education of Young Donald* (1967) Donald Horne invented the word 'sociography' to describe the kind of personal social history he was embarking on. In 1964 George Johnston, an expatriate returning after fourteen years abroad, published the autobiographical novel, *My Brother Jack*; he had started it on the Greek island of Hydra when, suffering from homesickness, he had set himself the task of re-creating a Melbourne street of his childhood. In its evocation of the period between the wars, *My Brother Jack* was well timed to exploit a demand for experiential history, and became a best seller. Two years later it was a great success as a television series which was seen as breaking new ground in its portrayal of twentieth century Australia. Johnston, Porter and Horne helped found a flourishing autobiographical tradition, which focused particularly on childhood.

Part of the appeal of these writers was the extent to which they encompassed the urban reality of Australian life, whether city or country town, which the legend-makers preferred to ignore. Painters, too, were finding more inspiration in their urban surroundings, although the images offered by artists as various as Noel Counihan, John Brack, Bob Dickerson and Jeffrey Smart were often sombre or menacing. The traditional landscape of bush and outback still retained a powerful attraction for artists, and one that was reinforced by the export of Australian art. When Nolan became fashionable in England, he raised certain expectations of the exotic harshness of the Australian landscape. Writing in the catalogue of the 1961 Whitechapel exhibition, Kenneth Clark praised Australian artists for looking at 'the harsh, lonely, inhospitable substance of their country'.[7] Curiously, the artist who has probably done most to transform the perception of the bush landscape, Fred Williams, initially met with an unenthusiastic response: his vision was not celebratory, and did not embrace myth in the manner of Nolan and Boyd.

While urban Australia had always been of interest to some writers, artists and commentators, it was suburbia which now seemed to be a perplexing concern. Patrick White, another returning expatriate, made his reputation with *The Tree of Man* (1955) and *Voss* (1957), novels which imbued the bush and outback with the qualities of myth. White records that a factor influencing his decision to return to Australia was 'the unexpected art world' he discovered, and he seemed to share some of the painters' preoccupations. Urban life, however, did not escape his attention, and he cast a sometime jaundiced eye on his suburban surroundings: his 1961 play, *The Season at Sarsaparilla*, was subtitled *A Charade of Suburbia*. Loathing the suburban environment to which he had condemned himself and his friend Manoly, White recalls how they gratefully depended 'on our Jewish migrant friends; they were our link with European culture, music in particular'.[8]

The year before *The Season at Sarsaparilla* the architect and writer Robin Boyd published *The Australian Ugliness*. Boyd's target was 'the disease of Featurism', which he saw as disfiguring urban Australia. The ugliness was only 'skin deep', but 'skin is as important as its admirers make it, and Australians make much of it. This is a country of many colourful, patterned, plastic veneers, of brick-veneer villas, and the White Australia Policy.' Boyd was not suggesting that Australia had a monopoly on Featurism, but this most suburban of societies fostered it. 'Modern Australia is not entirely suburb; there is still the outback and the nightclub, the woolshed dance and the art-film society; but it is mainly this half-way area, a cross-hatched smudge on the map round each capital city and larger town, in which may be found all the essential drabness and dignity of Australia.'[9]

At the time that Boyd was mulling over *The Australian Ugliness* the young actor Barry Humphries was launching the career of the high priestess of suburbia, Edna Everage. Humphries had his beady eye on Featurism too:

> The best Highett homes have hundreds of gnomes
> All scattered about on the grass
> There's wrought iron too, in a pale duck-egg blue
> And *acres* of sand-blasted glass

But Humphries also impeccably captured the suburban voice of Australia, whether in the shrilly cheerful cadences of Edna, or the phlegmatic monotone of Sandy Stone. Humphries based Sandy on 'a wiry old fellow' he encountered one winter's afternoon at Bondi Beach:

> This old character, in spite of his sturdy matter-of-fact mien,
> addressed me in a cracked falsetto which I immediately
> recognised as typical, funny and with just the right drawling
> intonation for a monologue which I had begun to write about a
> decent, humdrum little old man of the suburbs.

Although Humphries tellingly satirised suburbia – increasingly to the plaudits of its inhabitants – he also cast a poetic and affectionate eye on an urban environment which time and prosperity was eroding. Melbourne-filtered memories of old advertisements and jingles, and the names of suburbs and landmarks, could, when chanted in his sometime melancholy voice, take on the character of 'a nostalgic liturgy'.[10] Humphries was to save up his real venom for the new breed of middle-class 'trendies' which matured in the 1960s.

Boyd and Humphries, in their concern for city and suburb, reflected a shift in Australian perceptions. In 1970 the historian Hugh Stretton in *Ideas for Australian Cities* went one stage further with the bold assertion that 'the Australian preference for family life

10.3 Barry Humphries as (Dame) Edna Everage, who, starting out as an 'average' Moonee Ponds housewife (Humphries chose Moonee Ponds because of its euphonious name, not its social aptness), has gradually become a more extravagant theatrical creation. She is photographed here with Peter Coleman, then leader of the New South Wales Liberal Party. Coleman is editor of the conservative *Quadrant*, with which Humphries is also associated.

in private houses and gardens is probably intelligent. Instead of despising the suburbs we should work to improve them'. At the same time Patrick White's dyspeptic view of suburbia was giving way to a more generous appreciation of Sydney, a change encouraged by his move from outer suburban Castle Hill (Sarsaparilla) to inner suburban Centennial Park. White intended *The Vivisector* (1970) to be not only a portrait of an artist but also a portrait of his city – 'wet, boiling, superficial, brash, beautiful, ugly Sydney, developing during my lifetime from a sunlit village into this present-day parvenu bastard, compound of San Francisco and Chicago'.[11] The 'sunlit village' was, like other Australian cities, now a livelier and more diverse place, and the revitalising of the inner suburbs, which had influenced White's change of address, was one indication of this.

For the artist suburbia could be a focus for rebellion, yet at the same time not without its attractions. The Sydney painter, Brett Whiteley, recalls his family background as being 'Longueville, middle-class, overlooking yachts, tranquil, little squabbles about money'. As a child Whiteley prowled about 'in a Napoleonic rage', yet from the vantage point of middle age admits that the harbour suburb 'looks the most satisfactory place that a kid could be brought up in'.[12] The painter became a bohemian figure of flamboyant intensity: yet his work, which in a diversity of themes has included landscape, retains, particularly in its pallette, an affinity with the city of his birth.

Perhaps it has become more possible to appreciate the historical relationship between city and bush in Australian culture, and the sense in which each has exploited the contrast between them. Yet suburbia itself is, as Boyd called it, the 'half-way area'. Nothing more vividly captures the fragility of the environmental accommodation between city and bush than the summer explosion of bushfires, when the security and order of life in the outer suburbs are threatened by the invading force of elemental destruction. Remarkably, most of those who lose their houses in such bushfires rebuild in the ashes.

Whatever the attractions of the bush for city dwellers, there has been, among cultural critics, a continuing dissatisfaction with the European response to the Australian environment. Early colonial architecture, with its adaptation of the Georgian style, is often seen as being more successful environmentally than much that followed, while recent use of modern and post-modern styles has been characterised as slavishly international. In this context one might note the acclaim of Glen Murcutt's buildings, principally houses in both city and country. Murcutt's extensive use of corrugated iron, a building material much used but little regarded in Australia, has been hailed as imaginatively exploiting an Australian idiom. Philip Drew draws two interesting analogies in appraising Murcutt's work. He sees the essence of a 'bush architecture' in May Gibbs' books about the gumnut babies, whose houses were made from gum leaves in bird-nest form. But the ultimate compliment to Murcutt is the suggestion that his houses, combining strength and delicacy, share a sympathy with the environment characteristic of the Aborigines, summed up in a saying, 'to touch-this-earth-lightly'.[13] Yet Murcutt is a city-based architect for whom technology and invention are important tools.

The bush and the outback remain important in the Australian consciousness – they are always *there* – but there had been a gathering recognition that the artist need not feel compelled to draw inspiration from a particular concept of the environment. There has been a tendency for writers to seek different locales and issues. So, for example, some novelists like Christopher Koch and Blanche D'Alpuget have exploited the situation of the Australian living in south-east Asia, submerged in an alien culture, while others, like Xavier Herbert and Thomas Kenneally, have sought to encompass the Aboriginal experience.

The new sense of artistic diversity, reinforced by the ideological questioning generated by the counter-culture, made the promotion of cultural orthodoxy in the form of 'the Australian tradition' increasingly suspect. Did such a tradition in fact exist? How, for example, could the great procession of women writers, from Ada Cambridge to Christina Stead, be accommodated within a tradition which was so blatantly male in its proclaimed ethos? Might there not be alternative traditions, overlapping perhaps, or even unaware of each other? Perhaps women writers, contending with a male culture, constitute a tradition; or, likewise, those writers such as Henry Handel Richardson and Martin Boyd, who focused on the tension between metropolitan and provincial societies. Critics and historians not only set about recovering writers and artists who had been lost sight of, but began to reinterpret those who, like Lawson and Furphy, and the Heidelberg painters, had been central to 'the tradition'.

Interest was shown in regional variations within the culture. The historic rivalry between Sydney and Melbourne had long been a subject for jest, but different cultural traditions were now identified.

According to the poet Vincent Buckley, 'In Sydney if you have something to say you hold a party; in Melbourne you start a journal'.[14] The historian Manning Clark, whose work was to question radical nationalist assumptions, saw the Melbourne tradition as being more committed and more radical, while Sydney leant towards hedonism and pluralism. Outside of the two great capitals there has been a developing tendency to define more of a regional identity, as a sense of place has superseded more generalised perceptions of the Australian environment. Particularly has this been so of Western Australia, with its own brand of isolation. Art historian Bernard Smith detects something like a stylistic school of landscape painters there, while writers like Katharine Susannah Prichard, Randolph Stow, Dorothy Hewett and Elizabeth Jolley, whatever their contribution to the wider culture, have also been claimed for a local tradition.

Arts previously neglected in Australia have also seen a dramatic expansion. In music composers have at last established a presence, often helped by universities providing them with a base. Even in opera, that most traditional of forms, a beginning has been made with Barry Conyngham's *Fly* (1984), which concerns the inventor Lawrence Hargrave, and Richard Meale's *Voss* (1986), which, based on White's novel, uses a libretto by the poet and novelist, David Malouf. In dance, the Australian Ballet grew out of the company formed by Edouard Borovansky, a Czech dancer who, having come to Australia with the 1938 Russian Ballet company, and faced with the crisis in Europe, decided to stay. The Australian Ballet has aimed at planting the Anglo-Russian tradition of classical ballet in Australian soil, and has won a popular audience, but the newer contemporary dance groups, such as Graeme Murphy's Sydney Dance Company, have done more to exploit the athletic exuberance of Australian dancers in creating a repertoire. Both opera and ballet demonstrate the competing needs of international acceptance and indigenous expression, yet suggest that in a more sophisticated and diverse cultural environment both can be accommodated.

Performing artists are enabled by air travel to commute around the world in a way that was impossible for Melba and her contemporaries. Thus prima donna Joan Sutherland, maintaining homes in Sydney and Switzerland, is hardly an expatriate; and the same goes for many writers and artists who, even if domiciled abroad, return on a regular basis. The rise of the global village has done much to blunt the impact of expatriatism, and the decision to travel no longer carries the same connotation of escape or desertion.

10.4   Janet Vernon and Ross Philip's legs in Graeme Murphy's ballet for the Sydney Dance Company, 'Some Rooms': a striking image which relates to that very important room in the Australian home, the bathroom.

Greater ease of travel has been a liberating rather than a debilitating factor.

Just as the monocultural assumptions of the old immigration policy reflected an ideology of 'the Australian way of life', so in the attempt to proclaim one authentic cultural tradition there was an element of ideological compulsion. To some this tradition was all the more precious for the difficulty experienced, given the cultural cringe, in establishing it: they therefore resented attacks upon it as being culturally destructive. In the long view it can be better appreciated that a tradition cannot be imposed in this way, and that the recognition of diversity has already enriched the totality of the culture.

In *The Australian Legend* Russel Ward proposed a typical Australian who is rough and ready in his manners, an improviser, given to swearing, gambling and drinking, taciturn, sceptical of the value of religion and cultural pursuits, egalitarian, loyal to his mates and resentful of authority and tending to be a rolling stone. Donald Horne in *The Lucky Country*, which in its national self-analysis was one of the publishing successes of the 1960s, offered a different sort of symbol: 'The image of Australia is of a man in an open-necked shirt solemnly enjoying an icecream. His kiddy is beside him.'[15] Although both images were notably male, Horne's figure was a far cry from the itinerant bushman who had served as Ward's model.

Ward and Horne were engaged in different sorts of enterprise, yet both were making observations about the character and appearance of Australianness. Packaging and labelling national character is a dangerous exercise, because it seeks to impose a structural unity where none may exist. But it is reasonable to ask what qualities have been discerned as being central to the Australian experience and outlook. This is not a matter of defining a national type, but of suggesting the emotional range of the Australian people, and where, within that range, the important congruences are to be located. It is made more complex – and interesting – by the realisation that with changes in society these congruences might shift, different circumstances serving to highlight different emotional responses. Poetic licence might allow us to talk of an Australian psyche, but if so it must be remembered that this psyche is itself an historical process.

A. A. Phillips' 'cultural cringe' cleverly identified the emotional complexity of the colonial relationship – how the fawning insecurity of the cringe direct was inseparably linked to the braggart bravado of the cringe inverted. It was common for Australians to anxiously seek the approval of visitors to the country, and to be more than a little offended if it were withheld. The immigrant writer, Mary Rose Liverani, recalled how in the 1950s it seemed that Australians 'were always demanding support. Isn't that right? And if they didn't get it, they became peevish.' The upward inflexion at the end of a phrase, which has become a feature of colloquial Australian speech, implies the need for reassurance. The novelist Shirley Hazzard, returning from abroad, characterised Australians as a 'savage, derisive, insecure people'.[16]

Insecurity had long been evident in self-consciousness about the Australian accent, but here attitudes were, by the 1960s, fast changing. When *The Summer of the Seventeenth Doll* was first performed in 1956, the challenge to Australian actors of portraying cane-cutters and barmaids was met very much in terms of traditional 'character' accents. But as Australian plays became a staple part of the theatrical repertoire, actors and audiences adjusted to the wider realities of Australian speech. The resurgence of the film industry in the 1970s did much to complete the process of acceptance.

The often remarked characteristic of a resentment towards authority presents greater difficulties in interpretation. Precociousness and a lack of discipline were commonly discerned in colonial children, and postwar migrants were sometimes appalled by the laxity of Australian parents. On the other hand concern about rebelliousness and bad manners in children and adults was offset, in Australian eyes, by compensating qualities of self-reliance and resourcefulness. It is easy enough to suggest historical roots for this tension between authority and independence in the experience of convictism in a colonial environment, but the monuments of national mythology, such as the digger, which had been built upon the perception of such qualities often obscure the contemporary reality. In many ways Australians are a remarkably law-abiding and compliant people, not given to spontaneous revolt, and suspicious of anarchic impulses. Anti-authoritarianism is conveyed more through a scepticism of outlook which conditions obedience. It is the appearance and trappings of authority which are the target for resentment – hence the careful lack of enthusiasm of soldiers for saluting officers, and the sort of crowd mentality which feels no need to intervene in a fracas in support of beleaguered police. If authority is resented, it is simply because there is an acceptance, however cynical, that ultimately it must be obeyed.

This ambivalence towards authority may help explain the function of humour in Australian society. The Australian sense of humour can be raucous and aggressive as well as deadpan and underplayed, but is usually characterised by irreverence and at times an almost surreal mordancy. 'Sardonic' is the adjective often used to characterise the favoured attitude. From the nineteenth century the art of the political cartoonist has flourished, and leaders have had to accustom themselves to the constant threat of public ridicule. More recently, the insidious mimicry of Max Gillies on stage and television has done much to make the charisma of Hawke a laughing stock. It goes without saying that such mocking must be accepted with good grace.

All this relates to the tradition of social egalitarianism. It has already been argued that this egalitarianism did not represent a rejection of the realities of class, but a means of coming to terms with them. It remains, however, an important influence on social relationships and manners. Whilst in formal situations Australians are capable of a self-conscious decorum which can easily become pomposity, in ordinary social encounters a deliberate breeziness predominates. The relentless cheerfulness which D. H. Lawrence noted was still clearly evident to Mary Rose Liverani thirty years later. Whilst this mateyness is sincere enough in its origins, it can develop a mechanical quality, as in the casual greeting, 'How are you?', which does not expect a response.

The sense of Australian society being casual and relaxed provides the context for the phenomenon of the 'ocker' and 'ockerism'. Beginning life, it seems, as a nickname for Oscar, by the 1970s the ocker was representative of a brand of genial boorishness, perhaps first personified by Barry Humphries in his cartoon character, 'Bazza' McKenzie. The ocker embodies some of the characteristics of Russel Ward's bushman in a debased suburban form. A product of affluence, the ocker could be an affable, pot-bellied boozer; though always easygoing, he could also be a bit of a smart aleck, drawing on the larrikin tradition, as in the early television persona of Paul Hogan. Hogan's original image was urban working-class, his garb that of a site worker (he himself had been a rigger on the Sydney Harbour Bridge): only in the film 'Crocodile Dundee' did he appropriate the older bush stereotype.

The identification of the ocker began as an exercise in social satire, but 'ockerism' in a broader sense came to be seen as a kind of cultural malaise. Migrants, of course, had long observed to themselves the cheerful rowdiness of much Australian society, particularly in its male form. One Greek commented that Australians were 'good people ... good hearted', but, explaining that he did not like to worry his relatives in Greece by criticising Australia, confessed: 'I write that we work all the time, but the Australians have more fun. I tell them that there are nice Australians, but we don't meet them. I don't say that they are all drinkers and gamblers with broken homes'. The surface geniality of the ocker disguises the fact that he has the mentality of an addict, and there is an edge of desperation to what Xavier Herbert calls 'The Great Australian Thirst'. Perhaps this helps explain the Australian soldier's bravery in battle, which has been described as having its source in 'an energy akin to drunkenness'.[17]

Ockerism, then, could be perceived as potentially destructive, but it could also be employed as a cultural metaphor. In 1974 Max Harris saw Hawke, then president of the Australian Council of Trade Unions, as being an ocker politician:

> The rasp, the ready aggression, the appearance of being on the look-out for an intellectual punch-up, is an atavistic survival of the old-style Australian ockerdom. It suggests that barely concealed and grotesque Australian sense of insecurity for which we were once notorious, and which is being joyfully assessed overseas as still inherent in the national character.[18]

Hawke's style has since mellowed, but the hint of the larrikin and lair is still there. Yet Harris's concern about the 'overseas' view suggests his own insecurity, the kind which is expressed in criticism of Barry Humphries and Paul Hogan for presenting the wrong sort of image of Australia abroad.

Although women were not seen as being exempt from some aspects of ockerism, as a phenomenon it was largely male in character. With women emerging from the home into the workforce, and with the rise of divorce and *de facto* relationships suggesting that patriarchy was under attack, ockerism could be seen as a rearguard reassertion of male dominance in the social sphere, the expression of a determined ebullience in the face of new uncertainties.

The widespread concern, serious or satirical, expressed about ockerism nevertheless suggests that it was far from universal: it was a comment made by one element in society about another. It was a concern clearly related to the perceived effects of prosperity. Donald Horne's image of the man in an open-necked shirt solemnly licking an ice-cream, his kiddy at his side, draws on a more enclosed, less boisterous suburban tradition, which could encompass Humphries' Sandy Stone. The common ground between the two lies in the pursuit of pleasure, the belief, as Horne puts it, 'that every-one has the right to a good time'. Such an attitude encourages a certain tolerance, and perhaps helps explain Dennis Altman's assessment that although Australia was 'superficially . . . extraordi-narily repressive of sexuality', nevertheless 'in reality I suspect Australians are less hung-up about sex than either the Americans or English'.[19]

The outward amiability of Australian life draws attention to the deeper emotional reticence which has already been remarked upon. Good humour and mateyness become a protection against intimacy. 'So many Australians are made uneasy if one feels intensely', writes Patrick White, 'whether in writing, life, politics'. In the 1950s J. D. Pringle claimed to have been told by a Greek taxi-driver: 'In Europe I used to feel things. I was happy; I was sad; I was angry; I was miserable. Here in Australia I never feel anything. I have lost my feelings. There is no deep feeling anywhere.'[20] A character in Murray Bail's 1980 novel, *Homesickness*, confesses that 'We have rather empty feelings. I think we even find love difficult.' It could even be hazarded that the early emergence of Australian painting as a viable cultural medium reflects a preference for the visual, which avoids the need for emotion to be expressed in language. As another character in *Homesickness* puts it: 'We don't speak very well. Have you noticed how the Americans are so descriptive and confident? Our sentences are shorter. Our thoughts break off. We don't seem comfortable talking. I don't know why. Have you noticed we make silly quips, even when someone asks the time?'[21] It is as if the capacity for emotion is restricted by the failure to find an appropriate lan-guage for its expression.

Yet here, too, it is possible to detect change. The very raising of the question seems to reflect a desire to shed, or at least relax, traditional constraint. The other side to Hawke's ocker image has been a relatively unselfconscious expression of his emotions. When in 1984 Hawke, acknowledging his daughter's drug problem, wept at a televised press conference, there was some astonishment, but a sympathetic public reaction seemed to suggest that the event had a wider psychological importance. So, too, tennis player Paul McNamee felt able to confess that his long-standing doubles part-nership with Peter Macnamara had been an emotionally demanding relationship, involving tears and rows. The European infusion into the community must also in time affect attitudes to the propriety of expressing emotion. It might also be surmised that the greater participation of women in public life would have a liberating impact, though there is always the danger that the female pioneers will feel the need to conform to the male stereotype.

The ultimate fear is that at the centre of the Australian experience there is – nothing. The image of Australia as the continent with a dead heart has been a tempting metaphor for the national condition. So, in McAuley's much quoted stanza:

> Where once was a sea is now a salty sunken desert,
> A futile heart within a fair periphery;
> The people are hard-eyed, kindly, with nothing inside them.
> The men are independent but you could not call them free.[22]

Australian society is seen as being materialist in its values, inimical to the life of the spirit. According to this view religion in Australia, although important, has emphasised observance rather than spirituality, while a secular society has been dominated by what McAuley calls 'the state-school mind'. Australian democracy has encouraged a suspicion of excellence, and the pursuit of pleasure has obliterated the satisfaction of inner needs. In this context one might recall the recurring fears expressed by those in authority about community morale, from the days of the penal settlement to the crisis of the Second World War.

A colonial society, of course, is in its very creation concerned with the material, but the peculiarity of Australian origins has assumed the nature of, if not a blight, then at least an enigma. The barrenness of exile was an essential part of the Australian experience, yet it was an exile which could afford comfort and pleasure. According to one view the confrontation with the environment has been a quest, a purifying ordeal: yet, even from the beginning, the environment was also to be embraced, as a source of relaxation and renewal.

The concern about a lack of spiritual core often sits uneasily with a bemused admiration for the simplicity, and even dignity, of Australian hedonism. Horne's image of the man with ice-cream in hand is presented under the heading of 'innocent happiness'. Peter Porter concludes a poem about 'the democratic hero', the racehorse Phar Lap, who lives on, stuffed, in the Melbourne Museum:

> It is Australian innocence to love
> The naturally excessive and be proud
> Of a thoroughbred bay gelding who ran fast.

In Jessica Anderson's *Tirra Lirra By The River* Nora Porteous more ambivalently speaks of 'the contradictions of our home society – its rawness and weak gentility, its innocence and deep deceptions'.[23] Michael Gow's *Away*, hailed as an important play when first performed in 1986, enshrines the annual summer quest for pleasure in a Shakespearean web of magic, and seems almost a celebration of 'innocent happiness'.

Yet *Away* is also concerned with pain and suffering, and with the 1960s trauma of Vietnam, and could be interpreted as attempting to explore the nexus between material pleasure and spiritual fulfilment. Certainly, much artistic and intellectual effort in the postwar period has gone into probing beneath the materialist surface of Australian life: if the novels of Patrick White have been evidence of this, then so too has the epic history of Manning Clark. There was even an element of optimism in the observation of a character in *Voss* that 'our inherent mediocrity as a people' was not 'a final and irrevocable state', but rather 'a creative source of endless variety and subtlety'.[24] Although White and Clark have provoked some uneasiness, both have nevertheless been accorded a heroic status in Australian culture.

Likewise, the inheritance of convictism, so long ignored or obscured, has now in large measure been accepted. Genealogy flourishes as enthusiasts search for a 'first-fleeter' among their ancestors; descendants are no longer embarrassed to own to a convict in the family tree. In 1987 the reception accorded Robert Hughes' widely publicised history of transportation, *The Fatal Shore*, confirmed the new poise: that the book sold well in Britain and the United States was seen as evidence of a flattering interest in culturally fashionable Australia, rather than a cause for embarrassment. In coming to terms with their history, Australians may now be better able to acknowledge their emotional needs.

It is not as if Australian history has been a simple story of material progress and the perfecting of a hedonistic 'way of life'. On the contrary, it is a story which, from the inhumanity of penal servitude to the agony of the Great War and Depression, has encompassed a brand of suffering sometimes giving rise to anger, but more commonly characterised by a stoic cynicism. Indeed, the pursuit of pleasure could be seen as the great Australian anaesthetic, designed to obliterate emotional pain: an acquired habit which compensates for the disappointments of 'real life'.

All this takes on a new significance given the economic decline of the 1980s. It has become a truism that Australia is a 'lucky country' which has run out of luck. But when Donald Horne invented this term, he was not referring to the luck of its resources, whether minerals or beaches, but rather to 'the idea of Australia as a derived society', and particularly 'the luck lived on by the second-rate, provincial-minded "elites"' which 'were reared in an era of self-congratulation on "national achievements" that came mainly from foreign innovation'.[25] In the present climate 'national achievements' are much less easily won, and the economic crisis has become a crisis of self-confidence.

For Aborigines, of course, the reflections of white Australians on their psyche and culture are of only marginal relevance. However much *their* self-confidence has been damaged by two hundred years of white settlement, Aborigines can also view the newcomers with some disdain. They know that there can be no doubts about the spiritual strength of their own culture, and that their appreciation of the environment needs no justification. Whilst Aborigines might welcome the greater interest taken by white Australians in their art and mythology, they might nevertheless wonder whether the 'convergence' of European and Aboriginal cultures hoped for by a champion such as Bernard Smith is necessarily in their interest.

As Australia faces an uncertain future, its history takes on a new importance, and the past is ransacked for appropriate 'lessons'. The advance of history to the forefront of the Australian consciousness means that while at one level it has gained acceptance, at another level it has become the basis for contemporary argument and dispute. When different interests and groups plunder the past for their own purposes, what sort of vision of the future is possible? Yet having assembled the infrastructure of a more diverse and sophisticated culture, Australia is at least better equipped to exploit its dilemmas and divisions creatively. When Vance Palmer conjured up 'the Australia of all who truly belong here' it carried the innuendo that there were some who didn't. Perhaps in visualising the future we need to assume a broader sense of belonging, one that can encompass a diversity of traditions, and while recognising the peculiar 'belonging' of the Aborigines, still acknowledge the claims of the most recent immigrants. The uncertainty of the future offers the opportunity to invent one.

References

Chapter 1

1. George Tinamin quoted in Phillip Toyne and Daniel Vachon, *Growing Up the Country* (Melbourne, 1984), p. 5.
2. W. E. H. Stanner, *On Aboriginal Religion* (Sydney, no date), p. 155.
3. Josephine Flood, *Archaeology of the Dreamtime* (Sydney, 1983), p. 213.
4. Dampier quoted in C. M. H. Clarke (ed.), *Sources of Australian History* (Melbourne, 1957), p. 25; Cook, pp. 54–5.

Chapter 2

1. All these quotations come from John Cobley, *Sydney Cove 1788* (London, 1962), pp. 19–33.
2. M. B. and C. B. Schedvin, 'The Nomadic Tribes of Urban Britain', *Historical Studies*, 18/71, October 1978, p. 258.
3. *Australian Dictionary of Biography*, vol. 1, p. 539.
4. Brian H. Fletcher, *Ralph Darling* (Melbourne, 1984), p. 73; Shirley Roberts, *Charles Hotham* (Melbourne, 1985), p. 89.
5. *Australian Dictionary of Biography*, vol. 2, p. 398.
6. *Oxford Dictionary of Quotations*.
7. *Historical Records of Australia*, 1/1, p. 56.
8. Quoted, Marnie Bassett, *The Hentys* (Melbourne, 1954), pp. 35–6; Geoffrey Bolton, 'The Idea of a Colonial Gentry', *Historical Studies*, 13/51, October 1968, p. 318; Paul de Serville, *Port Phillip Gentlemen* (Melbourne, 1980), p. 204.
9. Quoted, Bruce Knox (ed.), *The Queensland Years of Robert Herbert, Premier* (Brisbane, 1977), p. 3.
10. M. F. Lloyd Prichard (ed.), *The Collected Works of Edward Gibbon Wakefield* (London, 1969), p. 115.

11. Quoted, H. J. M. Johnston, *British Emigration Policy 1815–1830* (Oxford, 1972), p. 168.
12. Quoted, Geoffrey Sherrington, *Australia's Immigrants* (Sydney, 1980), p. 40.
13. Prichard, *op. cit.*, p. 165.
14. Douglas Pike, *Paradise of Dissent* (London, 1951), p. 138.
15. Geoffrey Serle, *The Golden Age* (Melbourne, 1963), prefatory quotation.
16. *Ibid.*, p. 65.

Chapter 3

1. *The Voyage of Governor Phillip to Botany Bay* (facsimile, Sydney, 1970), p. 69.
2. Tench and Bigge quoted in Tom Perry, 'Climate and Settlement in Australia 1700–1930: Some Theoretical Considerations', in John Andrews (ed.), *Frontiers and Men* (Melbourne, 1966), pp. 143, 144; Sturt quoted in Bernard Smith, *European Vision and the South Pacific 1769–1850* (London, 1960), p. 212; settler quoted in D. N. Jeans, *An Historical Geography of New South Wales to 1901* (Sydney, 1972), p. 61.
3. Bernard Smith (ed.), *Documents on Art and Taste in Australia* (Melbourne, 1975), p. 11.
4. Ann Moyal (ed.), *Scientists in Nineteenth-Century Australia* (Melbourne, 1976), p. 20.
5. *Ibid.*, p. 25.
6. *Ibid.*, p. 67.
7. John Cobley, *Sydney Cove 1788* (London, 1962), p. 38.
8. Alan Frost, 'What Created, What Perceived? Early Responses to New South Wales', *Australian Literary Studies*, 7/2, October 1975, p. 199.
9. Patrick O'Farrell, *Letters from Irish Australia 1825–1929* (Sydney, 1984), p. 35.
10. Michael Williams, *The Making of the South Australian Landscape* (London, 1974), p. 15.
11. *The Voyage of the 'Beagle'* (Geneva, 1968), p. 431.
12. *Ralph Rashleigh* (Sydney, 1952), p. 68.
13. Geoffrey Serle, *The Golden Age* (Melbourne, 1963), p. 369.
14. Smith, *Documents* p. 35.
15. Mrs Charles Perry, endorsing the view of 'a certain Frenchman', in James Grant and Geoffrey Serle (eds.), *The Melbourne Scene 1803–1956* (Melbourne, 1957), p. 59.

16. Darwin, *op. cit.*, p. 441; Field quoted in Smith, *Documents*, p. 38; Mitchell quoted in Kathleen Fitzpatrick (ed.), *Australian Explorers* (London, 1958), p. 138; Scott quoted in Karen Moon, 'Aesthetic Qualities of the South Australian Landscape', *Flinders Journal of History and Politics*, 2, July 1970, p. 23.

17. Field quoted in Smith, *Documents*, p. 37; Darwin, *op. cit.*, p. 437; Henning quoted in David Adams (ed.), *The Letters of Rachel Henning* (Melbourne, 1969), p. 66.

18. South Australian colonist quoted in Moon, *op. cit.*, p. 25; Eyre quoted in Fitzpatrick, *op. cit.*, p. 177.

19. Darwin, *op. cit.*, pp. 433–4.

20. Lucy Frost (ed.), *No Place for a Nervous Lady* (Melbourne, 1984), p. 46.

21. *Australian Dictionary of Biography*, vol. 2, p. 85.

22. Fitzpatrick, *op. cit.*, p. 38.

23. *Ibid.*, pp. 347 (Stuart), 211 (Leichardt).

24. All quotations from Fitzpatrick, *op. cit.*: Forrest, p. 455; Warburton, p. 431; Giles, pp. 496, 488; Grey, p. 169; member of Sturt's party, p. 305; Wills, pp. 372, 370.

25. *Ibid.*, p. 252.

26. A. T. Yarwood and M. J. Knowling, *Race Relations in Australia* (Sydney, 1982), p. 35.

27. Grant and Serle, *op. cit.*, p. 20.

28. M. F. Christie, *Aborigines in Colonial Victoria 1835–86* (Sydney, 1979) p. 39.

29. Yarwood and Knowling, *op. cit.*, p. 80.

30. Darwin, *op. cit.*, p. 435.

31. Douglas Sladen (ed.), *Australian Ballads and other Poems* (London, no date), p. 232.

32. J. M. Powell, *Environmental Management in Australia 1788–1914* (Melbourne, 1976), p. 45.

33. Russel Ward, *The Australian Legend* (Melbourne, 1958), p. 13.

34. George Essex Evans, 'The Women of the West', in Brian Elliot and Adrian Mitchell (eds.), *Bards in the Wilderness* (Melbourne, 1970), p. 123.

35. Smith, *Documents*, pp. 135–6.

36. Sladen, *op. cit.*, p. 154.

37. Sydney, 1963 [1908], p. 7.

38. *The Prose Works of Henry Lawson* vol. 1 (Sydney, 1935), pp. 32–3.

39. 'Clancy of the Overflow' in Douglas Stewart and Nancy Keesing (eds.), *Bush Songs, Ballads and Other Verse* (Sydney, 1967), p. 201.

Chapter 4

1. C. M. H. Clark (ed.), *Sources of Australian History* (Melbourne, 1957), p. 203.
2. J. G. Steele, *Brisbane Town in Convict Days: 1824–1842* (Brisbane, 1975), p. 144.
3. Jean Woolmington (ed.), *Religion in Early Australia* (Sydney, 1976), p. 15.
4. Lloyd Robson, *A History of Tasmania*, vol. 1 (Melbourne, 1983), p. 72.
5. John Manning Ward, *James Macarthur* (Sydney, 1981), p. 26.
6. Clark, *op. cit.*, pp. 208, 214.
7. J. M. D. Hardwick (ed.), *Emigrants in Motley* (London, 1954), p. 109.
8. P. Cunningham, *Two Years in New South Wales*, vol. 2 (London, 1827), p. 53.
9. *Ibid.*, p. 56.
10. *Town Life in Australia* (facsimile, Melbourne, 1973), p. 83.
11. *My Life's Story* (Sydney, 1923), p. 146.
12. Geoffrey Serle, *The Golden Age* (Melbourne, 1962), p. 351.
13. From work in progress by Marc Askew.
14. *Australian Dictionary of Biography*, vol. 2, p. 136.
15. R. N. Ebbels (ed.), *The Australian Labor Movement 1850–1907* (Melbourne, 1960), p. 61.
16. Adrian Mitchell (ed.), *Charles Harpur* (Melbourne, 1973), p. 176.
17. Re. Brooke, see Serle, *op. cit.*, p. 363; the Keans, see Hardwick, *op. cit.*, pp. 98–9.
18. Margaret Williams, *Australia on the Popular Stage 1829–1929* (Melbourne, 1983), p. 63.
19. Leonie Sandercock and Ian Turner, *Up Where, Cazaly?* (Sydney, 1981), p. 19.
20. Harry Furniss quoted in Jane Clark and Bridget Whitelaw, *Golden Summers* (Melbourne, 1985), p. 127.
21. Kean quoted in Hardwick, *op. cit.*, p. 170; Webb quoted in John Rickard, *Class and Politics* (Canberra, 1976), p. 61; Higinbotham quoted in *Australian Dictionary of Biography*, vol. 4, p. 391.
22. Selby quoted in Lucy Frost (ed.), *No Place for a Nervous Lady* (Melbourne, 1984), p. 156; Mapleson quoted in Susannah Mapleson (ed.), *A Lifetime of Letters* (no date), p. 10; the Irishman quoted in Patrick O'Farrell, *Letters from Irish Australia 1825–1929* (Sydney, 1984), p. 53.

23. Ross Fitzgerald, *From the Dreaming to 1915* (Brisbane, 1982), p. 277.

24. Clark and Whitelaw, *op. cit.*, p. 129.

Chapter 5

1. John Rickard, *H. B. Higgins* (Sydney, 1984): the premier, p. 108; the politician, p. 111.

2. Max Chamberlain, 'The Wilmansruist affair: a defence of the 5th Victorian Mounted Rifles', *Journal of the Australian War Memorial*, 6, April 1985, p. 47.

3. Peter Burness, 'The Australian Horse: a cavalry squadron in the South African War', *ibid.*, p. 43.

4. Brian McKinlay (ed.), *School Days* (Melbourne, 1985), pp. 11–12.

5. Stewart Firth and Jeanette Hoorn, 'From Empire Day to Cracker Night', in Peter Spearritt and David Walker (eds.), *Australian Popular Culture* (Sydney, 1979), p. 24.

6. John Barrett, *Falling In* (Sydney, 1979), p. 66.

7. David Walker, '"War, women and the Bush" the novels of Mary Grant Bruce and Ethel Turner', *Historical Studies*, 18/71, October 1978, p. 301.

8. Higgins quoted in Rickard, *op. cit.*, p. 131; Parkes quoted in J. A. La Nauze, *The Making of The Australian Constitution* (Melbourne, 1972), p. 11; Deakin quoted in C. M. H. Clark (ed.), *Sources of Australian History* (Melbourne, 1957), pp. 497, 495; Watson quoted in R. N. Ebbels (ed.), *The Australian Labor Movement 1850–1907* (Melbourne, 1960), p. 234.

9. Margaret Williams, *Australia on the Popular Stage 1829–1929* (Melbourne, 1983), p. 240.

10. Michael Cannon (ed.), *That Damned Democrat* (Melbourne, 1981), p. 69.

11. Munro Ferguson quoted in Christopher Cunneen, *King's Men* (Sydney, 1983), p. 118; Fisher quoted in F. K. Crowley (ed.), *Modern Australia in Documents 1901–1939* (Melbourne, 1973), p. 214.

12. Bartlett quoted in Kevin Fewster, 'Ellis Ashmead Bartlett and the Making of the Anzac Legend', *Journal of Australian Studies*, 10, June 1982, p. 20; Masefield, *Gallipoli* (London, 1916), pp. 149, 25.

13. R. Ely, 'The First Anzac Day', *Journal of Australian Studies*, 17, November 1985, p. 55.

14. F. M. Cutlack (ed.), *War Letters of General Monash* (Sydney, 1934), pp. 112–13.
15. D. N. Jeans, 'The Making of the Anzac Memorial, Sydney', *Australia 1938*, 4, November 1981, p. 53.
16. *The Story of Anzac* (Sydney, 1921), p. 46.
17. Sydney, 1916, pp. 29, 117 and dustjacket.
18. *Argus*, 12 November 1934.
19. *Ibid.*
20. *The Education of Young Donald* (Melbourne, 1968), p. 57.
21. J. T. Laird (ed.), *Other Banners* (Canberra, 1971), pp. 127–8.
22. Colin Thiele, *Heyson of Hahndorf* (Adelaide, 1968), p. 312.
23. Richard White, *Inventing Australia* (Sydney, 1981), p. 118.
24. John Barnes (ed.) *The Writer in Australia* (Melbourne, 1969), pp. 201–2.
25. *Ibid.*, p. 192.
26. Sydney, 1923, Preface.
27. pp. 15–16.
28. David Walker, *Dream and Disillusion* (Canberra, 1976), p. 186.
29. Menzies diary quoted in *Age*, 24 July 1982; R. J. W. Selleck, *Frank Tate* (Melbourne, 1982), p. 174.
30. Selleck, *op. cit.*, p. 176.
31. 'My Country' quoted in Brian Elliot and Adrian Mitchell (eds.), *Bards in the Wilderness* (Melbourne, 1970), p. 215.
32. Barnes, *op. cit.*, p. 210.
33. A. A. Phillips, *The Australian Tradition* (Melbourne, 1958), p. 112.
34. *The Distant View* (Sydney, 1943), p. 242.
35. A. D. Hope, *Collected Poems 1930–1965* (Sydney, 1966), p. 13.

Chapter 6

1. R. N. Ebbels (ed.), *The Australian Labor Movement 1850–1907* (Melbourne, 1960), p. 166.
2. *Socialism Without Doctrine*, translated by Russel Ward (Sydney, 1973 [1901]).
3. Thorold Waters, *Much Besides Music* (Melbourne, 1951), p. 8.
4. Cameron Hazlehurst, *Menzies Observed* (Sydney, 1979), p. 155.
5. L. J. Louis and Ian Turner (eds.), *The Depression of the 1930s* (Melbourne, 1968), p. 179.
6. Mrs Brookes quoted in Peter Loveday, 'Anti-political Political Thought', in Judy Mackinolty (ed.), *The Wasted Years* (Sydney, 1981), p. 136; Menzies quoted in Hazlehurst, *op. cit.*, p. 74;

McMahon Ball quoted in W. G. K. Duncan (ed.), *Trends in Australian Politics* (Sydney, 1935), p. 142.

7. J. A. McCallum, 'The Economic Bases of Australian Politics', in Duncan, *op. cit.*, p. 56; *Whither Away?* (Sydney, 1934), pp. 11–12, 76.

8. On the King and Empire Alliance see Robert Darroch, *D. H. Lawrence in Australia* (Melbourne, 1981), p. 48; on the police strike see Andrew Moore, 'Guns across the Yarra', in Sydney Labour History Group, *What Rough Beast?* (Sydney, 1982), p. 222.

9. *The Rallying Point* (Melbourne, 1965), p. 26.

10. *Ibid.*, pp. 6, 72.

11. Campbell on Fascism discussed in Keith Amos, *The New Guard Movement 1931–1935* (Melbourne, 1976), p. 100; on the New Guard see *The Rallying Point*, p. 178.

12. *A New Province for Law and Order* (London, 1922).

13. John Rickard, *H. B. Higgins* (Sydney, 1984), p. 172.

14. *Ibid.*, p. 171.

15. *Ibid.*, p. 195.

16. Stuart Macintyre, *Winners and Losers* (Sydney, 1985), p. 65.

17. London, 1964, p. 146.

18. John Lonie, 'From Liberal to Liberal', in Graeme Duncan (ed.) *Critical Essays in Australian Politics* (Melbourne, 1978), p. 70.

Chapter 7

1. Royal Commission on the Decline of the Birth Rate and on the Mortality of Infants in New South Wales, *New South Wales Parliamentary Papers*, 1904 (Second Session), notes from Grant McBurnie.

2. Robin Boyd, *Australia's Home* (Melbourne, 1952), p. 76.

3. *Ibid.*, p. 77.

4. Donald Horne, *The Education of Young Donald* (Sydney, 1967), p. 138.

5. Ackermann, *Australia From a Woman's Point of View* (Sydney, 1981 [1913]), p. 77; Sabine Willis, 'Homes are Divine Workshops', in Elizabeth Windschuttle (ed.), *Women, Class and History* (Melbourne, 1980), pp. 188–9.

6. *The Prose Works of Henry Lawson*, vol. 2 (Sydney, 1935), pp. 90, 10; Barry Andrews, 'Ginger Meggs: His Story', in Susan Dermody, John Docker, and Drusilla Modjeska (eds.), *Nellie Melba, Ginger Meggs and Friends* (Malmsbury, 1982), 223–4.

7. *My Brother Jack* (London, 1964), p. 39; Horne, *op. cit.*, p. 169.

8. Janet McCalman, *Struggletown* (Melbourne, 1984), p. 260.
9. John Horgan (ed.), *The Golden Years of Ginger Meggs* (Adelaide, 1978), p. 24.
10. John Hetherington, *Norman Lindsay* (Melbourne, 1973), p. 117.
11. On dancing see McCalman, *op. cit.*, p. 147; the critic is Adrian Mitchell on 'Fiction' in Leonie Kramer (ed.), *The Oxford History of Australian Literature* (Melbourne, 1981), p. 114; Nettie Palmer quoted in David Walker, *Dream and Disillusion* (Canberra, 1976), p. 176.
12. Colin Thiele, *Heysen of Hahndorf* (Adelaide, 1968), p. 299.
13. *Kangaroo* (London, 1950 [1923]), pp. 304, 379.
14. Rhonda Wilson (ed.), *Good Talk* (Melbourne, 1984), pp. 5–6.
15. Marilyn Lake, *The Limits of Hope* (Melbourne, 1987), pp. 143, 174.
16. On Catholic schools see Edmund Campion, *Rockchoppers* (Melbourne, 1982), p. 68; on Richmond, McCalman, *op. cit.*, p. 72.
17. Horne, *op. cit.*, p. 24.
18. Denis O'Brien, *The Weekly* (Sydney, 1982), p. 14.
19. Hilary L. Rubinstein, *The Jews in Victoria* (Sydney, 1986), p. 165.
20. John Rickard, *H. B. Higgins* (Sydney, 1984), p. 282.
21. Jack Horner, 'Aborigines and the Sesquicentenary', in *Australia 1938*, 3, December 1980, pp. 44, 49.
22. 'The Aborigines', in J. C. G. Kevin (ed.), *Some Australians Take Stock* (London, 1939), p. 35.
23. *The Boy Adeodatus* (Melbourne, 1984), p. 255.
24. 14 May 1938.
25. F. K. Crowley (ed.), *Modern Australia in Documents 1901–1939* (Melbourne, 1973), pp. 117–19.

Chapter 8

1. F. K. Crowley (ed.), *Modern Australia in Documents 1939–1970* (Melbourne, 1973), pp. 1–2.
2. Alan Watt, *The Evolution of Australia's Foreign Policy 1938–1965* (London, 1967), pp. 14, 26.
3. Crowley, *op. cit.*, p. 39.
4. The historian, W. J. Hudson, *Casey* (Melbourne, 1986), p. 134; Lloyd Ross, *John Curtin* (Melbourne, 1977), pp. 99, 386.
5. Crowley, *op. cit.*, pp. 50–2.
6. Hudson, *op. cit.*, p. 134.
7. Peter Spearritt, 'The Queen and Her Australian Subjects', *Australian Cultural History*, 5, 1986, pp. 81, 83.
8. Menzies, *Afternoon Light* (Melbourne, 1967), p. 164.

9. Hudson, *op. cit.*, p. 246.
10. Crowley, *op. cit.*, p. 479.
11. *Ibid.*, p. 513.
12. Peter King (ed.), *Australia's Vietnam* (Sydney, 1983), p. 12.
13. Russel Ward, *A Nation for a Continent* (Melbourne, 1977), p. 386.
14. Melbourne, 1985, p. 53.
15. *Ibid.*, p. 101.

Chapter 9

1. F. K. Crowley (ed.), *Modern Australia in Documents 1939–1970* (Melbourne, 1973), p. 61.
2. Janice Wilton and Richard Bosworth, *Old Worlds and New Australia* (Melbourne, 1984), p. 9.
3. A. A. Calwell, *Be Just and Fear Not* (Melbourne, 1972), p. 109.
4. 'The Australian Nation', in George Caiger (ed.), *The Australian Way of Life* (London, 1953), p. 16.
5. *They're a Weird Mob*, p. 204; Snedden quoted in Wilton and Bosworth, *op. cit.*, p. 17.
6. Patrick O'Farrell, *Documents in Australian Catholic History*, vol. 2, (London, 1969), p. 390.
7. Hilary Kent and John Merritt, 'The Cold War and the Melbourne Olympic Games', in Ann Curthoys and John Merritt (eds.), *Better Dead Than Red* (Sydney, 1986), pp. 170, 182–3.
8. F. K. Crowley, *op. cit.*, p. 509.
9. *The Whitlam Government 1972–1975* (Melbourne, 1985), p. 457.
10. J. A. La Nauze, *The Making of the Australian Constitution* (Melbourne, 1972), p. 326.
11. p. 330.
12. Mart Cowley, *The Boys in the Band* (New York, 1968), p. 41.
13. *Coming Out in the Seventies* (Sydney, 1979), p. 24.
14. Frank Crowley, *Tough Times* (Melbourne, 1986), p. 296.
15. Harry M. Miller, *My Story* (Melbourne, 1983), pp. 176, 177.
16. Prefatory note.
17. Craig McGregor, *People, Politics and Pop* (Sydney, 1968), p. 118.
18. *Age*, 31 January 1987.
19. Sydney, 1984, p. 19.

Chapter 10

1. The historian, Richard White, *Inventing Australia* (Sydney, 1981), p. viii; Palmer quoted, Donald Horne, *The Lucky Country* (Melbourne, 1974 [1964]), p. 221.

2. Richard Haese, *Rebels and Precursors* (Melbourne, 1981), pp. 96–7.

3. The basic documents cited are in Max Harris (ed.), *Ern Malley's Poems* (Adelaide, 1971); the critic is Vivian Smith on 'Poetry' in Leonie Kramer (ed.), *The Oxford History of Australian Literature* (Melbourne, 1981), p. 371.

4. McCauley quoted in Leonie Kramer, 'The Late James McAuley', *Quadrant*, 30/11, November 1986, p. 69; on Wright see Smith, *op. cit.*, p. 392.

5. Haese, *op. cit.*, pp. 269, 283–4.

6. J. M. Main, 'Painting', in A. F. Davies and S. Encel (eds.), *Australian Society* (Melbourne, 1965), p. 179.

7. Gary Catalano, *The Years of Hope* (Melbourne, 1981), p. 88.

8. *Flaws in the Glass* (London, 1981), pp. 135, 140.

9. Melbourne, 1960, pp. 9, 61.

10. Humphries, *A Nice Night's Entertainment* (London, 1981), pp. 31, 14; Peter O'Shaughnessy recalls the 'nostalgic liturgy', *Age*, 26 January 1985.

11. Stretton (Melbourne, 1975 [1970]), p. 5; White, *Flaws in the Glass*, p. 151.

12. Interviewed by Phillip Adams, *Tension*, 11, January–February 1987, p. 8.

13. *Leaves of Iron* (Sydney, 1985), p. 54.

14. Lynne Strahan, *Just City and the Mirrors* (Melbourne, 1984), p. 78.

15. *Op. cit.*, p. 21.

16. Liverani, *The Winter Sparrows* (Melbourne, 1975), p. 312; Hazzard quoted in *Sydney Morning Herald*, 18 August 1984.

17. The Greek quoted in Eve Isaacs, *Greek Children in Sydney* (Canberra, 1976), p. 72; on Xavier Herbert and bravery see Veronica Brady, *A Crucible of Prophets* (Sydney, 1981), p. 97.

18. *Ockers* (Adelaide, 1974), p. 18.

19. *Coming Out in the Seventies* (Sydney, 1979), p. 24.

20. *Australian Accent* (London, 1961), p. 36.

21. Quoted in Nicholas Jose, 'Cultural Identity', in Stephen R. Graubard (ed.), *Australia: The Daedalus Symposium* (Sydney, 1985), p. 311.

22. *Collected Poems 1936–1970* (Sydney, 1971), pp. 6, 87.

23. Porter in David Campbell (ed.), *Modern Australian Poetry* (Melbourne, 1970), p. 248; Anderson (Melbourne, 1980 [1978]), p. 83.

24. (London, 1957), p. 476.

25. *Death of the Lucky Country* (Melbourne, 1976), pp. 93–4.

Bibliography

This bibliography outlines the main published sources on which the book is based: it is also intended to furnish suggestions for future reading. It does not seem appropriate, for a short history such as this, to point the reader towards manuscript sources or unpublished theses; but in any case the sheer volume of Australian history now being published makes a guide to it sufficient of a task. It is interesting to note how many of the works cited here have appeared since 1980. This is, therefore, a select bibliography which seeks only to identify the principal works relevant to the themes discussed. Once a book has been cited, a second reference gives only the author and *op. cit.* or short title. Chapter endnotes locate the precise source of any direct quotations in the text.

General

There are now numerous published collections of documents, but those used most in this history have been, for the nineteenth century, **C. M. H. Clark**'s *Sources of Australian History* (Melbourne 1957) and, for the twentieth century, **F. K. Crowley**'s two volumes, *Modern Australia in Documents 1901–1938* and *1939–1970* (Melbourne 1973). Both collections make for interesting reading.

Also much used has been the *Australian Dictionary of Biography* (Melbourne 1966–), the first six volumes of which cover the period up to 1890. A further four volumes for the 1890–1939 period have, at the time of writing, taken us as far as the letter N(er).

Australia's bicentenary has occasioned a flurry of publishing, but two projects are worthy of note. The historical profession has generated a formidable ten-volume, multi-authored history, entitled *Australians: A Historical Library* (Sydney 1987–). The publishers have chosen an epic format with handsome production and copious illustrations; marketing at $A695 it is clearly designed to be an imposing presence on the suburban bookshelf. Although not designed for casual reading, *Australians* is an important and valuable publication. Five volumes provide a treasure trove of information – *A Historical Atlas*, *A Historical Dictionary*, *Events and Places*, *Historical Statistics* and *A Guide to Sources*. The five narrative volumes make an innovative attempt to depict the totality of Australian society at particular points in its history, through 'slicing' at arbitrary fifty-year intervals. The first volume,

Australians to 1788, while concerned with the broad sweep of Aboriginal history, also focuses on the moment of contact with the Europeans. The next three volumes focus on *1838*, *1888* and *1938*, while the last, *Australians from 1939*, to some extent foresakes the method to cover the contemporary period. The scale and price of *Australians* rules it out for many a reader, but as a library resource it is invaluable.

A more modest but, correspondingly, a more digestible bicentennial summation is being offered with the five-volume *Oxford History of Australia*. At this moment (1987) only **Stuart Macintyre**'s volume 4, *The Succeeding Age*, which covers the period 1901–42, has appeared.

A major overview of Australian history is presented by **C. M. H. (Manning) Clark**'s *A History of Australia* (Melbourne), the first volume of which appeared in 1962. Five volumes have now brought the story to 1915; a sixth is promised to conclude it. Clark's history, tragic in its vision and prophetic in its style, has its admirers and detractors, but in its stress on religion and culture has done much to transform the writing of Australian history.

A number of specialist histories have contributed to this book and would be useful to a reader seeking more detailed information. **Geoffrey Serle**'s *From Deserts The Prophets Come* (Melbourne 1973) set out to be a history of 'high' culture in Australia; it was republished in 1987, in an expanded, illustrated format, as *The Creative Spirit in Australia: A Cultural History*. **Bernard Smith**'s *Australian Painting 1788–1970* (Melbourne 1971 [1962]) is a standard text and a masterly commentary; for music there is **Roger Covell**'s *Australia's Music: Themes of a New Society* (Melbourne 1967); and for architecture, **J. M. Freeland**, *Architecture in Australia: A History* (Melbourne 1968). *The Oxford History of Australian Literature*, ed. **Leonie Kramer** (Melbourne 1981), is a valuable guide, even if one does not always agree with the priorities of its contributors. I have less confidence in **Leslie Rees**'s *A History of Australian Drama*, 2 vols (Sydney 1978), but it is at least useful.

Chapter 1: Aborigines

There are several introductions to traditional Aboriginal society. **A. P. Elkin**'s *The Australian Aborigines* (Sydney 1938), has been through a number of editions: it was a pioneering work, but needs to be seen in the context of its time. **R. M.** and **C. H. Berndts**'s substantial *The World of the First Australians* (Sydney 1964) is dedicated to Elkin, and claims to be 'complementary and supplementary' to *The Australian Aborigines*. **Kenneth Maddock**'s *The Australian Aborigines: A Portrait of their Society* (Melbourne 1974 [1972]), is a much slimmer paperback which describes 'some of the general features of Aboriginal society', but confines itself to 'what is living in the Aboriginal tradition'. **Geoffrey Blainey**'s popular *Triumph of the Nomads: A History of Ancient Australia* (Melbourne 1975) focuses very much on the material culture of the Aborigines. The most recent contribution is a collection edited by **W. H. Edwards**, *Traditional Aboriginal Society: A Reader* (Melbourne 1987): it, like *Australians to 1788* (edited by **D. J. Mulvaney** and **J. Peter White**), appeared too late to be consulted in the writing of this book.

In the area of religion, myth and art, which are central preoccupations of this chapter, I have drawn on: **Louis A. Allen**, *Time Before Mourning: Art and Myth of the Australian Aborigines* (New York 1974); **Ronald M. Berndt**, *Australian Aboriginal Religion* (Leiden 1974); **Ronald M. Berndt**, *Djanggawul: An Aboriginal Religious Cult of North-Eastern Arnhem Land* (London 1952); **Ronald M. Berndt** and **E. S. Phillips** (eds), *The Australian Aboriginal Heritage* (Sydney 1978 [1973]); **Ronald M. Berndt** and **Catherine H. Berndt** with John E. Stanton, *Australian Aboriginal Art: A Visual Perspective* (Sydney 1982); **Ira R. Buchler** and **Kenneth Maddock** (eds), *The Rainbow Serpent: A Chromatic Piece* (The Hague 1978); **Mercea Eliade**, *Australian Religions: An introduction* (Cornell 1973); **W. E. H. Stanner**, *On Aboriginal Religion* (Sydney, no date); **Peter J. Ucko** (ed.), *Form in Indigenous Art: Schematisation in the Art of Aboriginal Australia and Prehistoric Europe* (Canberra 1977).

Also useful were: **Diane Bell**, *Daughters of the Dreaming* (Sydney 1983); **M. F. Christie**, *Aborigines in Colonial Victoria 1835–86* (Sydney 1979); **Josephine Flood**, *Archaeology of the Dreamtime* (Sydney 1983); **L. R. Hiatt** (ed.), *Australian Aboriginal Concepts* (Canberra 1978); **M. J. Meggitt**, *Desert People: A Study of the Walbiri Aborigines of Central Australia* (Chicago 1965[1962]); **Gezá Róheim**, *Psychoanalysis and Anthropology: Culture, Personality and the Unconscious* (New York 1968 [1950]); **Lyndall Ryan**, *The Aboriginal Tasmanians* (Brisbane 1981); **W. E. H. Stanner**, *After the Dreaming: Black and White Australians – An Anthropologist's View* (Sydney 1969).

Chapter 2: Immigrants

The only brief, historical survey of immigration is **Geoffrey Sherrington**'s *Australia's Immigrants 1788–1978* (Sydney 1980). However, **Richard Broome**'s *The Victorians: Arriving* (Sydney 1984), is a history of Victoria in terms of immigration.

Much has been written about the controversy concerning the origins of New South Wales: some of the contributions to the debate are brought together in **Ged Martin** (ed.), *The Founding of Australia: The Argument about Australia's Origins* (Sydney 1978).

On the origins of the convicts, see in particular **L. L. Robson**, *The Convict Settlers of Australia: An Enquiry into the Origin and Character of the Convicts Transported to New South Wales and Van Diemen's Land 1787–1852* (Melbourne 1965); also **A. G. L. Shaw**, *Convicts and the Colonies: A Study of Penal Transportation from Great Britain and Ireland to Australia and Other Parts of the British Empire* (London 1966); and **M. B.** and **C. B. Schedvin**, 'The Nomadic Tribes of Urban Britain', *Historical Studies*, 18/71, October 1978, p. 258.

On the soldiers, see **T. G. Parsons**, 'The Social Composition of the Men of the New South Wales Corps', *Journal of the Royal Australian Historical Society*, 50/4, 1964, p. 297.

Changing British attitudes to emigration are charted in **H. J. M. Johnston**, *British Emigration Policy 1815–1830* (Oxford 1972) and **David S. Macmillan**, *Scotland and Australia 1788–1850: Emigration, Commerce and Investment* (Oxford 1967).

The standard history of the founding of South Australia is **Douglas Pike**'s *Paradise of Dissent* (London 1951). **Geoffrey Serle**'s *The Golden Age* (Melbourne 1963), although confined to Victoria, depicts the gold diggers:

see also his article, 'The Gold Generation', *Victorian Historical Magazine*, 41/1, February 1970, p. 265.

The Irish have recently had the benefit of two studies: **Patrick O'Farrell**, *The Irish in Australia* (Sydney 1986), and **Chris McConville**, *Croppies, Celts and Catholics: The Irish in Australia* (Melbourne 1987). The Scots are less well-served with **Malcolm D. Prentiss**, *The Scots in Australia: A Study of New South Wales, Victoria and Queensland, 1788–1900* (Sydney 1983). However, for a local study, see **Don Watson**'s evocative *Caledonia Australis: Scottish Highlanders on the Frontier of Australia* (Sydney 1984). See also **J. F. Faull**, *The Cornish in Australia* (Melbourne 1983).

What has come to be known as the 'fragment' thesis derives from **Louis Hartz**, *The Founding of New Societies: Studies in the History of the United States, Latin America, South Africa, Canada and Australia* (New York 1964).

Chapter 3: The Environment

The most serviceable introductions to environmental history are **Geoffrey Bolton**, *Spoils and Spoilers: Australians Make Their Environment 1788–1980* (Sydney 1981) and **J. M. Powell**, *Environmental Management in Australia 1788–1914* (Melbourne 1976).

Concerning perceptions of the colonial environment I have drawn on: **John Andrews** (ed.), *Frontiers and Men* (Melbourne 1966); **Robert Dixon**, *The Course of Empire: Neo-Classical Culture in New South Wales 1788–1860* (Melbourne 1986); **Alan Frost**, 'What Created, What Perceived? Early Responses to New South Wales', *Australian Literary Studies*, 7/2, October 1975, p. 199; **D. N. Jeans**, *An Historical Geography of New South Wales to 1901* (Sydney 1972); **Karen Moon**, 'Aesthetic Qualities of the South Australian Landscape', *Flinders Journal of History and Politics*, 2 July 1970, p. 23; **Bernard Smith**, *European Vision and the South Pacific 1769–1850* (London 1960); **Michael Williams**, *The Making of the South Australian Landscape* (London 1974).

Several collections of documents provide interesting and informative reading. **Bernard Smith**'s *Documents on Arts and Taste in Australia* (Melbourne 1975), brings together some aesthetic appraisals of the environment. For the response of the explorers I have depended heavily on **Kathleen Fitzpatrick**'s selection of extracts from their journals, *Australian Explorers* (London 1958); for scientists there is **Ann Moyal**'s *Scientists in Nineteenth-Century Australia* (Melbourne 1976). Also useful are **James Grant** and **Geoffrey Serle** (eds), *The Melbourne Scene 1803–1956* (Melbourne 1957), and **Alan Birch** and **David Macmillan** (eds), *The Sydney Scene, 1788–1960* (Melbourne 1962).

For a history of architecture, see J. M. Freeland, *op. cit.*; the introduction of new flora and fauna is dealt with by **Eric Rolls** in *They All Ran Wild: The Animals and Plants that Plague Australia* (Sydney 1984).

There is a growing corpus of literature on Aboriginal–European contact. General accounts are offered by **Richard Broome**, *Aboriginal Australians: Black Response to White Dominance 1788–1980* (Sydney 1982) and **A. T. Yarwood** and **M. Knowling**, *Race Relations in Australia: A History* (Sydney 1982). **Henry Reynolds** makes a notable attempt to reconstruct the Aboriginal perspective in *The Other Side of the Frontier* (Melbourne 1982). For contact in Victoria, see M. F. Christie, *op. cit.*, and for the fate of the Tasmanians, Lyndall Ryan, *op. cit.*

Much imaginative ink has been spilt on Ned Kelly. For a sober inter-pretation which places the bushranger in his social context, see **John McQuilton**, *The Kelly Outbreak 1878–1880: The Geographical Dimension of Social Banditry* (Melbourne 1979).

Two recent studies throw fresh light on nineteenth-century painting: **Tim Bonyhardy** reappraises the so-called 'colonial' painters in *Images in Opposition: Australian Landscape Painting 1801–1890* (Melbourne 1985), while **Leigh Astbury** offers an historical reinterpretation of the celebrated Heidel-berg painters in *City Bushmen: The Heidelberg School and the Rural Mythology* (Melbourne 1985).

The ideological dimension of the *Bulletin* school is exposed by **Richard White** in *Inventing Australia: Images and Identity 1688–1980* (Sydney 1981), and also by **Graeme Davison** in 'Sydney and the Bush: an Urban Context for the Australian Legend', *Historical Studies*, 18/71, October 1978, p. 191.

Manning Clark offers a biographical 'hymn of praise', *In Search of Henry Lawson* (Melbourne 1978). **Xavier Pons** presents a more critical, if clinical view in *Out of Eden: Henry Lawson's Life and Works – A Psychoanalytic View* (Sydney 1984).

Chapter 4: Society

This chapter covers a vast territory, and the caveat that this is a select bibliography applies especially here.

On convictism I am indebted to **J. B. Hirst**'s *Convict Society and its Enemies: A History of Early New South Wales* (Sydney 1983). **Robert Hughes**'s *The Fatal Shore* (London 1987) is an eminently readable survey of the blood and gore of convictism, but pays only lip service to the historical consensus that this represented the exception rather than the rule. In addition to Hirst, I have drawn upon: **Alan Atkinson**, 'Four Patterns of Convict Protest', *Labour History*, 37, November 1979, p. 28; **Portia Robinson**, *The Hatch and Brood of Time: A Study of the First Generation of White Australians 1788–1828* (Melbourne 1985); **Lloyd Robson**, *A History of Tasmania*, Vol. 1. *Van Diemen's Land from the Earliest Times to 1855* (Melbourne 1983); A. G. L. Shaw, *op. cit.*; **Anne Summers**, *Damned Whores and God's Police: The Colonization of Women in Australia* (Melbourne 1975).

Family history, it might be said, is still in its infancy, but there is the collection of essays edited by **Patricia Grimshaw**, **Chris McConville** and **Ellen McEwan**, *Families in Colonial Australia* (Sydney 1985). Portia Robinson, *op. cit.*, is relevant to the first native-born generation. On children more generally there is little, but the Royal Historical Society of Victoria's collec-tion, *The Colonial Child*, ed. **Guy Featherstone** (Melbourne 1981), is a useful beginning.

Geoffrey Serle's *The Golden Age* describes Eureka; there is also the *Historical Studies Eureka Supplement* (2nd edn), (Melbourne 1965). The best case study of colonial politics is **P. Loveday** and **A. W. Martin**, *Parliament Factions and Parties: The First Thirty Years of Responsible Government in New South Wales, 1856–1889* (Melbourne 1966).

On moral improvement and education the reader is referred to **Alan**

Barcan, *A History of Australian Education* (Melbourne 1980); **George Nadel**, *Australia's Colonial Culture: Ideas, Men and Institutions in Mid-Nineteenth Century Eastern Australia* (Harvard 1957); **Michael Roe**, *The Quest for Authority in Eastern Australia 1825–51* (Melbourne 1965).

The Catholic Church has been relatively well served by historians. **Patrick O'Farrell** has not only written *The Catholic Church in Australia: A Short History 1788–1967* (Melbourne 1968), but also edited two volumes of *Documents in Australian Catholic History* (Melbourne 1969). There are no equivalent volumes for Anglican and Protestant churches, though for South Australia, 'the paradise of dissent', there are two studies, **Arnold D. Hunt**, *This Side of Heaven: A History of Methodism in South Australia* (Adelaide 1985); and **David Hilliard**, *Godliness and Good Order: A History of the Anglican Church in South Australia* (Adelaide 1986). Secularism and sectarianism are analysed in **J. S. Gregory**, *Church and State: Changing Government Policies Towards Religion in Australia; with particular reference to Victoria since Separation* (Melbourne 1973).

Robin Gollan's *Radical and Working-Class Politics: A Study of Eastern Australia, 1850–1910* (Melbourne 1960) is still the best introduction to the growth of trade unionism, supported by **R. N. Ebbels'** document collection, *The Australian Labor Movement 1850–1907* (Melbourne 1960). The professions and their organisations are still to be written about, but they do receive some attention from **Graeme Davison** in *The Rise and Fall of Marvellous Melbourne* (Melbourne 1978).

For writers, see Serle, *From Deserts the Prophets Come*; for painters, Smith, *Australian Painting*; music, Covell, *op. cit.* The world of popular theatre is entertainingly described by **Margaret Williams**, *Australia on the Popular Stage 1829–1929* (Melbourne 1983), and the early days of colonial opera by Harold Love, *The Golden Age of Australian Opera: W. S. Lyster and His Companies 1861–1880* (Sydney 1981).

Up Where, Cazaly? The Great Australian Game by **Leonie Sandercock** and **Ian Turner** (Sydney 1981) is a history of Australian Rules football. A useful introduction to the history of sport in Australia is provided by **W. F. Mandle**, 'Games People Played: Cricket and Football in England and Victoria in the Late Nineteenth Century', *Historical Studies*, 15/60, April 1973, p. 511.

The standard work on Australian economic development in the second half of the nineteenth century, which gives particular prominence to the role of urbanisation, is **N. G. Butlin**, *Investment in Australian Economic Development 1861–1900* (Cambridge 1964). Social and geographic mobility were the topic of an issue of the journal *Australia 1888*, 2, August 1979.

I have dealt with the 1890s in *Class and Politics: New South Wales, Victoria and the Early Commonwealth 1890–1910* (Canberra 1976). Racist sentiment is described by **Andrew Markus**, *Fear and Hatred: Purifying Australia and California 1850–1901* (Sydney 1979). For an authoritative account of the federal debate, see **J. A. La Nauze**, *The Making of the Australian Constitution* (Melbourne 1972).

Chapter 5: Loyalties

The 'changing but unbroken thread of British–Australian sentiment' is the subject of **Gavin Souter**, *Lion and Kangaroo: The Initiation of Australia 1901–1919* (Sydney 1976); he includes a chapter on Wilmansruist. Responses to the Boer War are analysed by **C. N. Connolly** in two articles in *Historical Studies*, 'Manufacturing "Spontaneity": the Australian Offers of Troops for the Boer War' (70, April 1978, p. 106), and 'Class, Birthplace and Loyalty: Australian Attitudes to the Boer War' (71, October 1978, p. 210). For Empire Day, see **Stewart Firth** and **Jeanette Hoorn**, 'From Empire Day to Cracker Night' in **Peter Spearritt** and **David Walker** (eds), *Australian Popular Culture* (Sydney 1979); and for 'boy conscription', **John Barrett**, *Falling In* (Sydney 1979). The policies of the early Commonwealth, including White Australia, are surveyed in **R. Norris**, *The Emergent Commonwealth, Australian Federation: Expectation and Fulfilment 1889–1910* (Melbourne 1975).

For a general account of the home front during the First World War, see **Michael McKernan**, *The Australian People and the Great War* (Melbourne 1980). **Bill Gammage** vividly recounts the experience of soldiers, using diaries and letters, in *The Broken Years: Australian Soldiers in the Great War* (Canberra 1974). Of central importance, both as a history and a source of Anzac values, is *The Official History of Australia in the War of 1914–18* (Sydney 1921–42). The editor, C. E. W. Bean, himself wrote six volumes, two on Gallipoli and four on France. **Richard White** neatly depicts the emergence of the digger myth in *Inventing Australia*. Sir John Monash is the subject of an impressive biography by **Geoffrey Serle**, *John Monash: A Biography* (Melbourne 1982).

The emergence of Anzac ceremonies and their significance as ritual are discussed in: **Richard Ely**, 'The First Anzac Day: Invented or Discovered?' and **Lee Sackett**, 'Marching into the Past: Anzac Day Celebrations in Adelaide', *Journal of Australian Studies*, 17, November 1985, pp. 41 and 18; **Philip Kitley**, 'Anzac Day Ritual', *ibid.*, 4, 1979, p. 58; **Mary Wilson**, 'The Making of Melbourne's Anzac Day', *Australian Journal of Politics and History*, 20/2, August 1974, p. 197.

For a selection of literary responses to the War, see **J. T. Laird** (ed.), *Other Banners: An Anthology of Australian Literature of the First World War* (Canberra 1971). **May Gibbs's** gumnut baby stories are brought together in *The Complete Adventures of Snugglepot and Cuddlepie* (Sydney 1946); likewise **Dorothy Wall**, *The Complete Adventures of Blinky Bill* (Sydney 1939). **Margriet Bonnin** writes on 'Ion Idriess: "Rich Australiana"' in **Susan Dermody**, **John Docker** and **Drusilla Modjeska** (eds), *Nellie Melba, Ginger Meggs and Friends: Essays in Australian Cultural History* (Malmsbury 1982).

The problems facing nationalist writers of the period are the focus of **David Walker**'s important study, *Dream and Disillusion: A Search for Australian Cultural Identity* (Canberra 1976). For Norman Lindsay and his followers see **John Hetherington**, *Norman Lindsay: The Embattled Olympian* (Melbourne 1973), and for the particular situation of women writers, **Drusilla Modjeska**, *Exiles at Home: Australian Women Writers 1925–1945* (Sydney 1981). Some relevant documents are to be found in **John Barnes** (ed.), *The Writer in Australia: A Collection of Literary Documents 1856 to 1964* (Melbourne 1969).

Concerning the 'federation villa' and 'Colonial Revival' architecture, I have drawn on **Conrad Hamann**, 'Nationalism and Reform in Australian Architecture 1880–1920', *Historical Studies*, 18/72, April 1979, p. 393.

There is, as yet, no real biography of Menzies, but **Cameron Hazle-**

hurst's *Menzies Observed* (Sydney 1979) is useful. On the governor-general as an imperial appointment, see **Christopher Cunneen**, *Kings' Men: Australian Governors-General from Hopetoun to Isaacs* (Sydney 1983).

Cricket enthusiasts are directed to **Ric Sissons** and **Brian Stoddart**, *Cricket and Empire: The 1932–33 Bodyline Tour of Australia* (Sydney 1984).

There is little which treats of accent in its cultural context. **Sidney J. Baker**'s *The Australian Language* (Sydney 1945), attempts some sort of historical perspective, but concludes nevertheless that 'our accent is bad'. **A. G. Mitchell**'s *The Pronunciation of English in Australia* (Sydney 1946), was an early (or, from another perspective, late) attempt to overcome the inferiority complex about accent.

Chapter 6: Political institutions

Twentieth-century political history is outlined in **Fred Alexander**, *Australia Since Federation: A Narrative and Critical Analysis* (Melbourne 1976 [1967]) and **Russel Ward**, *A Nation for a Continent: The History of Australia 1901–1975* (Melbourne 1977).

For a recent reassessment of egalitarianism, see **John Hirst**, 'Egalitarianism', *Australian Cultural History*, 5, 1986, p. 12.

Much has been written about the labour movement and Labor Party (as it spells itself), but here is a representative selection: **Verity Burgmann**, *'In Our Time': Socialism and the Rise of Labor 1885–1905* (Sydney 1985); **Robin Gollan**, *Revolutionaries and Reformists: Communism and the Australian Labour Movement 1920–1955* (Canberra 1975); **Peter Love**, *Labor and the Money Power: Australian Labour Populism 1890–1950* (Melbourne 1984); **D. J. Murphy** (ed.), *Labor in Politics: The State Labor Parties in Australia 1880–1920* (Brisbane 1975); **John Rickard**, *Class and Politics*. Lang is a figure who has commanded much attention, but note especially **Bede Nairn**'s recent biography *The 'Big Fella': Jack Lang and the Australian Labor Party 1891–1949* (Melbourne 1986); and the essays edited by **Heather Radi** and **Peter Spearritt**, *Jack Lang* (Sydney 1977).

Anti-labor is less well served historically, but note **John Lonie**, 'From Liberal to Liberal: The Emergence of the Liberal Party and Australian Capitalism, 1900–45' in **Graeme Duncan** (ed.), *Critical Essays in Australian Politics* (Melbourne 1978); **B. D. Graham**, *The Formation of the Australian Country Parties* (Canberra 1966); **P. Loveday**, **A. W. Martin** and **R. S. Parker** (eds), *The Emergence of the Australian Party System* (Sydney 1977); Rickard, *op. cit.* For Bruce, see **Cecil Edwards**, *Bruce of Melbourne: Man of Two Worlds* (London 1965). Lyons has no biography, but the memoir of **Dame Enid Lyons** is instructive: *So We Take Comfort* (London 1965).

The politics of the extreme right, particularly during the Depression, have attracted some interest. **Peter Loveday** discusses 'Anti-political Political Thought' in **Judy MacKinolty** (ed.), *The Wasted Years: Australia's Great Depression* (Sydney 1981). **Robert Darroch** speculates on the historical sources for *Kangaroo* in his undocumented *D. H. Lawrence in Australia* (Melbourne 1981). **Keith Amos** analyses *The New Guard Movement 1931–1935* (Melbourne 1976); the reminiscences of the Guard's chief commander, **Eric Campbell**, are also fascinating, if disingenuous at times – *The Rallying Point: My Story of The New Guard* (Melbourne 1965). **L. J. Louis** and **Ian Turner** bring together some documents on politics outside parliament (including

Douglas Credit and the Riverina Movement) in *The Depression of the 1930s* (Melbourne 1968).

I have written about the origins and early development of the industrial arbitration system in both *Class and Politics* and *H. B. Higgins: The Rebel as Judge* (Sydney 1984). On attitudes to employment and welfare, see **Stuart Macintyre**, *Winners and Losers: The Pursuit of Social Justice in Australian History* (Sydney 1985).

On federation and the role of the High Court, see **Geoffrey Sawer**, *Australian Federalism in the Courts* (Melbourne 1967) and **Leslie Zines**, *The High Court and the Constitution* (Sydney 1981).

The secession movement in Western Australia is discussed in **F. K. Crowley**, *Australia's Western Third: A History of Western Australia* (Melbourne 1960).

Chapter 7: Relationships and pursuits

Neville Hicks gives an authoritative account of the Royal Commission on the Decline of the Birth Rate in *'This Sin and Scandal': Australia's Population Debate 1891–1911* (Canberra 1978). Ginger Meggs is expertly dissected by **Barry Andrews** in 'Ginger Meggs: His Story', in Dermody, Docker and Modjeska, *op. cit.*

Much work remains to be done on home and family, but on the architecture of the suburban house **Robin Boyd**'s *Australia's Home* (Melbourne 1952) is still essential, while **Kerreen M. Reiger**'s *The Disenchantment of the Home: Modernizing the Australian Family 1880–1940* (Melbourne 1985) is a major contribution to characterising the changing ideology of the family in its suburban setting.

Mateship and sexuality are even more difficult subjects which necessarily invite impressionistic interpretation. Much of the conventional wisdom about mateship in Australia derives from **Russel Ward**, *The Australian Legend* (Melbourne 1958), but as history it has been challenged: see, for example, the special issue of *Historical Studies*, The Australian Legend Revisited, 18/71, October 1978, which was both a salute to Ward and a reassessment of his thesis. **Janet McCalman**, *Struggletown: Public and Private Life in Richmond 1900–1965* (Melbourne 1984) is a social history of a predominantly working-class community which offers important clues to the male and female cultures of this period.

There is a very interesting bunch of autobiographies, and autobiographical novels, mostly published after 1960, which describe the growing-up experience of the period between the Wars. Four of these, by Hal Porter, George Johnston, Graham McInnes and Donald Horne, are discussed in **Patrick Morgan**'s suggestive article, 'Keeping It In The Family', *Quadrant*, 18/3, May–June 1974, p. 10.

The emergence of urban history in recent years has been a belated recognition of its relevance to such an urbanised society as Australia. Works relevant to this period include: **Jill Roe** (ed.), *Twentieth-Century Sydney: Studies in Urban and Social History* (Sydney 1980); **Peter Spearritt**, *Sydney Since the Twenties* (Sydney 1978); **C. T. Stannage**, *The People of Perth: A Social History of Western Australia's Capital City* (Perth 1979). On soldier settlers and rural hardship I am indebted to **Marilyn Lake**, *The Limits of Hope* (Melbourne 1987).

As for education, Barcan's *A History of Australian Education* attempts the difficult task of covering six state systems as well as the private sector; see also **J. Cleverley** and **J. Lawrey** (eds), *Australian Education in the Twentieth Century* (Melbourne 1972).

Keith Dunstan's *Wowsers* (Sydney 1974) is an entertaining historical tour of the phenomenon, but for a more serious attempt to explain the source of wowserism in colonial Protestantism there are two New South Wales studies, **J. D. Bollen**, *Protestantism and Social Reform in New South Wales 1890–1900* (Melbourne 1972), and **Richard Broome**, *Treasure in Earthern Vessels: Protestant Christianity in New South Wales Society 1900–1914* (Brisbane 1980).

For food, see **Michael Symons**, *One Continuous Picnic: A History of Eating in Australia* (Adelaide 1982); for radio, **K. S. Inglis**, *This is The ABC: The Australian Broadcasting Commission 1932–1983* (Melbourne 1983), and **Lesley Johnston**, '"Sing 'em Muck Clara": Highbrow versus Lowbrow on Early Australian Radio', *Meanjin*, 41/2, June 1982, p. 210; for cinemas, **Diane Collins**, 'The 1920s Picture Palace', in Dermody, Docker and Modjeska, *op. cit.*, p. 60; for dancing and popular music, **Andrew Bisset**, *Black Roots, White Flowers: A History of Jazz in Australia* (Sydney 1979); on magazines, **Denis O'Brien**, *The Weekly* (Melbourne 1982), and **Richard White**, 'The Importance of Being *Man*', in Spearritt and Walker, *op. cit.*, p. 145.

Geoffrey Sherrington's *Australia's Immigrants* briefly surveys the pattern of immigration in these years. In *The Destruction of Aboriginal Society* (Canberra 1970), **C. D. Rowley** charts the frontier experience in the context of government policy. Elkin is the subject of a recent biography in **Tigger Wise**, *The Self-Made Anthropologist: A life of A. P. Elkin* (Sydney 1985).

Richard Haese's *Rebels and Precursors: The Revolutionary Years of Australian Art* (Melbourne 1981) looks at the emerging 'contemporary art' scene of the 1930s and also captures something of the bohemian atmosphere. Concerning women writers, see Modjeska, *op. cit.*, and women painters, **Janine Burke**, *Australian Women Artists 1840–1940* (Melbourne 1980).

Chapter 8: Dependence

For the postwar period there is a plethora of often unprocessed material, but, understandably, a shortage of historical works suitable for the lay reader. Suggested reading is, therefore, uneven, and there are some noticeable gaps. Once again, books such as Alexander, *op. cit.*, and Ward, *A Nation for a Continent*, give some sort of overall coverage.

Foreign policy has, however, attracted attention from its practitioners, historians, political scientists and commentators. **Alan Watt**, a former head of the Department of External Affairs (as it was then called), attempted first to fill the gap with *The Evolution of Australia's Foreign Policy 1938–1965* (London 1967): it is still a useful introduction, though the author's bias, as reflected in his lack of sympathy for Evatt, needs to be taken into account. **John Hammond Moore** brings together contributions from a number of writers in *The American Alliance: Australia, New Zealand and the United States 1940–1970* (Melbourne 1970): writing then Moore thought it 'probable' that

trans-Pacific ties would become stronger, not weaker. A more critical perspective is offered by **J. A. Camilleri**, *Australian–American Relations: The Web
of Dependence* (Melbourne 1980). Curtin is the subject of a dutiful study by
Lloyd Ross, *John Curtin: A Biography* (Melbourne 1977). **W. J. Hudson**'s
Casey (Melbourne 1986) is an excellent biography of this most interesting
Anglo-Australian, and throws much light on the making of foreign policy at
the political level.

The Second World War has generated another multi-volume official
history, *Australia in the War of 1939–1945*, though it has not had the impact of
its predecessor. **Paul Hasluck**'s two volumes on the home front, *The Government and the People, 1939–41* and *1942–5* (Canberra 1952 and 1970) are important. **John Robertson**'s *Australia at War 1939–1945* (Sydney 1984), is a useful
and well-researched short history.

The Royal 'tour' of 1954 is nicely described and compared with the
'visit' of 1963 by **Peter Spearritt**, 'Royal Progress: The Queen and Her
Australian Subjects', *Australian Cultural History*, 5, 1986, p. 75.

As already mentioned, Menzies has still to be accorded a full biography. The kind of hostility which Menzies and his political domination of
postwar Australia could arouse amongst some intellectuals is reflected in
Donald Horne's bitter analysis in Chapter 8 of *The Lucky Country* (Melbourne 1974 [1964]).

Kevin Fewster explores the postwar tennis boom and the American
connexion in 'Advantage Australia: Davis Cup Tennis 1950–1959', *Sporting
Traditions*, 2/1, November 1985, p. 47.

Two books serve as an introduction to Australia's Vietnam commit-
ment: **Peter King** (ed.), *Australia's Vietnam: Australia in the Second Indo-China
War* (Sydney 1983) and **Michael Sexton**, *War for the Asking: Australia's
Vietnam Secrets* (Melbourne 1981).

Frank Crowley presents 'an historical overview' of the 1970s in *Tough
Times: Australia in the Seventies* (Melbourne 1986). **Whitlam**, described by his
publisher as 'a literate and visionary statesman', has given us a 750-page
explication and defence of the achievements of his government at home and
abroad: *The Whitlam Government 1972–1975* (Melbourne 1985).

The quest for national identity has provoked a considerable literature of
dubious quality: **Richard White**'s *Inventing Australia* is an exception.

Chapter 9: Diversity

The impact of American troops on the Australian community is splendidly
documented in **E. Daniel** and **Annette Potts**, *Yanks Down Under 1941–45:
The American Impact on Australia* (Melbourne 1985).

Immigration has given rise to many books and articles often with a
sociological flavour. **Janis Wilton** and **Richard Bosworth** provide a valuable
historical introduction to both the policy and experience of immigration in
Old Worlds and New Australia: The Post-war Migrant Experience (Melbourne
1984). The literature of postwar immigration is usefully surveyed by
Andrew Markus in **G. Osborne** and **W. F. Mandle**, *New History: Studying
Australia Today* (Sydney 1982). Note, however, **Richard Broome**'s *The Victorians: Arriving*, which has three chapters on postwar immigration to Victoria. On the Greek community I have drawn on **Eva Isaacs**, *Greek Children*

in Sydney (Canberra 1976). For 'The Australian Way of Life' see **Richard White**'s article, *Historical Studies*, 18/73, October 1979, p. 528.

The works on religion by O'Farrell, Hunt and Hilliard, referred to under Chapter 4, are also relevant here, as well as **Edmund Campion**, *Rock-choppers: Growing up Catholic in Australia* (Melbourne 1982). See also **A. W. Black** and **P. E. Glasner** (eds), *Practice and Belief: Studies in the Sociology of Australian Religion* (Sydney 1983). For a critical view of censorship, see **Geoffrey Dutton** and **Max Harris** (eds), *Australia's Censorship Crisis* (Melbourne 1970).

Australia's First Cold War is the title of two volumes edited by **Ann Curthoys** and **John Merritt**. The first volume, 1945–1953, is *Society, Communism and Culture* (Sydney 1984); the second, 1945–1959, *Better Dead Than Red* (Sydney 1986). I have drawn particularly on the chapter from the latter by **Hilary Kent** and **John Merritt**, 'The Cold War and the Melbourne Olympic Games'. The Labor schism is amply narrated by **Robert Murray**, *The Split: Australian Labor in the Fifties* (Melbourne 1970).

On the plight of the Aborigines see **Richard Broome**'s *Aboriginal Australians* and Yarwood and Knowling, *op. cit.*

Frank Crowley's *Tough Times* deals, amongst other things, with protest and liberation in the 1970s. For an example of the personal impact of women's liberation see **Joyce Nicholson**, '"Sisterhood is Powerful": A Memoir' in **Marilyn Lake** and **Farley Kelly** (eds), *Double Time: Women in Victoria – 150 Years* (Melbourne 1985); concerning homosexual liberation, see **Dennis Altmann**, *Coming Out in the Seventies* (Sydney 1979). The flavour and ambience of the counter-culture is captured in **Frank Moorhouse**'s 'mosaic', *Days of Wine and Rage* (Melbourne 1980), while **Craig McGregor** concentrates more on the world of swinging popular culture, *People, Politics and Pop: Australians in the Sixties* (Sydney 1968). On the playwrights who emerged from the counter-culture, see **Peter Fitzpatrick**, *After 'The Doll': Australian Drama Since 1955* (Melbourne 1979).

The controversy of the Whitlam years and the dismissal of 1975 has continued in the literature it has generated. Whitlam's own account of his government has already been noted; see also **Michael Sexton**, *Illusion of Power: The Fate of a Reform Government* (Sydney 1979). **Sir John Kerr** justified his position in *Matters of Judgment: An Autobiography* (Melbourne 1978). The irrepressible Whitlam quickly responded with *The Truth of the Matter* (Melbourne 1979).

The immigration controversy of 1984–85 gave rise to **Geoffrey Blainey**, *All for Australia* (Sydney 1984), and **Andrew Markus** and **M. C. Ricklefs**, *Surrender Australia? Essays in the Study and Use of History: Geoffrey Blainey and Asian Immigration* (Sydney 1985).

Chapter 10: Vision

Although most of its material is from pre-Second World War Australia, **Ian Turner**'s *The Australian Dream: A Collection of Anticipations about Australia from Captain Cook to the Present Day* (Melbourne 1968), is perhaps the only attempt to present historically Australian perceptions of the future.

The origins and history of *Meanjin* are the subject of **Lynne Strahan**'s *Just City and The Mirrors: Meanjin Quarterly and the Intellectual Front, 1940–*

1965 (Melbourne 1984). Both the Dobell and *Angry Penguins* affairs are dealt with by Haese, *op. cit.*; on the latter see also **Max Harris** (ed.), *Ern Malley's Poems* (Adelaide 1971). For art in the 1960s, **Gary Catalano**, *The Years of Hope: Australian Art and Criticism 1959–1968* (Melbourne 1980).

One can learn something of the postwar evolution of Australian history from **Rob Pascoe**, *The Manufacture of Australian History* (Melbourne 1979), but he insists on imposing a typology which is not always helpful.

Garry Kinnane's *George Johnston: A Biography* (Melbourne 1986) can now be compared with **Johnston**'s autobiographical *My Brother Jack* (London 1964), and its two sequels, *Clean Straw for Nothing* (London 1969) and *A Cartload of Clay* (Sydney 1971). **Patrick White**'s *Flaws in the Glass* (Melbourne 1981) offers some autobiographical insights.

Some of **Barry Humphries'** most famous sketches are gathered together in *A Nice Night's Entertainment: Sketches and Monologues 1956–1981* (Sydney 1981). For a more than usually revealing interview with Humphries see **Jim Davidson**, 'A Fugitive Art', *Meanjin*, 2/1986, p. 149.

Glen Murcutt is the subject of **Philip Drew**'s study, *Leaves of Iron: Glen Murcutt, Pioneer of an Australian Architectural Form* (Sydney 1985).

On the historic rivalry between the cities, see the collection of essays with a cultural emphasis, **Jim Davidson**, *The Sydney–Melbourne Book* (Sydney 1986).

The growing interest in a sense of place is reflected in the publication of *The Oxford Literary Guide to Australia*, ed. **Peter Pierce** (Melbourne 1987).

Many books have attempted to dissect Australian society and comment on its values, and I hesitate to select any as being superior to the rest. However, for a 1950s view one might point to **John Douglas Pringle**'s urbane *Australian Accent* (London 1958). The most influential interpretation of the 1960s was undoubtedly Donald Horne's already cited *The Lucky Country*. For two recent profiles see **John McLaren** (ed.), *A Nation Apart: Essays in Honour of Andrew Fabinyi. Personal Views of Australia in the Eighties* (Melbourne 1983), and **Stephen R. Graubard** (ed.), *Australia: The Daedalus Symposium* (Sydney 1985).

Index